I was on my back with the signal panel on my chest, watching over my boot tops for the choppers. First I heard their rotors, then suddenly there they were, flying low and fast, the slick in the center with a gunship on either side. It's the arrival of the Valkyries, I thought, and decided they were the most beautiful sight I'd ever seen. The gunships opened up with everything they had, making one fast, deadly run along the edges of the clearing. Captain Conner brought the slick right into the mouth of our V, and the next thing I knew, I was diving into the chopper's open door.

I took one look around, saw that we were all there, and wildly waved a thumbs-up. "Go! Go! Go!" everyone was yelling, and we took off again like we'd been shot from a catapult. The door gunners were already firing nonstop. My point man suddenly saw something and opened up with his carbine. We had just flown over the treetops on the edge of the clearing when there were three large explosions in the center of the LZ. "Too late, suckers!" I screamed, suddenly laughing, realizing I'd lived through it once again. . . .

By Leigh Wade
Published by Ivy Books:

TAN PHU: Special Forces Team A-23 in Combat
THE PROTECTED WILL NEVER KNOW

THE PROTECTED WILL NEVER KNOW

Leigh Wade

IVY BOOKS • NEW YORK

This book is dedicated to the memory of
Boyd W. Anderson

An Ivy Book
Published by The Ballantine Publishing Group
Copyright © 1998 by Leigh Wade

http://www.randomhouse.com

Library of Congress Catalog Card Number: 97-94544

ISBN 0-8041-1713-6

Manufactured in the United States of America

First Edition: March 1998

10 9 8 7 6 5 4 3 2 1

You've never lived until you've almost died. For those who fight for it, life has a meaning the protected will never know.
                                        —Popular saying in SOG units

Hell, no! We won't go!! Ho-Ho-Ho Chi Minh is going to win!
                    —Antiwar chants,
                        especially popular on college campuses

You number-ten, dinky-dao!

                            —Vietnamese bar girls,
                                speaking to the author
                                on numerous occasions

Author's Note on Terminology

I realize that this book will be read by people with widely varied backgrounds and knowledge of the military. To aid those readers who have a limited knowledge of military terms and expressions, I have included a brief glossary at the back of the book. I recommend that the reader glance through it before beginning the book. It would probably benefit today's younger military readers to look through these terms also, because in the 1960s we may have used some terminology differently from the way it is used today.

Map 1. Republic of Vietnam

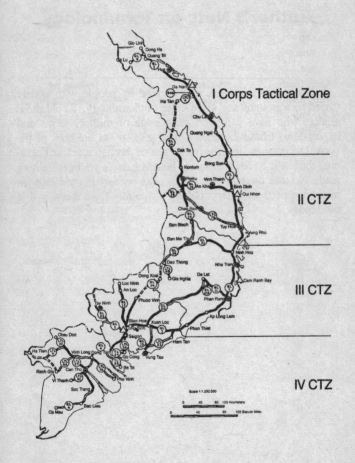

I Corps Tactical Zone

II CTZ

III CTZ

IV CTZ

Gio Linh
Dong Ha
Ca Lu
Quang Tri
Hue
Da Nang
Ha Tan
Chu Lai
Quang Ngai
Dak To
Bong Son
Kontum
Pleiku
Vinh Thanh
An Khe
Binh Dinh
Qui Nhon
Cheo Reo
Ban Blech
Ban Me Thuot
Tuy Hoa
Vung Rho
Ninh Hoa
Dao Thong
Dong Xoai
Gia Nghia
Da Lat
Nha Trang
Cam Ranh Bay
Loc Ninh
An Loc
Phuoc Vinh
Phan Rang
Tay Ninh
Bien Hoa
Xuan Loc
Ap Long Lam
Long Binh
Saigon
Phan Thiet
Chau Doc
Vinh Long
Dong Tam
Go Cong
Ba Tri
Vung Tau
Ham Tan
Ha Tien
Can Tho
Phu Vinh
Rach Gia
Vi Thanh
Soc Trang
Ca Mau
Bac Lieu

Scale 1:1,250,000

0   40   80   100 Kilometers
0   40   80   100 Statute Miles

Map 2. III Corps Tactical Zone, 1964–1971

U.S. Army Special Forces Camps in III CTZ, Vietnam, 1964–1971

1-Ben Soi
2-Bien Hoa
3-Bu Dop
4-Bu Ghia Map
5-Bunard
6-Chon Thanh
7-Dong Xoai
8-Duc Hoa
9-Duc Hue

10-Duc Phong
11-Go Dau Ha
12-Hiep Hoa
13-Ho Ngoc Tao-Tu Duc
14-Hon Quan
15-Katum
16-Loc Ninh
17-Long Hai
18-Long Thanh

19-Luong Hoa
20-Minh Thanh
21-Phuoc Vinh
22-Prek Klok
23-Quan Loi
24-Song Be
25-Soui Da
26-Tanh Linh
27-Tay Ninh
28-Thien Ngon
29-Tong Le Chon
30-Tra Cu
31-Trai Bi
32-Trang Sup
33-Xuan Loc
34-Chi Linh

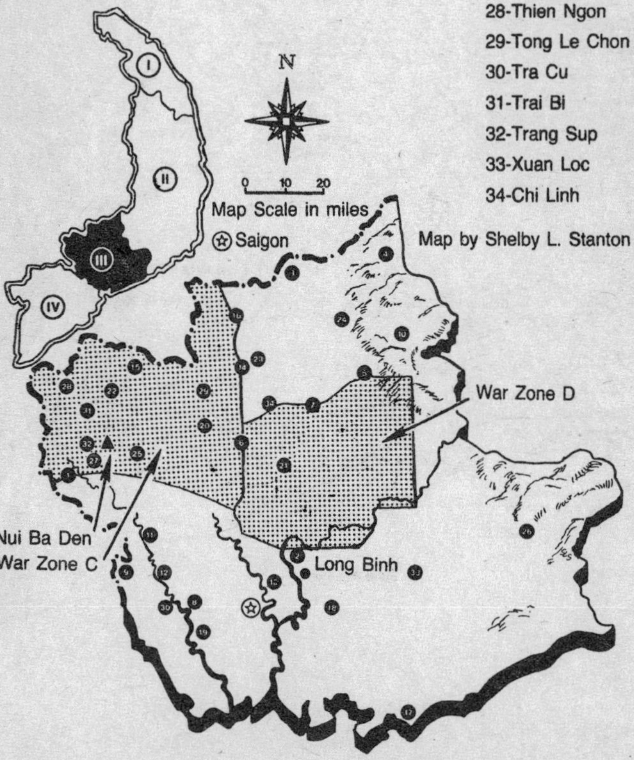

N

0   10   20

Map Scale in miles

Saigon

Map by Shelby L. Stanton

War Zone D

Nui Ba Den
War Zone C

Long Binh

Map 3. Coastal Binh Dinh Province

Note lonely location of Camp Vinh Thanh.

Prologue

It was September of 1966, shortly after my twenty-fourth birthday, and I was on my fourth tour in Vietnam. During the morning of D minus 3, our traveling circus arrived at the remote Special Forces camp named Dong Xoai. We set up our tents inside the camp perimeter, encircled them with concertina wire, and before evening, our mission support site was operational.

We were still in an embryonic stage in those days, so our crew didn't take up much room. Besides our six recon teams, each consisting of two Americans and four indigenous, we had a commando company of a hundred men, our air assets, and the headquarters element.

Our hosts at Dong Xoai were very hospitable, and that night several of our guys sat around their team house and drank a few beers with them. There was an enemy probe around midnight, and we all went to our alert positions, but it didn't amount to anything. We woke up at sunrise the next morning and got our initial intel briefing at 0800.

It was already hot in the GP-medium we were using for the operations tent, and for security reasons the sides were rolled up only partway. With the recon team members, the commando company leaders, the pilots, and our staff all present, the tent was pretty crowded. That made it even hotter.

Those of us on the recon teams had the privilege of sitting in the front row. After a short pep talk by our commander, Lieutenant Colonel Reish, it was the S-3 officer's turn. Captain Werbiski walked over to the situation map and threw back the piece of camo cloth that covered it. It was our first look at our operational area, and from somewhere in the room I heard a faint groan.

There was one small blue rectangle that indicated camp Dong Xoai. About twenty kilometers to the south, surrounded by a

1

cluster of red enemy-unit indicators, lay our operational area. The S-3 told us our exact mission:

Each team would first do a map study of its assigned recon zones. After identifying possible infil and exfil LZs, team leaders and assistants would make an air reconnaissance of the respective areas of operation to verify the maps and make the final decision about which LZs to use. The teams would then draw up their final operational plans and present them to the commander and his staff on D minus 1.

After infiltrating by helicopter, each team would conduct a five-day ground reconnaissance of its assigned AOs, then exfiltrate by air. That is, that was how it would all work if things went as planned.

This was to be strictly a recon mission, and enemy contact was to be avoided if possible. If a team was compromised and could not evade the enemy and continue the mission, it could request an immediate, emergency exfiltration.

The only fire support available was Tac-air. We had, however, considerable capability in this respect. Besides our own helicopter gunships, the Air Force had prop-driven Skyraiders and jet fighter-bombers on call for us. "Best of all," the S-3 told us with a big smile, "if you find a worthwhile target, we can have a B-52 strike in on it two hours after we get you out of the area!" This last bit of information caused a ripple of approving murmurs from all attendees.

While I was being issued maps and overlays for our team, Anderson, the team's number two man, went to draw the radios and crypto material. Boyd Anderson, a big, strong buck sergeant (E5) from New Mexico, had only been in the unit for a couple of months, and this would be his first time to go in on the ground with a team. He and I had been training hard together since he'd been assigned to my team, and I'd gotten to know and like Andy a lot.

Anderson met me and the rest of the members from Team 5 back in our tent, and as the Cambodians kicked back on their cots, Andy and I spread out the maps and went to work. As we'd been told at the briefing, our team's area of operation, or AO, consisted only of four square kilometers. This doesn't sound like much, but in the terrain we would be working in, it was plenty big.

Right away I didn't like the looks of that AO. The southwest corner of our recon zone was bordered by what appeared to be a rather large stream or small river. As far as Andy and I could tell from the map, there were only two possible landing zones for infil/exfil. One of these LZs was right in the bend of the river; the other was up at the opposite corner to the northeast. The map indicated rugged terrain, and the S-2 had told us to expect double- and triple-canopy jungle.

"Look here, Andy," I said, pointing to the possible clearing in the crook of the river. "If we try to use this for an infiltration and get compromised going in—which is what's been happening a lot—we'll be in a corner. Trying to cross this river would be suicidal, so we'd be boxed in on two sides. I want room to run!"

Andy studied the map and nodded in agreement. "I guess we could try to go in on this LZ up in the northeast, then move in a zigzag pattern and use this one by the river for exfiltration. . . ."

"Of course, that would box us in the corner again," I said. "But we sure don't want to try to use the same damned landing zone to go in *and* out of . . . oh well, let's wait until the flyover tomorrow morning. Maybe it isn't as bad as the map makes it look."

"It's up to you, boss," Anderson told me with a grin and a pat on the back. "You lead, we'll follow!"

"Gee, thanks," I told him. "C'mon, let's go check our men's equipment one more time, then find some lunch."

We had three different types of indigenous troops in the unit, but none of them were Vietnamese. There were Chinese Nungs, who we used for camp defense, and Cambodians, who made up most of the recon teams. We also had Montagnards, who were primarily in the commando company.

They were all pretty good troops—the best we could find. Our recruiters had traveled all over the country skimming some of the best fighters off of different A-teams. The recruiters told prospects that they would be going to a high-risk unit, but that it paid well. In fact, the mercenaries on our recon teams made about three times more than their A-team counterparts and as much as a major in the regular Vietnamese Army.

I thought I had an especially good bunch of indigenous. The four of them were young, tough, and brash. They all hated the communists, weren't afraid of a good fight, and liked earning lots of money. Andy and I checked out their weapons and equipment for about the thousandth time, and as expected, everything was perfect.

Originally our unit had been preparing for a tricky mission that made necessary the use of all "sterile" equipment and weapons. We had rucksacks, binoculars, and such, which were manufactured in Japan and were not normal American Army–issue items. The recon teams had originally carried the old .30 caliber M-2 carbine (capable of full-auto fire), but later had been issued brand-new Swedish-K submachine guns in 9mm.

On this operation we were carrying a mixed bag of equipment, some of it standard issue, some of it not. Our indige were still carrying the Swedish-Ks, for example, while Andy and I had opted to go with the M-16.

Besides the normal web gear, magazine pouches, two canteens, and beaucoup ammo, each team member also carried a trench knife, a snap-link and piece of rope for a Swiss seat, several frag grenades, one red and one green smoke, an air/ground panel, and a signal mirror. The men carried enough dehydrated rations to last the duration of the mission, and as a creature comfort, each carried a small, plastic ground cloth. Each American on the team also had a miniature flare gun, and the team leaders carried High Standard .22 pistols with silencers. In addition to all of this, most of the teams also lugged one or two Claymore mines, but this was left to the discretion of the team leaders.

That afternoon, we checked the team radios again and studied the signal operating instructions (SOI) and brevity codes, memorizing as much of it as we could. On this mission we were using the types of radios and communications techniques that Project Delta had worked out over the last year or so.

Mainly through trial and error, Delta had determined that the only reliable way to communicate with deployed deep-penetration teams was by using an air-relay. The teams carried standard-issue FM radios—PRC-10s in the early days, PRC-25s as they came on line later—and HT-1 radios as backup. The air-relay flew far enough away from the team AOs so as not to give away the team's presence in the area but close enough to maintain good commo.

The teams each had several scheduled contacts to make, and if a contact was missed, it was assumed the team was in trouble and the commando company was sent in. The biggest trouble with the whole system was that at that time, the air-relays could not fly at night, so a team was strictly on its own from dusk to dawn.

Brevity codes had been worked out to minimize the time required to pass information. "Blue Dog" might mean "need water resupply," and "Red Bear" might mean "our shit's in the wind, need immediate exfiltration, help, get us the hell out of here!" Because on-line voice-encryption devices still weren't available in 1966, a simple alphabetical transposition cipher system was used to transmit longer messages.

After a quiet night, for once not interrupted by enemy activity, Andy and I grabbed a cup of coffee at the A-team mess hall in the morning, then went out to the landing pad. The sun was just coming up, and the crew chiefs were wiping dew off the chopper's windshields.

We'd be making the air recon on the same HU-1D, and with the same pilots who would be flying our infiltration. I had a quick conference with the pilots to go over the maps and pick out some checkpoints to look for on the way. By 0800 the engines were warmed up and we lifted off.

Andy and I each wore aviator helmets with earphones and microphones so we could communicate with the pilots on the intercom. We circled up to high altitude, then angled off in the direction of the AO.

I studied the ground through a pair of binoculars as we flew along, as this was the same flight pattern we would be using on the actual infiltration. The pilot pointed out various obvious terrain features. "We're two minutes out," he told me over the intercom. "That river intersection will be the last checkpoint."

We remained at high altitude and didn't stay in the area long for fear of giving ourselves away. We stayed long enough to see that the map was pretty accurate, though, and that my original qualms were justified.

The two possible LZs I had spotted on the map were in fact the only two in the AO. Our unit had good pilots, and they could get in and out of LZs just big enough to clear the rotors, but there were only two clearings in the whole area. The river on the SW corner of the AO was even larger than it appeared on the map and had plenty of water. Two other small streams meandered through the area.

I gave Andy a questioning look, he shrugged an okay, and I told the pilot we'd seen enough.

After that there wasn't much to do. Andy and I worked out our final plan that afternoon, keeping with the KISS ("Keep it simple, stupid!") principle. I used one of the interpreters to brief our indigenous team members on what was going to happen. It was late afternoon by the time I'd finished talking to the bored Cambodes, and I asked them if there were any questions. "What time chop-chop?" one of them asked, rubbing his growling stomach.

Our A-team hosts loaned us their fortified operations center for the brief-backs. The same people who had been at the initial briefing attended this one, along with a colonel from MACV and some guy in civvies. Each team leader stood up in turn and presented his team's plan of operation. We followed the standard briefing format, and the brief-backs were quite detailed and complete. At the end of each presentation there was a question-and-answer portion.

This was the first time I'd given a brief-back, because on my other operations I had always been the junior man. I was the youngest recon team leader, and although I had recently been promoted to staff sergeant (E6), I was also the lowest ranking. I did, however, have as much Vietnam combat experience as anyone in the room.

Giving the briefing didn't particularly bother me, because I'd taught a lot of classes since I'd been in Special Forces and tended to be a natural ham anyway. I introduced myself and Anderson, told the audience I was leader of RT-5, and launched into it. When I got to the part about the infiltration, I paused a moment and took a deep breath.

"There are only two possible LZs in our AO," I told them, pointing them out on the situation map. "This one in the northeast corner will be our primary infiltration LZ and our alternate for exfiltration. This clearing in the southwest will be our primary exfiltration LZ." I paused again, and Colonel Reish jumped right on it.

"If you can't get into your primary infiltration LZ, Sergeant Wade, will you use the one in the southwest as your alternate?"

"Sir, if we are unable to go in on the primary, I want to abort the mission," I told him.

There was a moment of silence that seemed to last a lot longer than it did, and all eyes swung to Reish.

"What are your reasons, Sergeant Wade? You realize this is not SOP," the commander said.

I explained to him and the others my fear of being compromised on infiltration and of having no room to evade the enemy if we went in on the LZ next to the river.

After hearing me out, the colonel thought it over for only a second, then agreed. "You are the team leader, the ground commander in this operation, Sergeant Wade. What you say goes."

My portion of the brief-back was finished with no further questions.

During the next two days Teams 1 through 4 successfully infiltrated as scheduled. After supper on the evening before our team was due to go in, Andy and I went over to the A-detachment's team house and watched a movie that had just come in by chopper that day. The story was about a guy who gets captured by savages in Africa, is stripped to a loincloth, then told to run while the bloodthirsty natives chase him for the whole movie. Andy and I would be on the ground in the AO the next night, and I hoped we wouldn't be in the same predicament as the poor bastard in the story!

At first light the next morning, all four of the previously committed teams made their regularly scheduled radio contacts and said they were continuing mission. Just before noon, Team 2 called in, said they were in trouble, and requested an immediate, emergency exfiltration.

Along with the two Americans from Team 6, Andy and I stood around the commo tent, monitoring the commo. We couldn't hear the radio transmissions from Team 2, but we could pick up what the pilots were saying.

Team 2 had made contact with the enemy, and although shots had been fired, so far the team had taken no casualties. The team popped a smoke grenade to indicate its exact position to the orbiting FAC (forward air control), who then gave them directions to the nearest possible exfiltration LZ. They were almost to the LZ when they were cut off and surrounded by the enemy.

The surrounded men took cover in a large bomb crater and began calling on Tac-air in hopes of blasting their way through to the LZ.

"Bird Dog, this is Fast Mover," the pilot of the F-100 said to the FAC. "I've got a flight of four and we're loaded with wall-to-wall napalm and twenty mike-mike [20mm cannon]. ETA about zero-two, over . . ."

"Roger that, Fast Mover, stand by. Break. Team Two, did you copy Fast Mover? . . . Roger . . . Roger. Break. Fast Mover, this is Bird Dog, I've got troops on the ground in contact with enemy twenty-five meters from their position. They want it as close as possible, over."

"Roger, Bird Dog," the jet pilot answered, "I monitored Team Two on fox-mike [FM] push. . . ."

The FAC made a low pass, taking several hits from small-arms fire, and marked the target with a rocket of white phosphorous. "Fast Mover, this is Bird Dog. I've marked with smoke, identify color, over."

"This is Fast Mover, roger, got your white willie pete, over."

"Affirmative, Fast Mover. Make your approach from north to south, keep all ordnance west of my mark, confirm, over."

"Roger, Bird Dog, understand. Break. Team Two, this is Fast Mover on fox-mike . . . keep your heads down, guys, we're comin' in hot. . . ."

The Air Force did a great job that day, pulling off the tricky job of delivering napalm very close to friendly troops without incinerating them along with the enemy. Team 2 successfully broke through the encirclement, got to the LZ, and was pulled out. The only casualties they suffered were two slightly burned by napalm.

I had a chance to talk briefly with the leader of that team right after they got back, and he told me what a close thing it had been. "They were dropping that crap *real* close," he told me, finishing a much deserved beer with one swallow. "When that nape went off it was so hot it sucked the air right out of my fucking lungs!"

The afternoon went quickly as Andy and I made last-minute preparations. We were keeping a close watch on the weather due to reports of thunderstorms in the area. Our infiltration was scheduled for last light and the timing had to be exact. The idea was to hit the ground and move off the LZ with just enough light remaining to allow quick and quiet movement to a position several hundred meters away from the infiltration point before holing up for the night.

The final weather decision was to be made half an hour before takeoff time. Forty-five minutes prior to that we got dressed, changing into the tiger-stripe camouflage uniforms we wore on operations. We made sure that items such as air/ground panels, signal mirrors, SOIs, and so forth were all in the prescribed pockets. Web gear and rucksacks were already loaded and ready to put on. On schedule, the S-3 Air came in and told us the mission was a go.

Nothing left to do then except douse down with insect repellent and go through the ritual of applying camouflage stick to all exposed skin. We used the repellent to soften the hard camouflage paste and make it easier to apply.

At five minutes to takeoff we heard the helicopter engines start and begin to warm up. "Time to *di-di*," I told my team. We put on our equipment, picked up our weapons, and walked out to the landing pad.

My team members took up their positions on the floor of the infiltration chopper, three men to a side, facing the open doors. Colonel Reish was there to watch us take off. I saluted him and gave thumbs-up to the pilot, and we were airborne, quickly reaching altitude and beginning our flight plan. In a few minutes the pilot turned to me, pointed to the ground, and held up one finger: checkpoint one.

It didn't take long to make the twenty-kilometer flight. We were exactly on schedule, and the sun was a big red ball just hitting the horizon when we passed the two-minute marker. The crew chief handed me his helmet so I could hear the pilot on the intercom.

"The FAC says it still looks good," the pilot said. "You guys ready?"

I nodded yes.

"Okay, we're starting our descent."

As we began a rapid drop to the LZ, I looked out the door of the chopper and watched the setting sun. I wondered if that would be the last sunset I'd ever get to see. Christ, I thought, how did I ever get myself into this mess . . . ?

PART I

A Romantic Interlude

An' if sometimes our conduck isn't all your fancy paints,
Why, single men in barricks don't grow into plaster saints.
— RUDYARD KIPLING

But the things you will learn from the Yellow an' Brown,
They'll 'elp you a lot with the White!
— RUDYARD KIPLING

Chapter 1

When I returned from my first combat tour in Vietnam, it was just before Christmas of 1963. I was near the end of my original enlistment in the Army, and although I'd never planned on an Army career, that first experience with Asia and with a real war had hooked me. The thought of going back to college and civilian life seemed pretty bland, so that spring I reenlisted.

Now it was June of '64, and I'd been up in San Fran for a few days visiting an old high school buddy. I'd stopped by to see him on my way to my temporary duty assignment at the Army Language School in Monterey, California. When I'd reenlisted at Fort Bragg, I requested transfer to either the 1st Special Forces (SF) Group on Okinawa or to language school, and when my orders came a few weeks later, I was happy to see that I'd been given both. Before proceeding to Okinawa, the orders read, I was to first attend the three-month Spoken Thai course.

I was driving an Austin Healey 3000, which I'd bought right after I returned from Vietnam. I'd been able to save most of the per diem the Army paid me while I was overseas, and I paid cash for the used Healey. It was the first car I'd ever owned, and I was proud of it even though it wasn't the most comfortable car in the world. On the way across the U.S. from North Carolina to the West Coast, a big semi had blown past me coming from the other direction. We'd both been doing about 100 miles an hour, I guess, and the ragtop on the Healey exploded off like I'd pushed the ejection button or something. It had a couple of rips in it, so I just left it folded after that, rain or shine. Hell, I told myself, if you want to drive a ragtop sports car, you got to learn to suffer a little.

Between Santa Cruz and Watsonville the traffic got heavier, and I had to slow down. I heard a rumble behind me, then a pack of Hell's Angels passed and quickly disappeared in the distance. One guy had on a chrome-plated Nazi helmet. Cool, I thought to myself, maybe I ought to buy a motorcycle and get rid of this stodgy old car.

After I went through the little burg of Marina, the traffic got even worse. The highway took me through the Fort Ord Army base, and rifle ranges lay on either side of the road. My mind had drifted off, wondering what my assignment at language school would be like, and when the machine guns suddenly started firing off to my left, I jerked so violently I almost went off the road. I still had a bad case of nerves from Nam, and unexpected gunshots or explosions tended to send me diving for cover.

It was Saturday, and the pretty seaside town of Monterey was packed with people. There were college kids from nearby schools, soldiers from Ord and the language school, and tourists from all over the country. Ten or twenty years before, Monterey had been a quiet little village dependent on commercial fishing and canning. Then writers like Steinbeck and Kerouac turned the place into a tourist attraction.

I put the Healey into low gear and chugged up the steep hill that led to my new temporary home at the Presidio. I signed in to my student company and lugged my duffel and B-4 bag up the stairs to my room. The barracks at language school were more like college dorms. Each student was assigned a two-man room that included a study table, lamp, and ashtray. I dumped my bags in the corner and noticed that my roommate had already moved his stuff in. He wasn't around, and wondering who I would be living with for the next three months, I went back down to the orderly room and asked for his name. I found out it was another SF guy named Larry Feuge, a man I didn't know.

Classes didn't start until Monday, so I had the weekend to look things over. I left the Healey in the lot and was wandering over to the NCO club when a car with two guys in it cruised by, stopped, and honked. I went over and saw that one of the men was a buddy of mine from the 5th Group named Carl Hargus. Carl introduced me to his companion, a short, heavyset fellow called Gunboat Smith.

Smitty was from the 7th Group and was an old Special Forces hand who had already served in the 10th SFG in Germany and the 1st on Okinawa. He had also attended language school once before, studying some weird European language like Romanian.

Smitty knew all the good drinking places around town, and he and Carl were heading down there to lift a few. I climbed in the backseat and went with them. We went to a place named Angilo's down on the end of Fisherman's Wharf. The bar faced a big glass wall, and as we guzzled a beer and watched the tourists aimlessly wandering up and down the pier, I got to know Gunboat.

Gunboat Smith was about ten years older than I, and several years older than Carl. He was a Korean War veteran who had served there with an armored unit. He'd gotten to that war in one of the early increments that were mauled during the retreat back to the Pusan Perimeter. Smitty was a never-been-married bachelor when I met him and had a reputation as a character. He was a staff sergeant, lived in the barracks, and was the only barracks rat I'd ever heard of who'd been allowed to keep a dog as a pet. It was a big, male Doberman named Fang, or something like that.

Back at Bragg, Fang and Smitty had lived in one of the cadre rooms up on the top floor of the old wooden barracks the 7th Group occupied at that time. Smitty left the animal in the room during the day while he was out training. "Never did have to worry about getting my room inspected while I was out," he told us with a grin. "Had to give old Fang away when I left Bragg, though. Ended up giving him to my company commander."

While we were sitting there, one of the Neuhause twins came in. I didn't know him, but Smitty introduced us. "What language you taking this time, George?" Carl asked him.

The Neuhause brothers were both making a career out of the 10th Group in Germany. They'd been over there twelve or fourteen years already when I met them. The Army had a policy at the time that a soldier could only spend six years in an overseas assignment before taking a permanent change of station back to the U.S. The way the Neuhause boys worked it, every six years they came back to language school for one of the one-year courses, then transfered back to Germany. This time they were taking Czech.

Smitty asked Neuhause how things were at the school.

" 'Bout like always," George said. "More SF guys here now than before, but mostly there's still just intel pukes. Lot of ASA fags."

"Still a lot of suicides?" Smitty asked.

At that time, academically the Army Language School was probably the toughest in the Army. To get assigned there you had to pass the Army Language Aptitude Test, and most people failed it. Then, once there, you were given three-hour homework assignments every night, and if you failed to keep up with the class, you were dropped. The pressure was so great that the school had a higher than normal suicide rate.

That evening when I returned to the barracks, my roommate was back. We introduced ourselves and shook hands. Larry was a young, single guy about my age, a medic. We talked about people we knew and exchanged bits of intel we'd been able to pick up about the school.

I told him that from what I'd heard, the school was supposed to be pretty intellectually challenging. Larry was unconcerned. Later, by accident, I found out that Larry had a General Technical score of 145. The GT is the Army's equivalent of IQ. Larry's score put him up in the genius range.

On Monday we started, and I got to meet the rest of the class. There were only seven of us. Besides Carl, Smitty, Larry, and me, there was another young medic just out of the SF qualification course, a young SF captain named Popham, and an old "leg" (nonairborne, not parachute qualified) infantry major. The only one in our class not headed for the 1st Group in Okinawa was the major, who was preparing for a MAAG (military advisory assistance group) assignment in Thailand, after which he planned to retire.

During the first hour, we were given a briefing and found out how the school operated. There were four Thai instructors, two men and two women, and they would rotate each hour in our class. Nothing but Thai would be spoken in class for the next three months. This was the immersion method, a technique pioneered at the Army Language School. We would be in class eight hours a day, and at the end of each day we'd be given a homework assignment.

The assignment was one or two paragraphs of Thai, written in phonetics, that we were to memorize. At the start of every day, each of us would have to stand in front of the class and recite the memorized material, with the instructor correcting our pronunciation. The rest of the day would be spent learning new material, which would then be incorporated into that evening's homework assignment.

It was expected that each night's homework would take from one to three hours to memorize. We'd have the weekends free, but would be given a longer assignment to memorize on Friday, and be expected to have it ready to recite on Monday morning.

At first the homework assignments weren't too long or too hard to memorize, so Larry and I went to town to rent a TV set for our room, which became a minidayroom for the rest of the enlisted guys in the class. The two officers were both married and lived off post with their families. It immediately became apparent who the good students in the class were.

I bet I *would* have been a serious student if it hadn't been for ol' Smitty. He was just a bad influence, that's all.

"Hey, Gunboat, let's run down to the wharf and get drunk," I'd say.

"Okay," he'd reply, "but give me a couple of hours or so to memorize this shit. I really blew it this morning."

"Oh, come on! We can get up a couple of hours early in the morning and memorize it before class. That waitress with the big tits is working tonight."

"Well . . ."

And away we'd go.

Smitty was from some little town in Tennessee near Memphis. His mother was a schoolteacher, and although Gunboat liked to play the country-bumpkin fool, he was smarter than many people thought. Smitty became one of my early mentors in Special Forces, and he taught me some important things: (1) war was okay, and was something a professional soldier looked forward to, not dreaded; (2) civilians were all assholes; (3) all noncombatants in the Army were assholes too.

The days and weeks went by, and although the homework assignments got longer and longer, somehow all of us managed to keep up with the school pace. Many a morning Gunboat and I and a couple of others would be out in the hall in front of the classroom, sweating and sick with hangovers, trying to memorize assignments we'd be required to recite within minutes.

One morning after one of our escapades, Smitty looked over at me as we sat in the classroom glumly waiting for the teacher to get there.

"Hey, Wade, what we need is a good little firefight to get our blood circulating," he said, trying to smile.

The old major had been watching us with his usual secret amusement. "Oh, I don't know," he said. "I think all it would take to wake me up would be for someone to shoot one little round!"

The uniform at the school was dress greens, but no one wore ribbons in those days unless required. All the old major wore was a CIB with a star on top and a Big Red One combat patch on his right shoulder. He always regarded the rowdy antics of the rest of us paratroopers with a sort of bemused, fatherly interest.

One day we had to have the class picture taken and were told to wear all our awards and decorations. Smitty had several rows of ribbons, a CIB, and Master Jump wings. I had wings, CIB, and two service ribbons. A couple of the guys in class had nothing but wings and maybe a marksmanship badge. The old major's awards and decorations started somewhere up around his left epaulette and ended down around his belt. He had so many clusters in his Purple Heart that you couldn't see the ribbon. The only award he didn't have was the parachute badge.

Smitty was the ranking NCO up on the third floor of the dorm and in charge of things, like making sure it got cleaned and that his young troops got down to morning formation on time. He was the only Special Forces guy on the floor, the rest of the men being Intelligence Corps and ASA. Smitty had been in combat-arms and paratroop units his entire career, and having to deal with the wimpy intel types was a new challenge for him.

One morning he came into class shaking his head. He said he'd asked one of his charges why he hadn't been at morning formation. The kid told Smitty he'd had a big fight with his roommate that morning, had been crying, and didn't want the rest of the men to see him with red, tear-filled eyes.

"So what did you do?" we asked the still fuming Gunboat.

"Well," Smitty said, "I chewed his ass up one side and down the other, and the kid started crying again. 'But Sergeant, you didn't listen to my *plea*,' he told me! Christ, I can't hardly stand this place!"

Somehow, we all managed to graduate, with Larry getting honors for top student. We decided to throw ourselves a big graduation party, which would involve renting a van, nominating Carl to stay sober and drive, and then, beginning at noon Saturday in San Jose, hit every cool drinking establishment down the coast, eventually ending up back at Monterey.

All of us thought this sounded like a good idea except for the old major, who politely said he thought he'd better stay home with his wife. We decided to wear our uniforms for this excursion, figuring to give the civilians a thrill. American soldiers wearing berets were still a novelty back in '64, and we figured we'd be able to attract more chicks.

Everything went off as planned, and we had a good time without getting in any trouble. About midnight we were in a very crowded, fun-filled place in Santa Cruz, and, feeling a little queasy, I wandered out to the boardwalk and walked to the end of a pier.

As I stood there, smoking and watching the dark ocean, I realized I'd been at that same spot once before—when I'd just finished basic training at Fort Ord and was on my first two-day pass. A bunch of us recruits, all about eighteen years old, had taken the bus up to Santa Cruz to find some excitement. It turned out to be a real bust. None of us were old enough to get in the bars, none of the girls would have anything to do with us because of our recruit uniforms and shaved heads, and there was nothing to do except wander up and down the boardwalk and ride the roller coaster.

Back then, right at sunset, I had walked out to the end of that same pier and watched as four kids about my age docked their little sailboat directly beneath me. There'd been two boys and two girls, each of them tan, windblown, laughing and having a great time. I overheard their conversation about the great party they were going to that night and had a fleeting fantasy that they would see me standing there alone, feel sorry for me, and ask me to go with them.

Of course, they went hurrying off to their sun- and fun-filled lives, leaving me to contemplate my own bleak future, getting on the bus the next morning and returning to the dreary barracks, the screaming sergeants, and the sand hills of Fort Ord.

I was jolted out of my memories by the sound of the van horn and someone yelling my name. It was time to head down the coast to the next place. I grinned to myself. Fuck the civilian bastards, I thought, paying final tribute to the kids in the boat and to all California Golden People in general.

Two days later I was on a plane heading for Okinawa and new adventures.

Chapter 2

In the early sixties Okinawa was a great place to be stationed, especially if you were young and single. I know a lot of old-timers will say that it was even better in the late 1950s, but I don't think it was ever any better than the years I was there.

Before WWII, Okinawa had been under the control and domination of the Japanese. The population had led an agrarian lifestyle, and the Japanese had done little to improve their living conditions.

During the American invasion in '45, widespread destruction occurred, pretty much demolishing what urban centers there were. After the war, during the American occupation and reconstruction of Japan, Okinawa had received American aid too. In the 1950s, after the Korean War, the island became more important to American defensive strategy in the Asian theater. Besides an important Air Force presence, the island also became home to a large number of Marines, Navy SeaBees, paratroopers of the Army's 503rd Combat Team, and the 1st Special Forces Group.

Although some agriculture, such as the raising of pineapples and sugarcane, remained important, by the time I got there in 1964 the main industry appeared to be pleasing the American GI. There were bars, restaurants, steam baths, and pawnshops galore—all the necessities for a good time. Hell, I thought I'd died and gone to heaven.

Okinawa was really the best of both worlds for a military man: not very expensive, but not as run-down as a typical Third World country. The American military still ran things then, and the currency was U.S. dollars rather than Japanese yen. A program was in effect to ensure that health and sanitation were not degraded by the many bars and restaurants. American troops were not allowed in establishments not prominently marked with a large "A" sign.

Prostitution was everywhere, of course, but was legalized and under government control. There were cases of venereal disease, mostly gonorrhea, but these were usually brought to the island by men returning from TDY (temporary duty) assignments to other Asian countries. Most barmaids, although not all, would go with a GI after closing hours, and many had long-term, live-in arrangements. There were several villages, such as New Koza, with bar/whorehouse establishments that specialized in "short-times." And, for those in a real hurry, there were places like the infamous Whisper Alley, where for two dollars one could purchase oral sex—or about anything else you had the stomach for.

Our plane from Travis landed at Kadena AFB in the late afternoon, and we were taken by bus to Chibana, which was just outside the gates. As soon as we got signed in, were assigned a bunk for the night, and had changed into civvies, Carl and Gunboat took me into the nearby town of Koza to show me a few of the sights.

We flagged down one of the many *skoshi* cabs that prowled the road right outside the compound and headed to see the bright lights. We went to the area around Gate Two and B.C. streets, the same places I'd visited the year before when I'd stopped through on the way to Vietnam. This time I got to become a lot more familiar with the place, hitting ten or twelve bars that night. I even ran into the little girl I'd gone home with on that previous visit, but she didn't remember me.

We finished off the night with steam baths and massages at one of the better establishments. On Okinawa most of these places were strictly on the up-and-up; that is, although the pretty little attendants would wash and massage you, that's *all* they'd do. The bars closed about midnight on the weekdays, but the restaurants stayed open for several hours after that. The three of us went into one and had some cream of mushroom soup, then headed back to the barracks.

The next day was spent in-processing, and I discovered that the 1st Group was spread out in different parts of the island. The headquarters was at Bishagawa, near Kadena. The line companies were split up, some at Sukiran, some at Machinato, and part of the unit was in Matsuda up at the north part of the island. Signal Company was located at Chibana, where we were temporarily being housed.

It was temporary for everyone but Carl and me, that is. Because we were both radio operators, we would be staying there awhile.

From scuttlebutt, we soon realized that we'd been screwed and that Sig-Co was *not* the place to be. Signal Company was made up mostly of non-SF-qualified personnel. Unlike the line units, most of the troops in Sig-Co were below the rank of sergeant and were young and inexperienced. Because of this, the company was run more like a unit one might find in the 82nd or 101st. Carl and I had been shanghaied into the outfit because they needed Morse code radio operators, of which there was a critical shortage throughout the 1st Group.

"I want to transfer to an A-team," I told the company first sergeant as soon as he finished welcoming Carl and me to the unit.

"You do a good job for us here, keep your nose clean, then maybe I'll see about a transfer in a few months. We've got a one-month TDY mission to Korea in a few weeks, and I need you two for that. Now get the hell out of my office!"

I was obviously not getting off on the right foot.

I fell right into the new routine of life on Okinawa. Compared to stateside duty at a place like Fort Bragg, life for an enlisted man on Okinawa was plush—especially if you were an NCO. Although I hated being assigned to Sig-Co, I really had it made while there and actually lived better than I later did down in the line units.

Because Sig-Co had so few NCOs, E-5s and above were assigned two-man rooms. For a few dollars a month we hired houseboys who not only washed our uniforms but cleaned the rooms and made the beds. Okinawan civilians were also working in the mess hall, and instead of going through a chow line, you just sat down, handed in a slip of paper with your order, and the food was brought to you by one of the cute little *nesans*.

As far as day-to-day work in Special Forces units on Okinawa, you were either preparing for an off-island TDY mission, performing such a mission, or back on-island, in goof-off mode while waiting for the next mission. While in goof-off status, my day went something like this:

Wake up at 0530, dress in exercise clothes, stagger downstairs, and do PT with the unit. After that I'd blow off breakfast, go back to my bunk, and sleep another hour until work call. After work call, several of us would get in someone's car and drive over to the Kadena AFB NCO club, where we would have a leisurely, two-hour breakfast, then hang around the PX until about noon.

At noon I'd make an appearance back at the unit and stand formation at 1300 hours, which was the last one of the day. If no one had anything for me to do, which was the usual case, I'd make up some excuse to leave the company area and again sneak off, maybe to go over to one of the clubs near the line units, where I could always find someone like Gunboat to hang out with. In the afternoon, just before the troops were released for the day, I'd show up back at the company again to let them know I was still alive and not in jail or something.

As soon as we were *officially* off duty, I'd run up to my room, rip off my uniform—leaving it in a pile on the floor for the houseboy to take care of—jump into civvies, and by 1800 hours I'd be down in the ville or over at the Topper NCO club sipping a cold one and bullshitting one of the little barmaids.

Carl and I had a couple of weeks of this before we began our premission training for Korea, then we had more to do. There were only three other Morse code operators in the unit, and one morning we were told to pack up our AN/GRC-109 radios, grab our rucks, and get on a 2½-ton truck for a ride up north.

It was actually a pleasant break. The truck dropped us off in the north training area, we moved off the road a short distance, set up our radios and poncho shelters, and spent a week in the woods practicing communicating back with the base-station guys at Chibana. We had a couple of cases of C-rations, and in typical SF fashion, we soon made contact with one of the Okinawa civilians in the area who, for a small fee, agreed to bring us shipments of ice, beer, and soft drinks each evening.

After we returned from this pleasant camping excursion, we spent another couple of weeks going to classes, filling out paperwork, and pulling maintenance on equipment.

An advanced party went over to Korea with a couple of our truck-mounted 26D radio rigs and established commo back with the island Special Forces Operational Base (SFOB). The advance party had been over there only a couple of days when they realized that some important crypto material had inadvertently been left behind. The crypto stuff had to be hand carried over by courier, and this led to a funny story that's one of my favorites from those days.

The 1st Group had a new commander at that time by the name of Francis J. Kelly. He was one of those very by-the-book type of officers, a strict disciplinarian who didn't appear to have much of a sense of humor. In other words, he was someone you didn't want to mess with.

Also at this time, we had a guy in Sig-Co who was the kind of troop you don't see much of in the new, modern Army. I'll just call him Randy, which isn't his real name. Randy was one of the oldest guys in the company, in his early thirties, I guess, and had been in the Army about fourteen years.

In an earlier part of his career, Randy had served with the Army

Security Agency and gone all the way up in rank, even enjoying a brief stint as a warrant officer. Then something went wrong, Randy started to drink . . . well, you know the rest of *that* story. By the time I knew him, Randy had worked his way down to Spec Four, was trying for private, and had a sake habit of one "typhoon-fifth" a day.

Sig-Co was shorthanded, and Randy not only had nothing to do, but also had managed to hang on to the top secret, crypto security clearance that was needed for courier duty. Well, they put Randy in his dress uniform, furnished him with a civilian airplane ticket, warned him on threat of death not to screw up, and with an attaché case handcuffed to his wrist, launched him in the direction of Korea.

He made it as far as Tokyo International, where he had a four-hour layover waiting for the plane to Seoul. There was a bar in the airport, and along with the drinks he'd downed on the short flight from Okinawa, Randy was soon feeling good. By some horrible quirk of fate, Colonel Kelly and several members of his staff were heading back to Okie after a quick inspection of the operation in Korea, and they had also stopped in the airport.

Randy, staggering past the coffee shop, happened to spy the commander sitting there. Delighted at seeing a fellow SF troop, he went in, walked up behind Kelly, and just as the colonel was raising his coffee cup to his lips, slapped him on the back. "Hey, Colonel, how ya doing? My name's Randy, one of your men from Signal Company!"

The members of the staff were horrified, and speechless. Kelly, slowly wiping the coffee from his face, turned to look at Randy. The colonel couldn't miss the fact that Randy was indeed in his unit, because he was wearing a beret, rather casually pushed to the back of his head.

Before Kelly could say anything, Randy threw his arm around the commander's shoulders and, breathing his alcoholic breath into Kelly's face, began to tell him some things that had been on his mind. "You know, Colonel, I hate to tell you this, but ever since you took over this outfit, things have gone to shit. Now, the way I see it, here's what you need to do to make this into a good group, the way it *used* to be. . . ." And Randy commenced to tell him.

The colonel relieved Randy of his courier duty and of his classified material, and ordered two members of his staff to arrest Randy and escort him back to Okinawa.

"Hell," Randy told me later, "I was only trying to help the guy out!"

Carl and I flew over to Kimpo air base outside of Seoul with the main element. We were trucked to the Korean SF headquarters area, which was a few kilometers south, and I got my first look at their troops. I was favorably impressed.

During the Korean War, the South Korean Army had turned in a lackluster performance, but in the years since the armistice, they'd transformed themselves into one of the best-trained, best-equipped, and most feared military organizations in Asia. Their SF were the cream of the Korean Army and had all the attributes of special operations units the world over: they were smart, tough, and self-confident to the point of arrogance.

Most of the training would be taking place farther south, and after Carl and I filled out another round of paperwork, we got on a C-123 and flew down to Taegu. One of our C-teams had an FOB (forward operations base) established in the local American compound, and we were assigned a bunk and told who to report to. Much to our delight, we discovered that there was actually nothing for us to do yet, and so for several days we explored the town and got acquainted with the NCO club.

It was a nice club, and our guys from Group had pretty much taken it over. Every afternoon, a military bus picked up any of the local females who wanted to come in and delivered them to the club. For the privilege of getting on post, the girls had to have their VD cards checked regularly, and they agreed to certain price controls for their services. At that time prices were actually still very cheap for everything in Korea, although us big-spending TDY Special Forces guys were doing our best to cause a bad case of inflation.

After a week of partying, I was glad when we were finally given our assignments and put to work. I was to be part of an umpire team, which consisted of an American captain from one of the infantry units up on the DMZ, a Korean Special Forces lieutenant, and a Korean corporal who was our driver. We would have a jeep with an AN/GRC-87 radio mounted in the back, and we would be attached and moving with a battalion of Korean infantry. My only real job was to make one Morse code radio contact each evening to tell everyone we were still okay.

This turned out to be one of those "good deals" that you sometimes stumbled into in Special Forces. What it amounted to for me was a three-week auto tour of the lovely coastal area around Pusan and Taegu. Since I was traveling with the two officers, I was afforded the same treatment they received, and since we were traveling with the Korean unit, the treatment we received was fit for a crown prince.

The weather was perfect. It was November, and the air was brisk and clear but not really cold. The battalion we were with moved every two or three days. We followed at our leisure in the jeep. By the time we arrived at the battalion bivouac, the Korean unit had already set up our tent, installed electric lights, unfolded our cots, and had the stove going. It took me fifteen minutes to string an antenna and make my radio contact, then I was off work for the day. Both of the officers I was with were good guys. They didn't have any real work to do either, and we all realized that we had it dicked.

The battalion only fought one mock battle, which occurred on the last night of the training exercise. We called it a draw between the regulars and the guerrillas, loaded our jeep the next morning, and headed back to Taegu. By the time we got there, most of the 1st Group had already packed up and returned to Okinawa. There were several trucks that had to be turned in at the depot back up in Seoul, however, and they were asking for volunteers to be part of the rear party and take care of it. Because this would give me a good chance to see Seoul, I volunteered.

It turned out to be a smart move. There were about ten men in the rear party, four or five of us young guys, the others unmarried, Old Asia Hands who knew all the ropes and were in no big hurry to get back to the island. There were no officers in our group, and the ranking man was a master sergeant from one of the line companies.

We made it to Seoul in one day, although back then the roads weren't all that great. The next morning we took the trucks to a place one of our NCOs knew about, where, for a half case of leftover C-rations, we had them steam-cleaned. By noon everything was turned back in to the depot, and we had nothing left to do for the next four days but the usual. We leaped into civvies and headed for town. . . .

Chapter 3

"We want to transfer to a line company so we can go back to Vietnam," Carl and I said in chorus. It was the day after we got back from Korea, and we were standing at parade rest in front of the first sergeant's desk.

One of the main reasons Carl and I had transferred to the 1st Group was because they were pulling most of the TDY missions to Vietnam. We'd just heard that our old group, the 5th, was being sent over there on a permanent basis. But we were trapped in Sig-Co on Okinawa.

"Sorry, I need you here," the first sergeant told us.

"You said you'd let us go after Korea," I told him.

"That's not what I said, and you damn well know it!" he replied. I could tell he was aggravated, because he'd started to scream. The company clerk peeked nervously around the edge of the door to see what was going on.

"Look, you two," Top said, fighting to regain his composure, "didn't you guys both just get out of Thai language training?"

We told him that was correct.

"Well, our annual exercise in Thailand is coming up in a few weeks. It lasts three months. Do that one for me, *then* I really will let you transfer. Now get the hell out of my sight!"

We found out that the exercise in Thailand, "Kitti-08," didn't start for two whole months, so we went back to goof-off mode. My Healey had arrived by boat while I was in Korea, and I decided to have some restoration work done on it. I had it painted bright red, got new black leather upholstery, with a black top and tonneau cover to match, all for about two hundred dollars. There was a British Motors dealership on the island whose mechanics had been trained in England, so I had some mechanical work done too. I quickly found out that the little red car was a big hit with girls down on B.C. Street.

Shortly after we got back from Korea, I received my first introduction to the drop zone on Okinawa, Yomitan DZ. I'd been hearing horror stories about it ever since I became a jumper, and now I got a chance to see it up close and personal. Yomitan was on an old runway, so a good deal of it was covered with broken, cracked cement. On either side of the cement lay fist-size rocks and pineapple fields. One side of the DZ was bordered by high-voltage power lines. Along the western end ran the main highway, and just beyond that was the ocean.

Colonel Kelly, the 1st Group's new commander, had broken his leg on one of his first jumps on Yomitan, and from then on elected to make only water jumps into the warm China Sea, which immediately earned him the nickname of "Splash" Kelly, which stuck for the rest of his career.

Except for a few bruises, I never got hurt jumping on Yomitan DZ. But I never got to where I really enjoyed jumping on it either.

I celebrated Christmas of '64 at the Topper NCO club, and saw in the New Year of 1965 down on B.C. Street. A wild time it was too. The streets and bars were jammed with revelers from all the services. I'd begun my own celebrating early in the evening, and as midnight approached, things became kind of blurry.

I remember walking into one of the bars just in time to catch the end of the stripper's routine. Only it wasn't the regular, professional dancer, but the seventeen-year-old daughter of some Air Force officer from Kadena. Everyone was yelling, laughing, and egging her on. Hell, she did a better job than the real stripper.

Yep, it was quite a night.

All the NCO clubs had slot machines, and I'd quickly developed a mild addiction to playing them. I wasn't as obsessed with the damned things as some of the guys, but I lost a lot of money. They don't call them "one-armed bandits" for nothing, you know. One afternoon I played a four-wheel dime machine for five hours straight, finally giving up in exhaustion. As soon as I sat down, another sergeant started playing the machine, and on his third dime, he hit four stars. After that I was so disgusted that I almost quit playing the stupid machines completely . . . almost.

My bacchanalian lifestyle on Okinawa was costing me a lot of money—more than I earned. I was an E5, drawing overseas pay and jump pay, but we still only got paid once a month in those days, and by the third week after payday, I'd be broke.

Luckily, many Okinawan entrepreneurs had anticipated this predicament, and the pawnshops did a thriving business. I only had two material possessions at that time: a Rolex watch and my Austin Healey. The first thing to go in hock each month would be the Rolex, which I pawned for twenty dollars.

If that didn't turn out to be enough, I would hock my car for two hundred dollars. All you had to do was give the shop your pink slip . . . you were allowed to keep and drive the car. At the first of each month, I had to pay off these debts or risk losing the items, so I was always behind economically. It took several TDY trips, which paid good per diem, to get me caught up.

Okinawa is really quite beautiful, with many uncrowded, unpolluted beaches and picnic areas. Often I'd take one of the barmaids with me and drive up the coast for a day of swimming, eating, and drinking on Moon Beach. In the evening, with the top down on the Healey and the balmy breezes blowing through our hair, we'd drive back down the winding coastal road, singing along with the music from the radio. I'd take her to her home, or to an Okinawa hotel, and we would spend a night surrounded by paper walls, discarded kimonos, futons, the sounds of tinkling wind chimes, and the fragrances of chrysanthemum and sandalwood.

The premission training for Kitti-08 finally started, giving Carl, me, and the three or four other Morse code operators something to do: classroom work, code-speed practice, and equipment maintenance.

One morning at oh-dark-thirty we climbed on C-130s, and late that afternoon we landed at an airfield on the outskirts of Lopburi, Thailand.

We were met by one or two American officers who had gone over on the advanced party. Soon several buses and trucks driven by Thais arrived, and after making sure our equipment was on the trucks, we loaded the buses and I got my first taste of Thai roadmanship and driving customs.

It was very exciting.

In the first place, the Thais drove on the left side of the road, British style. The roads were narrow, crowded with bicycles, mopeds, motorcycles, pedestrians, cars, trucks, buses, dogs, chickens, and small children. There didn't appear to be any speed limit, nor any other traffic laws as far as I could determine. Our driver sped along with great élan, honking his horn, bluffing his way through intersections, and running slower-moving vehicles off the road when necessary to pass. All this time he was looking back over his shoulder to talk to us in broken English, waving his arms, laughing, and yelling out the window at other motorists.

The Thai Army Special Forces were stationed at Camp Pawai, which was only a few kilometers outside of Lopburi. Miraculously, we arrived still in one piece, unloaded our equipment, and were assigned our billets, which were in one of the Thai barracks. We set up folding cots, laid our poncho liners on them, hung mosquito nets, and we were in business.

Compared to bivouacking in the field, these accommodations were pretty swank. The latrine was in a building out back and consisted of Oriental, squat-type crappers and a urinal. The shower facilities were in a separate building a little farther away. There was no hot water, but the climate was so mild it didn't matter.

We had our initial briefing that evening. Carl and I discovered that we would again have nothing to do for several weeks, until the first A-teams were infiltrated. Our job would be to communicate with the committed teams, transmitting and receiving on the powerful base station rigs. Until the teams jumped in, it was another case of "stay out of sight, check in now and then, and don't get in trouble."

We didn't need a lot of prompting. A bunch of us immediately caught a so-called *baht* bus right outside the front gate of the camp and headed for Lopburi.

Besides being an Army town, Lopburi is on the major north-south highway and train route. The town had once been a walled city, and portions of the old wall still remain, making it a minor tourist attraction and point of interest for foreign and domestic travelers. Because of this, there were many clubs, bars, restaurants, and houses of ill repute.

In other words, I had discovered another little bit of paradise.

In that winter of '65, there were still few Americans stationed in Thailand. Most of the ones there on permanent duty status were in engineer units working up in the north, or Air Force guys down around Bangkok. Although U.S. Special Forces had been training the Thai special units since the 1950s, we were still a novelty around Lopburi and had not yet worn out our welcome in the country; the Thais still liked us.

The Thais are a handsome people. They are of medium height; the men strong and well muscled, with no excess body fat, the women world-renowned for their beauty. The Thais are extremely polite, easygoing, and smile a lot, but both the men and the women are capable of dishing out some major ass-kicking if provoked.

Carl and I had an edge, of course, because we spoke the language pretty well. We weren't completely fluent by any means, but we spoke better Thai than ninety-nine percent of the other Americans in the country. We weren't proficient enough, say, to give a formal presentation at a state dinner, but with the taxi drivers, waitresses, bartenders, pimps, whores, gangsters, thugs, and soldiers we normally dealt with, we did quite well.

On that first visit to Lopburi, Carl and I were with a small group of Thai Special Forces NCOs who were acting as our guides and hosts. "First we show you Weeng-ping," one of the Thai sergeants told us with a leer and a wink.

The portion of the old wall that formed the gate to the city is still standing. A little road went directly from the center of Lopburi down to the wall and through the entrance. Immediately to one side of the gate, nestled up against the old wall, stood the famous Weeng-ping bar and short-time house.

The "house" itself was a wooden two story, and held about twenty separate rooms. The patrons sat at tables outdoors in the well-maintained courtyard and were waited on by the "hostesses," who brought beer, mixed drinks, or food. Colored electric lights were strung overhead, music played over speakers, and it was really very pleasant to sit there in the scented, tropical air while you made up your mind about which girl you liked.

Lopburi also had several conventional nightclubs that offered dancing. Or you could sit at one of the many sidewalk cafés as you ate, drank, and watched the flow and ebb of people on the street. Everything was still dirt cheap in Thailand then. If you ate at one of the places down by the train station or in the market, you could get a huge meal for ten *baht*, which equaled fifty cents.

The 1st Group's headquarters element, which had accompanied us as part of the advance party, seemed to have more than its share of young, naive, inexperienced troops. They provided Carl and me with much amusement.

One morning at roll call it was discovered that one of the young clerks was missing. The last time anyone had seen him was the night before, when he was reported to have been having a good old time of it down by the train station.

The local cops were alerted, and combined Thai-American Special Forces search teams were rushed out to look for him. About 1100 hours the missing man appeared on his own at the front gate. He was completely naked, covered with bug bites and scratches, and was trying to cover himself with a ratty piece of blanket he'd found somewhere.

He said the last thing he remembered was leaving the nightclub in the back of a *samlor* to go to some "special party" a Thai man and woman had enticed him to. He'd regained consciousness that morning on a canal bank, naked, sick, and lost, but he'd finally made his way by foot back to camp.

On another occasion I was on the upstairs balcony of the barracks, which happened to overlook the building where our cooks had set up shop. Suddenly I heard a yell and one of the cooks came running out, the back of his T-shirt on fire. Other cooks just stood frozen in shocked amazement as the kid ran straight to a nearby open well and, without the slightest hesitation, dove headfirst in it. There was a drop of about ten feet to the water.

A couple of the dazed witnesses finally got up enough nerve to go peer over the edge of the well to see if he was alive. About this time the burned cook began hollering—between gurgling sounds—for someone to save him, as he couldn't swim. One of the other cooks eventually got a rope down to the kid and he was rescued. I watched as they dragged him over the rim of the hole, and he looked so bedraggled and pitiful that everyone, including me, started laughing so hard that no one even bothered to ask the young man if he was okay.

I mentioned earlier that the latrine we were using was the same one the Thais used. The urinal was on one end, then a narrow passage ran down the center, with four partitioned but doorless stalls on either side. The "commodes" themselves were simply holes in the floor with obvious areas on either side of the openings where you could put your feet while you squatted, trying to get most of your load through the six-inch hole.

The Thais were in charge of maintaining all such facilities at Pawai, and frankly, they didn't do such a hot job of it. The latrine stank and was full of buzzing flies; the floor area around each squat-crapper was always stained and splattered with urine and fecal matter where people had missed.

One day I went in for my morning constitutional and happened to glance in one of the stalls as I passed. There was a young Spec Four finance clerk in there from the headquarters, trying to take a shit. He wasn't squatting over the hole in the obvious fashion, but *sitting* on it, his legs sticking out in front of him. In that position, he didn't fit very well in the stall. "They just don't make these things big enough for us long-legged Americans," he told me with a sheepish grin.

I never did bother to straighten him out, and wondered if that's how he used the latrine for the entire three months we were in the country.

After we'd been there a few weeks, I was given a four-day pass to go into Bangkok. I'd never been there before but had heard stories about it for years. As it turned out, none of my regular running mates, like Carl, was able to go, so I was with a group of headquarters men I didn't know very well.

We took the train for the trip to Bangkok, the trip being an experience in itself. Once in the city, I realized I was with a group of nerds. They all wanted to sightsee, take pictures, and go to such tourist attractions as the Floating Market and the Snake Farm, or to take a tour of the Buddhist temples.

We split up, and I started wandering around Bangkok by myself, looking for some action. In the early evening of my first day in town, I went in the first likely place I came to, a large nightclub with music and dancing. It was not a GI hangout, and I was the only other American in there. The Thais didn't mind my presence at all, and in fact were very happy to see me.

I homed in on a table of Thai females, assumed they were "working girls," and began dancing with one of them and buying her drinks. Her English was as limited as my Thai, but we were able to communicate pretty well. She told me her name was Naam. I fed her the usual lie, saying that I'd been recently assigned in Thailand. I said I was with a road construction battalion stationed at Lopburi. Naam told me she was a college student, a story I assumed was as phony as the one I'd told her.

We left that place after a while and went to some other joints she knew. About midnight I took her back to the hotel with me. When we took our clothes off and got in bed, she acted real shy, but I figured she was just new in the profession.

She asked me for no money that night, nor the next morning, but that was normal for Thai prostitutes. It was considered impolite to pump a customer for money, and payment was rendered when the man decided he was finished with the woman.

She still seemed to be acting a little out of character, however. Usually one of these bar girls would want to stay right with you during the day—probably so you wouldn't disappear and not pay her—but Naam told me she had to go to attend classes. She said she'd meet me back at the hotel coffee shop that afternoon, which is what happened. This routine continued for the next couple of days. Naam would leave in the morning, meet me again in the evening, and the two of us would then go have dinner, take in a movie, go to a nightclub, and spend the night at my hotel.

On the evening of the third day, Naam said she wanted to take me to dinner and introduce me to her family. I'd been through a similar scene with a girl I'd met in Vietnam, so I wasn't too surprised, although it still seemed very odd behavior for a prostitute. We went to a large Thai restaurant, and her people were all there: four older brothers, Mom, Dad, and Grandma.

We had a great evening, with many rounds of drinks, and a meal consisting of about twenty courses. The family all thought it was very nice that I could speak a little of their language. The four brothers, all big, strong bruisers who looked like they lifted weights, were especially interested in talking to me and telling me how much they cared for and protected their baby sister.

My last day in town rolled around, and that afternoon Naam came to the hotel room to say good-bye. She was acting weirder than usual, was all teary-eyed and sad to see me go. I gave her a little opal ring I'd purchased on drunken impulse the day before, and tried to give her money, but she vehemently refused it. I decided that Naam was a girl who definitely didn't have much future in her chosen profession and that she should find a new line of work.

She gave me her mailing address there in Bangkok and asked for mine. I went ahead and gave it to her: Sgt. Leigh F. Wade, RA 19-702-465, Camp Pawai, Lopburi, Thailand. She told me she would write to me and asked me to write to her. I said I would, and also told her more lies, saying I'd be back to see her in a month or so and that I was being transferred to Bangkok permanently in the near future.

Honestly, it wasn't until I got back to Pawai, sobered up, and got to thinking about it a little, that I began to realize that she probably really was just a college student. Then her letters began arriving, and I knew for sure.

Naam's English wasn't good enough to write the letters herself, so she had gone to a professional English-language letter writer to have them done. Her letters were poignant but unintentionally amusing.

"Dear Sergeant Wade," they would start off. Then followed the body of the letter, which was filled with ornate Victorian romantic language and phrases that had probably been copied out of books. Every letter ended the same way: "So I'll close for now, my love, but my heart will never close for you, Sergeant Leigh F. Wade, RA 19-702-465."

I didn't get another chance to visit Bangkok again during that training exercise, but Naam's letters continued until I returned to Okinawa.

To give us Morse operators something to do and to get us away from the area, we were assigned to check out the communications in the various AOs that the A-detachments would be working from. Each American operator was assigned to a team of three Thai commo sergeants, and with our AN/GRC-109s in our ruck-sacks, sent on our way.

No transportation was allotted us, and how we got to our assigned locations—all of which were some distance from Lop-buri—was left up to the individual teams. Some took the train, some caught hops on military aircraft, and some, like my bunch, elected to go by commercial bus.

Our AO was at Aranyaprathet, on the Thai-Cambodian border. In later years this area was to gain some notoriety as the site of one of the major holding camps for Cambodian refugees fleeing the slaughter of the Khmer Rouge, but that winter of '65 it was still an unknown, quiet town. Our trip took all day and was not very pleasant. The bus was hot and overcrowded, and the seats were narrow.

On arrival, we checked in at the local Thai Army base and were assigned very nice quarters. We had a three-bedroom bungalow all to ourselves, a unit that I later found out was usually reserved for visiting senior Thai officers. The three Thais set up their radio in one corner of the bungalow, while I set up in another. We strung some antennas and had no trouble establishing contact back to Pawai. We only had two scheduled contacts a day—one in the morning and one in the evening—so we had plenty of free time.

One of the Thai sergeants in our group was originally from that area, and he took the rest of us around to different homes, introducing us to his old friends. Each visit called for a mini-celebration and party that involved much Singha beer, and Mekong whiskey. My hosts all thought it was wonderful that I liked their local beverages so much, especially the Mekong, which most Americans didn't care for. Little did they know that in those days I'd drink whatever had an alcohol content, even kerosene.

The commo experiment lasted a week and was successful. By the end of this "field trip," I was getting a little bit worn around the edges from all the parties and socializing, though, and was glad to hear when we got back to Pawai that the A-detachments would arrive the next day and that it was almost time to go to work.

As I recall, we were committing six U.S. teams during that exercise. A couple of the detachments were combined Thai/American SF, a couple of the teams were all U.S., and the Thais were sending in a few all-Thai detachments. Some British SAS guys had also come up from down around Malaysia somewhere and were accompanying some of our units.

The U.S. teams flew in from Okinawa, had only a couple of days of free time, then went immediately into isolation. This is standard procedure for special operations units, and had been developed back in the old OSS days of WWII.

A team is chosen for a mission, is alerted to be ready, and then is locked up in an isolation area. Once the team goes into isolation, its members have no further contact with the outside world until the mission is completed and the team has been debriefed.

This is all done for reasons of security, of course. During the isolation phase, which can last anywhere from a couple of days to a couple of months, depending on how complicated the mission is, the team receives its classified mission, makes its plans, receives any specialized training or equipment, then presents its plan at a brief-back. If the commander and his staff accept the team's plan, the team prepares for immediate infiltration.

Although all Special Forces personnel are parachute qualified, they are also trained in, and utilize, all the other means of infiltrating a "denied" (enemy controlled) area. They can go in by boat, scuba, helicopter, civilian transportation, or simply walk. The most common infiltration method in '65 was still parachute, although helicopters were being used more and more, especially in Vietnam.

We established our radio shack for the base station in a room just off our sleeping quarters. Three of the big receivers from the 26D rigs were set up on a long table, along with three telegrapher keys. The transmitters were some distance away to eliminate interference, and were connected to the telegrapher keys by cable.

Each of the A-teams was only required to make one scheduled contact a day. We also monitored a "guard" frequency twenty-four hours, which could be used in case of actual emergency. Once a day we transmitted a blind, timed broadcast (BTB) that the teams would monitor to receive any info or new orders from headquarters. We established our shifts so that we had two operators on duty during the scheduled contacts with the teams, but otherwise we only kept one man on duty to monitor the guard frequency.

Things ran pretty smoothly, because the ranking commo sergeant over the entire operation was an old hand from the line unit and he let us run things the way we wanted. Carl was the ranking operator and set up the shifts so we had plenty of time off. The only fly in the ointment was the so-called signal officer.

The signal officer was one of those non-SF-qualified lieutenants who not only knew nothing about Special Forces operations, but nothing about communications. I think he was Quartermaster Corps or something like that. He'd been given the job as signal officer because no one else wanted to do it, and because the headquarters didn't know what else to do with him.

Instead of doing the smart thing and just staying out of the way to let things run, he thought he should, by God, *take command*. The guy constantly hung around the radio room, making comments, trying to act like he knew what he was doing, and generally making a pest out of himself.

I was a good Morse operator by that time, having worked the net in Vietnam on an A-team for six months, and was proud of it. To work the base station end of a radio net with deployed A-teams, you really needed to have previous experience working at the A-team level. Unless you had experienced what it was like trying to send a message in the field, huddled under a poncho, flashlight held in your teeth, and the guy cranking your generator grunting and whispering for you to hurry, you just wouldn't have the empathy required to do a good job.

One day I was on duty, receiving a very difficult message from one of the teams. The signal was weak and there was lots of interference. I prided myself on being able to get a team's message on the first try, with no requests for repeats. I had the earphones on so I could hear better, and it was taking all the concentration I had. Behind me all this time, pacing the floor, trying to give me advice on how to tune the receiver better, and asking, "What're they saying, what're they saying?" was the lieutenant.

As soon as I heard the team's final "out," I jumped up, ripped the earphones off my head, and handed them to the signal officer. "Here, sir, finish taking this message for me. I've got a case of the shits!" And I ran out of the room, leaving him standing there with a "Now what do I do?" look on his face.

After that, he stayed away and left us alone most of the time.

The A-teams were in the field for a couple of weeks, then were pulled out, and my work was basically done for that exercise. We started breaking down all the equipment while the teams were still getting their debriefings, and by the time they were released, we were ready to return to Okie.

We made a few jumps with the Thais, exchanged parachute wings with them, had one final drunken going-away party, then headed for home. I really enjoyed those three months in Thailand, and although I didn't know it then, in a couple of years I'd be back for a much longer stay.

PART II

Back to the War

And the measure of our torment is the measure of our youth.
God help us, for we knew the worst too young!
— RUDYARD KIPLING

Chapter 4

By the time we got back from Kitti-08, Carl and I had finished half of our eighteen-month tour of duty on Okinawa and it was time to put in our requests for our next assignments. It looked like we were going to be stuck in Sig-Co forever, so instead of requesting to stay with the 1st Group for another tour, as we'd originally planned, Carl and I put in our papers for transfer back to the 5th Group in Vietnam. Because of the chronic, critical shortage of radio operators there, we were told that we had a hundred percent chance of this request being approved.

We didn't even bother trying to bug the first sergeant anymore about transferring to an A-team, but simply lapsed into goof-off mode while awaiting the next development. It was a short wait.

"Hey, you two!" the company runner yelled at us. Carl and I were sneaking back toward the barracks, having just returned from a four-hour breakfast at the NCO club. "I've been looking all over for you. Where have you been?"

"It's Monday morning, isn't it?" Carl asked the PFC runner.

"Yeah, so?" said the runner.

"Well, we've been conducting Monday morning activities, of course," Carl told him. "What the hell do you want us for?"

"The first sergeant says for you to report to his office ASAP. He's got some sort of secret mission for you!"

We wasted no time getting over there.

"Are you two still wanting to go back to Nam?" he asked us without prelude as soon as we walked into his office.

"Sure thing, Top," we told him, suddenly interested.

"Good. You need to report over to the headquarters at Bish' at 1300 hours for a briefing by the group commander. Don't ask me what it is, because I don't know—it's highly classified. Hopefully you'll be gone a long time. Now go away."

As Carl has often reminded me, we were given this particular assignment as the result of something that had occurred two days before, during the Saturday morning inspection-in-ranks. Sig-Co was the only unit in the 1st Group that ever put its troops through these chickenshit, in-ranks inspections, and that was one of the reasons most of the men hated it there.

To prepare ourselves for the inspection, Carl and I had spent that Friday night down on B.C. Street drinking 151-proof rum chased with beer. We got back to the barracks on Saturday morning in just enough time to change into class A uniform and fall out on the parade ground. The sun was beating down, and we were a couple of sick dudes by the time the first sergeant started his inspection.

Carl was standing next to me in the back rank, and I could tell by his pale, sweaty skin that he was in even worse shape than I. The moment Top stopped in front of him to check his uniform, Carl puked all over the first sergeant's mirror-shined jump boots. Just to make matters even worse, I'd cracked up laughing.

So I guess we really shouldn't have been expecting the first sergeant to send us on one of those good deals the 1st Group was famous for. Still, it wasn't anything like we thought it might be.

When we got to the headquarters for our briefing, Carl and I discovered we were part of a group of sixteen other NCOs. There was a mixture of job specialties represented, but the majority were weapons men and medics. We all milled around outside, talking excitedly, trying to figure out what was going on.

The group sergeant major came out, told us to put out our smokes and file into the briefing room. As soon as we found seats, someone yelled, "Attention!" and Colonel Kelly strode to the podium.

"I want you to know that you men have all been handpicked for this mission," Kelly began, looking out at us with an almost fatherly expression. "You were selected because of your fine records, and because each of you here has prior experience in Vietnam."

"BOHICA* . . ." someone in the audience whispered loudly.

"As I'm sure you are all aware," the commander continued, pretending he hadn't heard, "the 503rd—now known as the 173rd—was shipped to Vietnam last week."

The colonel was interrupted by wild applause, cheers, catcalls,

*"Bend over, here it comes again!"

and laughter. After the sergeant major yelled, "At ease, goddamn it!" several times, Colonel Kelly was able to continue.

"The 173rd had very little prior warning before being shipped over, and as a consequence, they did not have time to fill several critical slots on their T.O. and E. The 173rd has asked us, their brother airborne unit, to help them out in their time of need. . . ." There was a low murmuring that sounded a lot like a growl coming from the audience now, as we all started figuring out what the score was.

"Now let me finish, men," the colonel continued hurriedly. "You will only be temporarily *attached* to the 173rd, and the assignment will be for no longer than ninety days—"

"Will we be drawing per diem?" one of our NCOs asked.

"Uh, I don't believe you will, because you will be well taken care of by the 173rd," the colonel said. There were more ugly rumblings from the group.

"I know this is asking a lot from you men," Kelly told us, "and this is strictly a volunteer assignment. I'm going to give you a short break so you will have a little time to think it over. I promise that if anyone decides he does not want to accept this challenging assignment, it will not affect his future career one bit."

The colonel left the room so we could talk it over in private. "Yeah," one of the sergeants behind me whispered, voice dripping with sarcasm, "if it won't affect our careers, what's the sergeant major doing back there with that pen and clipboard?"

In the end, perhaps needless to say, we all volunteered.

We landed on the large, recently improved runway at Bien Hoa, climbed out of the C-130, and stood blinking in the bright sunlight. The scene around us was one of pandemonium, reminding me of newsreels I'd seen of the Allied beachhead at Normandy. Trucks, armored personnel carriers, self-propelled artillery, jeeps, and an occasional Vietnamese on a motor scooter swarmed around like ants. There was even a large contingent of Australian troops moving in, their odd-looking equipment, uniforms, and vehicles causing them to stand out from the Americans.

A master sergeant from the 173rd had suddenly appeared out of the mad confusion and begun welcoming us to the unit. "All right, all you snake eaters, the 173rd commander orders that there won't be any damned berets in his unit, so ditch 'em and put on soft caps.

Also, while you're with us, you've got to wear our patch, so rip those goddamned SF patches off right now!"

" 'The 173rd will take *good* care of you,' " one of our guys said, doing a pretty good imitation of Colonel Kelly.

We had no problem with not wearing berets, because we never really wore them much in Vietnam anyway. The wool hats just weren't very practical or comfortable in the tropical heat. The patches were another matter, however. There was quite a lot of expense and hassle involved in removing the SF patches, sewing on theirs, only to reverse the process again in a few months when we went back to Okinawa. In the end the 173rd relented and compromised by only making us remove our patches but not requiring that we wear theirs.

The 173rd was one of the Army's best units, and the group of guys who originally deployed from Okinawa to Vietnam were especially well qualified and adapted for the task. They were a well-trained paratroop unit and most of their men were professional soldiers. Many of their members had served with the unit for years and could be considered Old Asia Hands. Although the 173rd had no prior experience in Vietnam, it had been deploying and training all over the rest of Southeast Asia for years. They were used to the Asian climate, the terrain, and the people.

Having said all of that, I've got to tell you that the 173rd's first few months in Vietnam appeared to Carl and me to be one huge gaggle-fuck.

The unit was bivouacked in a rubber plantation up on a low rise of ground just on the edge of the Bien Hoa airfield. The main group had been there about a week when our bunch from the 1st SF got there, and they'd dug some foxholes on the perimeter of the rubber trees. They'd cleared a nice field of fire out about fifty meters to a tree line where the vegetation got a lot thicker. The field kitchen, medical, and headquarters tents were all set up and operating, and on the perimeter they were attempting to build some better bunkers with overhead cover.

There had been no real enemy activity except for occasional harassment by snipers. The main problem was that it was raining a lot, and all the dug-in emplacements were beginning to fill up with water. There was a lot of mud. The food was lousy. There was no ice, no soft drinks, and no beer.

When we did our minimal in-processing, Carl and I once again found out we had no jobs. The rest of our crew from the 1st Group slid immediately into slots. It was no problem, for example, to find a position for a Special Forces light weapons NCO in an airborne infantry outfit. The 173rd was also eager to get our medics, who were the best trained in the Army. But when it came to assigning Carl and me, it was a different matter.

"You say you got the MOS of 05B4S?" their personnel sergeant said, scratching his head. "What the hell is an 05B4S?"

We told him it was a Special Forces, Morse-code-trained radio operator.

"I guess I could send you over to the signal platoon at headquarters company. They got some radio operators, but the job only calls for a rank of PFC. What they do is carry the PRC-10s on operations and kind of act as butt-boys for the officers. You guys know how to operate a PRC-10?"

We told him we thought we could probably figure them out.

The personnel sergeant gave us the name of the signal officer we were to report to, a Captain Goodwin, and sent us on our way.

"Why am I feeling more and more like we got the shaft?" I asked Carl as we picked our way through the mud, water puddles, and stacks of sodden equipment. There had just been a sudden downpour, and water was still dripping off the rubber tree leaves.

Captain Goodwin seemed like a nice guy, but he was overwhelmed with all the problems involved with getting the newly arrived unit up and operating. He was surprised to see us, told us he did not have any open commo slots at all and had not requested any radio operators from the 1st Special Forces or anywhere else. "I especially don't know why they'd send me a couple of NCOs," he told us.

The captain turned us over to a staff sergeant who took us out to the portion of the perimeter that Sig-Plat was responsible for. "You can set your tent back here in the trees, then at night you'll be responsible for manning that bunker up there on the line." He pointed to a partially completed emplacement that was half filled with water. "Your bunker looks like it needs some work, but you got nothing else to do around here anyway," he told us with a shrug. "See you guys later; let me know if I can help you find your way around."

"Set up our tent?" Carl asked me. "What fucking tent?" Although each man in a regular infantry unit was issued a shelter-half, in Special Forces we were issued two ponchos instead. Carl and I dropped our rucks, pulled out our four ponchos, and soon had a very spacious, dry place to live. Our poncho hooch soon became the envy of the regular infantrymen around us.

We didn't need the staff sergeant to help us find our way around either. Civilization was only a kilometer away down at the bottom of the hill. Not only was there the town of Bien Hoa itself, but also a large Air Force base, several MACV units, and the 5th Special Forces B-team.

The 173rd kept tight rein on its men, and only occasionally allowed one or two officers or senior NCOs to leave the bivouac area for visits to the air base. Otherwise, the 173rd's leaders knew that their entire unit would be down there screwing off. It took Carl and me about an hour to figure a way to beat the system. We checked in with Captain Goodwin, fed him some flimsy excuse as to why we needed authority to sign out a jeep and go into town, and were on our way. As soon as we left the 173rd area, we replaced our patrol caps with our berets.

Wearing our berets gave us the best of both worlds. To any patrolling NCOs or officers from the 173rd who were looking to catch AWOL screw-offs from their unit, we appeared to be members of the local Special Forces B-team. If by some odd chance someone from the B-detachment should ask us what we were doing, we could tell them we were attached to the 173rd!

After a few hours spent reconnoitering the area, we'd discovered all the PXs, open mess halls, restaurants, clubs, and bars within ten kilometers of the 173rd's bivouac.

Carl and I fell into a daily routine that wasn't too different from the one we had on Okinawa. Because we were up half of every night on perimeter watch, we'd sleep through breakfast. It was a pain in the ass to have to stand in the long mess line, only to be served cold, reconstituted eggs or greasy SOS. About 0900 we would go over and sign out Captain Goodwin's jeep, then drive down to the Bien Hoa Air Force base and have a decent meal at the NCO open mess.

We'd spend the rest of the morning hanging around the air base or over at the Special Forces club, then eat lunch in the B-team's mess hall. Around 1400 hours we'd go back to the 173rd area and spend most of the afternoon either working on our bunker, reading skin magazines, or sleeping. For supper we'd eat snack food we'd purchased down at the PX that day—something like crackers, Slim Jims, and a candy bar.

At night Carl and I took turns standing guard duty in our bunker on the perimeter. We rotated pulling either the 1900 hours–to-midnight or midnight-to-dawn watches. There was really not much enemy threat right there at Bien Hoa, but we did have occasional probes and harassment attacks. Because the 173rd was new to combat in Vietnam, they were trigger-happy as hell, and this added greatly to the excitement.

Almost every night there would be shooting on the perimeter, and most of the rounds were fired at imaginary targets. One night a trip flare went off, probably activated by some small animal, and one of the guys down the line from me threw a grenade. It was dark, and the grenade hit a small tree just in front of him, bounced back, and detonated about five meters from our own perimeter.

This brought about the usual wild fusillade of shooting, then the dreaded cry for a medic was passed along. Two men from headquarters had been wounded by frag from the grenade. The officers eventually got the shooting stopped and the wounded evacuated back to the field hospital. It was quiet again after that, and I heard this conversation from some men in positions next to me:

"Hey, who chucked that fucking 'nade?" one of them asked. There was a little pause before anyone answered.

"Victor Charlie chucked that 'nade," another soldier finally ventured. This answer amused me because the closest place a VC could have thrown from was the tree line fifty meters away.

After thinking things over for a while, the other voice said in a kind of awed wonder, "Man, Charlie sure can chuck 'nades!"

One morning one of the night ambush patrols had just returned and was standing in the chow line for breakfast. For some stupid reason, it had been ordered that 173rd medics could only carry pistols or twelve-gauge riot guns while on operations. This was because medics were supposedly noncombatants, and the 173rd thought this meant they could only be armed for self-defense, not offense. The medic who had accompanied this newly returned patrol was not familiar with the shotgun, and he was attempting to clear the weapon by jacking the rounds through the chamber. It went off, killing the man in front of him and wounding several more men standing in line.

Another morning, at about 0800, there was a huge explosion down on the air base. The blast was so powerful it shook the ground clear up where we were and created a mushroom cloud. Sirens went off, people started yelling, and up at the 173rd we all ran like hell for our alert positions. I actually wondered for a minute if a tactical nuke had been deployed.

After about ten minutes we were told to relax, that it had not been an enemy attack, only an accidental explosion. Of course, Carl and I immediately got the jeep and ran down there to check out the carnage. There was a lot of it to see.

Apparently one of the fighter-bombers with a full load of ordnance had somehow exploded while it was being prepared for a mission. Luckily for all concerned, only five or six people had been killed by the monster blast, but many more had been wounded by flying debris. One poor airman had been killed while lying on his bunk. A big piece of an engine had blown a hundred feet in the air, then come crashing through the tin roof of the barracks and landed right on top of the guy.

The rumor was that the man should not have been in his bunk at that time of the morning but had been sleeping late because of a hangover. "Aw, the wages of sin . . ." I said.

Captain Goodwin knew that Carl and I were spending a lot of time screwing off, of course, and we soon found out that he had an ulterior motive for letting us get away with going to town every day. One morning, after the captain had gotten caught up on his work a little, he told us we could use the jeep as usual, but that we had to take him with us.

Carl and I had no problem with this, as having an officer along gave us even better cover. We showed Goodwin all the good places we'd discovered, and after that the captain accompanied us on our excursions several times a week. The men in the unit got so used to seeing the captain with us that they soon began to refer to Carl and me as his bodyguards.

One day Carl and I were walking past a group of the young 173rd paratroopers as they sat sharpening their already razor-honed bayonets. One tough little Chicano Spec Four grinned at us and said, "Hey, man, who you two protecting Captain Goodwin from, the VC or *us*?"

I thought that was a good question.

By the time Carl and I had been living in the rubber plantation for about a month, we'd finally turned our bunker into a good fighting position. We managed to get the drainage working so it wasn't full of water and had constructed some solid overhead cover. We continued to pull our night duty on the line, and occasionally we accompanied the night ambush patrols.

* * *

The patrol leader was a sergeant first class. "We got ten men, including you two," he told Carl and me. "I'll give the operations order right after noon chow over at my hooch. I'll do an inspection at 1900 hours, just before dark, and we'll be going out the wire an hour later."

The sergeant seemed to hesitate a moment. "I suppose you two been on one of these night ambushes before, right?"

We said we had.

"This is my first real one," he told us. "You two are the only ones going who have prior combat experience. If you see me or anyone else doing anything that might fuck us up, let me know, okay?"

We assured him we would do that, and the patrol leader went off to notify the rest of his crew.

"Ten men seems a little too large a bunch, don't you think?" Carl asked me as soon as the NCO was out of earshot.

"I suppose it's really too big to do a lot of sneaking around, but on the other hand, we should have enough firepower to blast our way out of anything we run into," I said.

"I'm actually kind of looking forward to it," Carl said. "It will be a hell of a lot different than going out with our Vietnamese irregulars at an A-team camp. Shit, we won't even need an interpreter!"

"And the troops can all shoot," I added.

"Plus, we know they won't shoot at *us*!" Carl said.

When we gathered for the reading of the operations order, Carl and I got to meet the rest of the ambush patrol members. There was one staff sergeant, and the rest of the men were Sp.4s and PFCs. One of them was the bloodthirsty Chicano who had asked us who we were guarding Goodwin from.

To me and Carl, who were used to the hodgepodge of weapons and equipment carried by our CIDG troops, it seemed like our patrol was armed to the teeth. We had one M-60 machine gun, a man with an M-79 grenade launcher, two guys who were each lugging claymore mines, and another man who was bringing the trip flares. The rest of us, except for the medic, were carrying M-16s, several frag grenades, and extra ammo.

The SFC (E7) patrol leader was wearing a Ranger tab, and did a professional, thorough job of presenting the patrol order. It was a simple operation and a simple plan. We would leave our lines just after it got dark, move to a large trail that was about one kilometer from the battalion bivouac, set up our ambush, and wait for someone to stumble into it. We would be operating in a tactical free-fire zone, and anyone moving on the trails at night was considered to be Cong.

"We'll set up the ambush using the standard L formation," the patrol leader told us. "There's a slight bend in the trail, and that's where we'll put the M-60. That way the MG can fire down the long axis of the kill zone."

The patrol leader planned to initiate the ambush by firing one of the claymores, then the rest of us would blast 'em with what we had. Carl and I were given the specific job of searching any enemy bodies, and we were reminded to bring our flashlights for that purpose.

Whether or not we made contact, we would remain at the location until first light, then return to camp. Trying to come back in through our lines while it was still dark was dangerous, and we would only attempt it if we had to evac someone who was seriously wounded.

When he was finished, he asked if anyone had any questions.

"Have you checked out that radio?" I asked the young PFC who would be carrying the PRC-10.

He said he planned to do it that afternoon, and Carl advised him to also carry a spare battery and handset.

Carl and I had each brought a pair of tiger-stripe camouflage fatigues with us, but after discussing it with the patrol leader, we decided against wearing them. Everyone else would be wearing the standard OD jungle fatigues, and someone might mistake us for an enemy once we left the friendly lines.

At the prescribed time, the patrol members again gathered and the patrol leader quickly inspected everyone, looking for loose, noisy equipment, things that would reflect light, and so forth. We all had our shit in order, and he didn't find much wrong. When he was done, a captain came over, checked us again, and asked if there were any last-minute questions. We were good to go, and as darkness fell, we passed through our perimeter wire and faded into the nearby tree line.

Besides his aid bag, our combat medic was carrying only a .45 pistol. I'd noted the fact that the guy with the M-79 grenade launcher also had an M-16 slung across his back. As soon as we got into the trees and out of sight of camp, the medic took the extra M-16.

We didn't have any trouble getting to the ambush site. The patrol leader had walked the route during the day to recon it. The 173rd guys all moved in a professional manner, and it felt reassuring to be with other, well-trained Americans—even if they didn't have any combat experience yet—rather than with the Vietnamese irregulars I was used to.

Once at the ambush site, we got in position with a minimum amount of confusion. Carl and I were in the middle of the formation, which was strung out about ten meters off the trail. The M-60 was up to our right, along with the patrol leader, radio man, and medic. I could feel the tension in the air, and hoped that no one accidentally fired off a round to give things away. Figuring we had a long wait ahead of us, I tried to settle in and get comfortable.

I'd sat through several ambushes without ever making contact, and I wasn't expecting much to happen this night either. The moon was practically full, so there was quite a lot of light. About midnight I was almost asleep when I thought I saw something moving up the trail toward us. At first I thought it was my imagination, but then I felt Carl tense up on one side of me and heard the guy on the other side suddenly catch his breath.

I could hardly believe it. We were only one klick from this huge American paratroop unit, and here came three stupid bastards ditty-bopping right down the middle of the trail. Each was wearing some sort of odd-looking helmet and carrying a weapon. There was about ten feet between them, and by the time the last guy got in our kill zone, the first one was almost on top of the claymore when the patrol leader touched it off.

Blammo! The mine blasted the poor guy back about five feet, and he dropped in a heap. The machine gun ripped at least half a belt down the trail, and the rest of us let loose with our M-16s. Talk about three hunks of Swiss cheese! One of the Cong fell over on the opposite side of the trail where we had a trip-flare wire and set it off. We were too close for our man with the M-79 to shoot, so he lobbed one down the trail in the direction the enemy had come from just in case there were more we hadn't seen.

Each of the three enemy soldiers had probably been shot twenty or thirty times by the time the firing stopped. One of the dead men gave a final, spasmodic twitch of the legs, and our Chicano buddy put another half magazine into him.

Then Carl and I got to go out and root around in all the blood and gore. The trip flare was still burning, casting weird shadows as some of the smoke from it drifted across the trail. We discovered no secret documents telling of planned operations or anything like that. In fact, other than a few personal photos and a small amount of piasters, the dead men carried nothing of interest.

All three were dressed in standard black VC uniform, but each carried an AK-47 assault rifle, and this caused us to think they had probably been NVA. We took their weapons, helmets, and blood-soaked web gear back with us the next morning as trophies. I wouldn't be surprised if it all isn't hanging in someone's den right now.

No one in the 173rd hassled us, and we pretty much did anything we felt like, but it was still a miserable existence living in the mud and all of that.

One day Carl and I were sitting around the club at the Special Forces B-team down in Bien Hoa, and Carl got to talking with the signal officer. The officer was complaining about how shorthanded they were, and how their B-detachment Morse code operators were having to pull twelve-hour shifts. Carl told him that he and I were experienced radio operators and were sitting up on the hill attached to the 173rd with nothing much to do.

One thing led to another, and we worked out a deal between the B-detachment and Captain Goodwin. Carl and I would pull radio shifts for the B-team, and in return we would be allowed to move to their relatively luxurious quarters at the Train Compound. Captain Goodwin had no problem with this. But he told us that the 173rd had several larger-scale, battalion-size combat operations coming up soon, and that he wanted us to go on them with him. This sounded fine to Carl and me, as we were both anxious to see what a big operation would be like with an American unit anyway. In the meantime we would be out of the mud and doing something more useful with our time.

Compared to the conditions up at the rubber plantation, the living situation down at the B-team was very nice. We had folding cots to sleep on, a real shower with hot water, a good mess hall, and a club to drink in. Also, we were with our own people again and didn't feel like such outsiders.

I got my first look at the new radio Special Forces had recently started using at both the A-team and base station level. It was a civilian ham radio made by Collins and was quite an improvement over the old AN/GRC-109s. The Collins was a single side-band rig, operated on voice or Morse mode, and pushed a respectable 100 watts of power. A linear amplifier was available that added another 500 watts. The radio was a little tricky to tune, and as I would later find out, it really wasn't very well suited for the rough treatment it received down on the A-teams, but overall it was a great success.

With the addition of Carl and me to their roster, the B-team radio operators were able to return to pulling shifts of eight hours on and sixteen off. About every ten days or so we got a free day. The B-team was supporting six or seven A-teams, and several of them were in very hot areas, so there was usually a daily or, more often, a nightly crisis to deal with.

Although the big U.S. buildup of combat units had begun that winter, originally these units were not allowed to conduct offensive operations. For the first few months the combat units were in Vietnam, their mission was to guard certain populated areas like Bien Hoa. It was not until June 8 that President Johnson authorized the use of U.S. troops in direct combat.

In the meantime, Special Forces had expanded its role, and had its ass hung out at more precariously defended A-team camps than ever. This was a transitional phase for Special Forces. Although we had started developing our own mobile reaction units—called Mike Forces—they weren't operational yet either. During those weeks of June and July that Carl and I worked for the B-team, the A-detachment camps still had to depend solely on the ARVN if they needed reinforcements.

Chapter 5

Carl and I accompanied the first couple of large offensive operations the 173rd conducted in Vietnam. Going into combat with this American outfit was a big thrill for me, and was something I had only fantasized about two years before, down in Camp Tan Phu in the Delta. It was a hell of a lot different operating with a group of professional, highly trained, heavily armed U.S. paratroopers than it was fighting with our own ragtag CIDG (Civilian Irregular Defense Group) troops. Hell, everyone spoke English, for one thing, and I didn't have to worry that half the unit were secretly VC. But probably the most comforting thing was knowing that when the shit hit the fan, the Americans wouldn't all run off and leave my ass in a sling the way our own irregulars often did.

The unit had been equipped with the M-16 rifle just prior to being sent to Vietnam, and the 173rd was the first major ground combat unit to carry the weapon there. Along with the new M-60 machine guns and the M-79 grenade launchers, the lightweight M-16s with full-auto capability gave the paratroopers tremendous firepower.

The 173rd also had its own field artillery, air-transportable 105 howitzers, plus an integral aviation unit with its UH-1B slicks and armed gunships.

The new tactical voice radio known as the PRC-25 was coming on line, but the 173rd originally rotated from Okinawa with the old PRC-10s. The 173rd wasn't having any more luck with the PRC-10s than Special Forces had, so at first their commo was piss poor. To make up for this lack of radio communications, they were still attempting to utilize landline telephones while in the defense. Because of the terrain and the very fluid nature of combat in Vietnam, wire was impractical and was eventually used only in permanent or semipermanent fortifications.

* * *

We had only been working at the B-team for a couple of weeks when Captain Goodwin drove down in the jeep and told Carl and me to get ready for the coming operation. When we got back up to the rubber plantation, everyone was excitedly running around, trying to recover their lost or loaned-out equipment, screaming "Airborne!" and "All the way!" in response to every order, and in general preparing for war.

This was a battalion operation, and we'd be going farther from the base camp than we'd ever gone. The president had only authorized Americans to perform these large offensive operations several days before, but the unit had been planning for such an eventuality since it arrived.

We would move by motor convoy the next morning to our staging area, which was up on the edge of War Zone D. From the staging area we were to sweep up into the AO, check out some suspected enemy concentrations, then loop back toward the south again and eventually come out on the road where we'd be picked up and trucked back to camp. The operation would last five days and nights if we encountered no real resistance. If we got into a fight, of course, we planned to slug it out for as long as it took to demolish the enemy. No one, including Carl and me, even considered the possibility that the other side might win such a confrontation.

We had the same attitude a big, strong but slow guy has when he's fighting a fast, tricky little opponent. If we could just get our hands on those slippery little bastards, we muttered to ourselves, we'd really teach 'em to mess with us!

The oddest thing about the operation, as far as Carl and I were concerned, was that neither of us had any real responsibility. This was a big change from the situation we faced when fighting with the CIDG. Down on the A-teams, we'd found ourselves involved with every phase of the operations, from the planning to the after-action reports. We asked the captain several times if there was something he wanted us to do, but he told us just to stick near him and his command group.

The convoy movement to the staging area had tons of security. There were numerous "bird-dog" aircraft in the air, several armed helicopters scouted the route ahead of us, and we passed a number of armored vehicles parked at strategic locations along the way. We weren't taking any chances with ambushes.

When we got to the staging area, we discovered that it had

already been secured. Evidently, a pathfinder unit had been inserted by chopper the evening before to ensure there'd be no nasty surprises awaiting those of us in the main unit when we got there.

So far, so good. Everything was going according to the book—the *American* book—and I was becoming more and more at ease.

Because of the limited assets of the ARVN, and particularly of our CIDG, those of us in Special Forces had always been forced to cut corners and take many chances with all our combat operations. Had this been an ARVN movement, for example, we'd have all piled on a few broken-down, overcrowded trucks and driven like hell to the dismount point, getting lost and stopping with mechanical problems several times on the way. There would have been no aircraft of any kind overhead, no security along the route, and no security party to meet us once we arrived. Once at the staging area, we most likely would have bivouacked for the night while the Vietnamese leaders argued over what to do next. This would have given the Cong plenty of time to get ready for us, and upon finally leaving the area the next morning, we'd probably have run into an ambush.

Compared to one of those abortions, this first large combat operation of the 173rd was running like clockwork. Not that there weren't a *few* foul-ups and moments of screaming and mass confusion, of course. But these things happen in even the best of units.

Members of the intelligence and recon (I&R) platoon, along with the pathfinder unit, were already pushing into the jungle-covered hills by the time the main body had dismounted the trucks and formed up. There would be no hesitation getting the operation under way, I was glad to see. Carl and I fell in behind the captain and we began slogging our way into the tough terrain.

Other than the standard web gear and a light combat pack, I wasn't carrying much, but my steel helmet was starting to irritate me. I'd never had to wear a helmet while on an operation with our CIDG, and the unaccustomed weight of the thing was already causing my neck muscles to tire.

The troops were psyched up before, but as yet no shots had been fired, and they began to relax. I knew exactly what they were thinking and pretty soon I began to hear a few of them vocalizing it.

"What a bunch of crap!" someone muttered.

"I thought we were gonna kick some butt," someone else said. "Shit, this is just like it was in Thailand a couple of years ago."

"It's the same old shit, just another fucking phony war," the first guy said.

About an hour later, around noon, the platoon in front of us came under fire. I didn't think the enemy unit was very large, probably no more than ten or twelve men. I could tell most of the fire was outgoing, but if you didn't know what was happening, it sounded a lot worse than it was.

We were only about fifty meters from where all the shooting was taking place, but in the thick jungle terrain we couldn't see what was happening. We were close enough so that a lot of the rounds sprayed by both sides were coming our way and popping overhead. Occasional bits of foliage and tree bark were shot loose and came fluttering down. Something blew up pretty damned close to us, sending hunks of frag whizzing by with that horrible buzz-saw sound. I actually suspected it was one of our own M-79 rounds, or maybe a hand grenade, but it was hard to tell; it could have been an enemy rocket-propelled grenade, or worse yet, the beginning of a mortar attack.

It's a weird situation being shot at like that in dense jungle. On the one hand, you want to get as low as possible and really hug the damn ground—especially when the indirect fire (mortars or artillery) starts coming in. Unfortunately, if you're in the full prone position, you can't see any damn thing, and if the enemy rushes, he'll be right on top of you before you can react.

All the NCOs were yelling to their men, trying to get reports from them about casualties, enemy situation, and all of that. Everyone with any kind of radio was frantically talking at once, jamming the frequencies, feverishly trying to find out what the hell was going on. I was in a low crouch behind a big tree, trying to peek around it now and then to identify a target. I glanced behind me and saw one of the guys who'd been bellyaching about not having enough combat action. I was perversely satisfied to see that his white face held a look of mild terror.

Although anytime someone is shooting at you, you could call it a serious situation, I knew that this wasn't a really *critical* one. I was used to being in this sort of position while with only a couple of platoons of CIDG—a situation that really *could* get critical in a hurry. But in this case I was smack in the middle of an American paratroop battalion, and as far as I could determine, we were being attacked only by a squad.

Unfortunately, the thing I was dreading happened at about that time. One of our M-60 machine gun crews started blasting off rounds blindly through the jungle, and their fire was in the general direction of our own troops to our front. Thinking they were under attack from the flank, these guys naturally began shooting back at us, and now there was really some shit flying!

By then I'd assumed the *full* prone position behind my tree. . . .

A couple of NCOs finally got the internal firefight stopped, and I don't think anyone got hit by friendly fire. The whole action was over in about five minutes. I'm sure the enemy had probably departed the scene after the first few shots, but they managed to inflict some casualties. Word drifted back to us that one of our guys—whose name I didn't know—was KIA, and a couple of others were wounded. Progress of the operation halted for about an hour while the dead and wounded were carried to the nearest open area that could be utilized as an LZ. Dustoff dropped in, picked up the load, and zoomed off.

I wandered back to where the two macho guys who'd been bitching about the lack of action now sat smoking cigarettes. They had quickly recovered not only their composure, but also their tough-guy attitudes.

"I just wish the assholes would have tried to hit us instead of first platoon," one of them said.

"They'd have been in for a real surprise if they had," the second one answered.

We gobbled down some C-rats while we had the chance and refilled our canteens. While the medevac was going on, we'd also taken the opportunity to pick up a few five-gallon cans of water. Sufficient drinking water was always a problem.

Around 1300 hours we got under way again, everyone now feeling like hardened combat veterans. We were moving at a slow, careful pace, not pushing it too hard. This first operation was as much to acclimatize and toughen up the unit as it was for anything else. Most of the men had gotten out of shape while lying around the rubber plantation for two months.

We stopped several more times while other elements, both in front of and behind us, got in firefights with small enemy units. War Zone D was always a good place to find some enemy, and in that summer of '65, large NVA units had already moved into the area.

I checked my compass now and then, trying to keep track of our location. The captain had the only map, so I could only figure out our general position. I was used to knowing at all times where we were and where we were heading, and I felt very uncomfortable being out of the know. I was also used to having full access to the radio, and it was hard for me not to run over, grab the handset, and take over when the captain or some other officer was talking on it and not communicating as efficiently as I knew it could be done.

In a way, having no responsibility other than that of an ordinary rifleman was easy. On the other hand, I was used to having some say-so in things and liked to know what the hell was going on. I suppose my anxiety was similar to what a guy who's used to doing all the driving experiences when he lets his wife or girl-friend take the wheel of his new car for the first time.

The type of terrain we were moving through was as new to me as it was to everyone else. My previous experience had been down in the Mekong Delta, which was flat and consisted of mostly open rice paddy. The stuff we were in now was double- and triple-canopy rain forest with only an occasional cleared area. There weren't many flat areas either, and it seemed that we were constantly either climbing up muddy, slippery slopes or sliding and falling down the other side. It was hotter than hell, of course, humid too, and not a breath of breeze made it to us through the tangled undergrowth.

I could tell that commo with either our other elements on the ground or with the rear area was not good. Evidently, the radio net back with the main headquarters at Bien Hoa was being conducted through the FAC that constantly flew overhead. We had an Air Force forward ground control NCO with us who was also in constant radio contact, using his small VHF radio, and it appeared to me that this had become our main means of communicating with the rear. Several times during the operation we heard that the 173rd commander himself was in one of the aircraft overhead, personally overseeing things.

We moved until dusk, then went into a 360-degree, battalion defensive position on the tops of several low hills. Each company had its own hill, and each hill was connected with landline commo. We were close enough so we could also depend on the PRC-10 radios for backup.

Someone gave the order to dig in, and we all reluctantly began hacking away at the rocky, root-filled ground. It soon became apparent we weren't getting anywhere, and that to dig good, chest-deep holes would take all night. We ended up scratching out some shallow prone positions, and hoped we wouldn't get mortared.

Carl and I didn't have any men to oversee, but out of habit we wandered around with the captain and the platoon sergeant, checking out the perimeter. Everything looked pretty good. The M-60s were positioned in good locations that covered the obvious approach routes, and the gun crews had even attempted to drive in aiming stakes. Some trip flares had been put out about thirty meters in front of the position, and these were covered by both the MGs and claymores. After some discussion it was decided that establishing a forward listening post was not practical. We didn't want to worry about friendlies out in front of the lines.

No one was very interested in eating, but Carl and I tried to whip up something with the C-rats that was halfway appetizing. The more of the stuff we ate, the less our packs would weigh. We used the smokeless heat tablets to warm up a mixture consisting of one can of beans and franks and one can of beef and potatoes, all liberally doused with Tabasco sauce. We managed to gag down a few bites each, then threw it all away.

The night was fairly uneventful. The unit was keeping a 25 percent alert, and a roster was established so that everyone pulled an hour or so of guard while the rest tried to sleep. Carl and I had been forgotten in the confusion, and somehow no one remembered to put us on the roster. We still didn't get a whole lot of sleep, of course, and around midnight a flare went off over on one of the other hills, setting off one of those shoot-'em-ups—all outgoing fire—that I'd grown accustomed to while down at Tan Phu in 1963.

During the next couple of days, we pushed deeper up into War Zone D, but made no other enemy contact at all. I suppose the earlier probing attacks and small ambushes had been just to feel us out and discover what kind of firepower we had. Our troops started getting bored and sloppy again, figuring we had won the war, I guess. Then, on the fourth day of the operation, after we'd made our loop and started back to the south, heading for home, we ran into our heaviest opposition.

Evidently, the I&R platoon, which had been acting as a forward scouting element, ran into an enemy unit of unknown size and was pinned down. The rifle company directly behind had maneuvered up to aid the I&R platoon and had themselves come under heavy fire from another, larger enemy unit that was on some higher ground to their right flank. The rest of us in the trailing companies came under simultaneous probing attacks on both flanks.

When this battle first kicked off, it seemed a repeat of the types of actions we'd had the first day. No one, including me, was very concerned. We could hear the firefight between the I&R platoon and the enemy, and as we lay in our hastily taken defensive perimeter, waiting for it to be over, guys were almost in a festive mood.

"Kill the fuckers!" one guy said.

"Blast 'em, and let's get on with it, I want a hot shower!" said another.

In a few minutes, however, we heard the battle increase in intensity, and soon began taking fire ourselves. The mood changed dramatically. For the first time on the operation I became really worried, and got that knot in my stomach I usually had while in combat with our Vietnamese irregulars. The situation, I knew, could quickly deteriorate into something pretty bad.

I heard someone nearby yelling for a medic and realized our platoon had taken its first casualty. Wanting to know what kind of crap we'd gotten into, I crawled into the center of our perimeter, where the captain, sitting behind the trunk of a large fallen tree, was talking on the radio. Carl was already there, along with a couple of lieutenants and senior NCOs who were waiting for orders.

When he got off the radio, the captain gave a quick briefing on the situation. At that time, all he knew was that the lead elements of the battalion were in heavy contact and that all the other companies were under the same sporadic fire we were taking. We had helicopter gunships and Air Force fighter-bombers on the way, he told us, and we should be prepared for a possible heavy assault ourselves.

Carl and I crawled back to the perimeter and took up firing positions on either side of a tree.

The other men in the platoon had also realized the gravity of the situation we were in and now had grim, resigned looks on their faces. A fog of acrid gun smoke hung close to the ground in the still, humid air. Some heavy shooting broke out to the right of where Carl and I lay, and this time much of it was incoming. I heard the thunk of our M-79 blooper, followed immediately by the sharp crack of the 40mm round. Whatever the target, it hadn't been far away. There were curses and another cry for a medic.

An enemy RPD (Russian light machine gun) ripped off a burst

of ten in our direction, immediately followed by several short bursts of AK fire. It all went over our heads but was close enough to make Carl and me roll completely back behind the tree trunk. Behind the tree we were safe from direct fire but also blind. What if they charged? It takes a lot of guts to stick your head out from behind cover when someone is shooting at you.

There was a pause in the enemy fire, and I moved back to a firing position. I couldn't see deeper than ten feet through the tangle of leaves and branches, and although many of the other men on each side of me were blazing away, I saw nothing to shoot at. I'd originally learned to shoot as a civilian youth and had done a lot of hunting. Due both to the fact that ammunition was expensive, and for reasons of safety, it had been drilled into me from an early age that you shouldn't shoot unless you could identify your target.

I finally decided what the hell, and holding my M-16 as low to the ground as the twenty-round magazine would allow, I popped off eighteen rounds of semiautomatic, spacing the shots in an arch to my front. I detected no response from the enemy, and so didn't know if I'd done any good or not, but as I changed magazines, I felt a lot better anyway.

I realized I had been aware of the *whop-whop* of Huey rotors overhead for some time, and now began hearing the explosions of rockets and the rattle of their 7.62 machine guns. Occasionally I caught a glimpse of one through the triple canopy as it flew low above us. Then the sound of the choppers faded, to be replaced with the whistling, roaring sound of F-100s as they rolled in, dropping napalm and strafing with their 20mm cannon.

The arrival of the aircraft improved everyone's mood immediately. We were no longer taking fire ourselves, and most of the other small arms fire we were still hearing up and down the column was obviously friendly. The ground shook as one of the jets began dropping 750-pound bombs. The men around me started to grin again. This battle was obviously over, and we'd won.

It took several hours to sort everything out and make sure that the enemy had indeed retreated. There were numerous friendly dead and wounded who needed to be evacuated. Most of our casualties were from the lead company and the I&R platoon. We searched the abandoned enemy positions and recovered a few weapons, some equipment, and several badly mangled and burned bodies that had been killed during the air strikes.

We formed our night bivouac earlier than usual, not too far from the battle site. Word passed around that from intelligence recovered on the battlefield, the enemy unit we'd fought was indeed North Vietnamese Army regulars, not Viet Cong.

The next day we walked back to the highway with no further incidents, got on the waiting trucks, and with much joking, singing, and laughter, returned to the relative security of Bien Hoa.

After that first big operation, Carl and I talked with one of the Sig-Plat NCOs who claimed to be Morse code–qualified. We went to Captain Goodwin and told him that if we could find some local unit to loan us an AN/GRC-109 or even one of the older AN/GRC-87s, we could use the equipment to establish a direct communications link from these operations to the base headquarters at Bien Hoa. This would give the commanders another means of communicating with the rear other than having to depend on an air-to-ground relay. Goodwin gave the idea his blessing, and Carl and I began looking for someone to loan us a radio.

The B-team down in Bien Hoa didn't have any 109s to spare, but we found a brand-new AN/GRC-87 at the local MACV adviser's outfit. "Sure, take it," the major in charge told us. "Keep the damned thing if you want, we have no one that even knows how to use it."

When Captain Goodwin came by the B-team to take us back up the hill for the next operation, he was pretty excited. This one was going to be the biggest operation the 173rd had yet run and would involve two infantry battalions, elements of the airborne artillery battalion, and all the choppers of their 335th Aviation Company.

Our battalion, 2/503rd, and the other battalion—I believe it was 3/503rd—were to be airlifted by chopper to LZs some distance north of Bien Hoa, up in War Zone D. Several batteries of 105s would also be brought in by chopper to act as direct fire support. We were making a combat air assault, and our battalion was the lead element. Headquarters Company, of which Sig-Plat was a part, would be on the second lift.

By sunrise of the following day the entire battalion was down at the runway. The UH-1B assault choppers were lined up on either side of the tarmac. It was the most helicopters I'd yet seen in one bunch before, and was really impressive. We broke down into chalks and lifts and stood or sat on the dew-covered grass at the edge of the runway as we waited to get under way.

Other than a mass parachute combat assault, there is probably nothing in the world as electrifying as a large-scale air assault by chopper. I've talked to other vets, who agree that the closest a movie has come to depicting the experience is the scene in *Apocalypse Now* where they go in to the strains of "The Ride of the Valkyries."

As far as I know, this operation Carl and I went on with the 173rd was the first large-scale air assault performed by a regular American combat unit in Vietnam. Although the 173rd had plenty of experience with parachutes, until then most of their members had little or no experience with helicopters. For many of those guys, this air assault was their first ever ride in a chopper!

The duty of spearheading our battalion's assault was given to one of the rifle companies. The battalion commander and part of his staff had elected to go in with it. These were the guys who would get shot to pieces if it turned out to be a hot LZ. The rest of us watched them loading up, and there was so much adrenaline in the air that it seemed a spark would have set off an explosion.

Each lift consisted of about twenty Huey "slicks" and was accompanied by five or six armed choppers. All those engines and rotors made a lot of noise in the previously quiet morning, and the downwash from the props plastered our uniforms against us as we stood, waving and yelling encouragement to the lead group. The first lift took off in formation, rose to altitude, and headed north across the river to War Zone D.

The battalion XO (executive officer) was the commander of our lift. He'd gone out to the chopper to see off the battalion commander, and now came hurriedly walking back toward us, checking his watch. "We load in four minutes," I heard him yell to the headquarters commander. "Get 'em saddled up!"

Carl and I were going in on separate birds, each of us having been given the honor of being the first one out the door when we got there. I got in the UH-1B, looked around to make sure the other men on my stick were there, shook my head yes to the crew chief, and we took off.

It wasn't a real long flight, and seemed even shorter than it was. We were airborne and on the way to the objective when the spearhead element hit the LZ, and I remember checking my watch and seeing that they should be on the ground already.

Although the battalion XO was in direct contact with the battalion commander's lead element, the rest of us had no way of knowing if they'd run into a shitstorm or not, nor did we know what kind of reception to expect ourselves. I saw the choppers from the first lift flying past us, going back to pick up the next load of troops, and I tried to count them. Were there a few missing?

I had no time to think much about it because the door gunners on our UH-1B started checking their M-60 machine guns, and I knew we were almost there. I tried to crane my neck and see around the pilot to look through the windshield. We were dropping toward the ground quickly and I didn't have much time to see anything . . . smoke rising from the edge of the tree line, one of the armed choppers firing rockets, a UH-1B sitting on the ground, several groups of men running, others huddled behind cover. . . .

The door gunner on my side suddenly opened up at something. Then the chopper flared out five feet above the grassy earth, and before I knew it I was already on the ground, running in a crouch to get clear of the rest of the men jumping out right behind me.

The UH-1Bs all flew away as quickly as they'd flown in, and I noticed the sudden stillness around me. It was very similar to the quiet you notice right after your chute opens. I could hear some shooting over on the edge of the LZ, the yells of NCOs trying to round up their troops, and even the buzzing of insects in the grass.

There was the occasional nasty crack of incoming small arms fire, but nothing really too bad . . . nothing like an LZ surrounded by dug-in machine guns and bombarded with mortar fire, which is what I'd been dreading.

I checked my compass and led my group of seven men off the LZ toward the rally point. I spotted Carl and Captain Goodwin already moving in the same direction and followed along behind them. The LZ was covered with waist-high elephant grass, and it was not easy going, especially with the eighty-pound ruck I was carrying.

The rest of the troops were carrying only the usual load of ammo, water, and light combat field packs. On this operation, Carl and I were carrying our Special Forces rucksacks because they were the only thing big enough to hold the damn AN/GRC-87 and its components. Besides the receiver/transmitter itself, we also had to carry the hand-crank generator, antenna wire, odds and ends of connector cables, and a couple of dry cell batteries. That crap is heavy, Jack!

I caught up with Carl and the captain at the rally point, which was near one corner of the LZ in a small gully. A temporary command center had already been established. A field switchboard was in operation and several men were trying to communicate on PRC-10s. Another man was using one of the new PRC-25s and seemed to be having much more luck. The battalion commander and his staff were off to one side, huddled around a map.

I found out that the lead element had encountered only light resistance on the initial assault. The enemy force, which was estimated to have been not larger than platoon size, had quickly been overwhelmed. We'd taken a few casualties, but everything was going smoothly so far, and as soon as the remainder of the troops got there, we would be pushing into the jungle toward our first objective.

I saw the Chicano Spec Four sitting in the shade with his back to the gully. He was cleaning his nails with his bayonet and looking bored. "Big fucking deal," he told me as I walked past.

I went over to where a PRC-10 operator was cussing his inability to contact one of the line companies. The line company had moved into the jungle and was several kilometers distant. Carl and I had put together some field-expedient "jungle antennas," which usually helped boost the range of the 10s. I got one out of my ruck and plugged the positive and negative leads into the radio's antenna connection. There was a small tree right up above us on the edge of the gully. I left my ruck next to the radioman, climbed as high up in the tree as I could get, and started to hang the antenna to a branch.

Pop-bang! A round missed my head by about an inch. I immediately let go of the limb I was hanging from and dropped to the ground. Screw that idea!

About ten minutes later we got a message from one of the line companies. It said to pass along the warning to watch out for VC snipers up in the trees. One of their guys had just killed one. "Got the bastard with one shot . . . saw him fall out of the tree!" the excited radio operator told me.

By 1000 hours that morning the air assault was complete, all elements were on the ground, and all initial objectives had been reached and secured. The sun was well up in the sky, and it looked like it was going to be nice and hot. We got into our order of march and pressed into the jungle, commencing our sweep.

The terrain was particularly rugged, even worse than what we'd encountered the first time. We were under double canopy some of the time, and the vegetation wasn't so bad there. But there were many streams and small rivers to cross, and around their banks the growth was denser. There were lots of steep hills to negotiate too. By the time we took our lunch break, Carl and I were already whipped from lugging that damn AN/GRC-87.

While the other guys kicked back, relaxing and eating their field rations, Carl and I strung out a doublet antenna, got the radio hooked up to the hand-crank generator, and began trying to contact Bien Hoa. We'd flipped a coin to see who got to crank and who got to operate the radio, and Carl got the generator. I sent my initial call exactly on the scheduled time, and the base must have received our signal loud and clear, because he came right back with an answer.

Goodwin had come over to watch our experiment, and he and Carl both smiled when I told them we had commo. We'd prepared a short, unimportant message to send, and after the guy back at Bien Hoa said he was ready, I tapped it out on the leg key, sending slowly at about twelve words per minute. There was a pause at the other end. The pause got longer. Finally the guy at the other end came back on the air. *Ditty-dumdum-ditty,* he sent, which is the Morse signal to repeat. "Repeat? Repeat what, the whole fucking message?" I snarled.

Carl started cranking, sweat pouring down his face, and I sent the message again, this time going even slower, dropping my speed down to about six words per minute. Of course, the slower I sent the message, the longer poor Carl had to crank.

Ditty-dumdum-ditty, came the response once again.

"One more fucking time," I told Carl and the captain. Carl looked about ready to collapse, and Goodwin was nice enough to relieve him at the generator. This time I sent the message as slowly as it could be sent without it becoming completely unintelligible.

Ditty-dumdum-ditty, the base station said.

"He thinks he finally got it that time," I lied, jerking off the earphones. "Let's tear this shit down and grab something to eat." As we were taking down the antenna, I whispered the truth to Carl.

He shrugged. "Oh, well," he said, "at least it worked in theory!"

Just as we finished packing the heavy radio and generator away in our rucks, we got the word to prepare to move out once again.

"Good thing we haven't really worked up an appetite yet, huh?" I told Carl as we slogged our way down off the low hill.

We were pushing through the jungle with our two battalions moving more or less abreast and parallel to one another. The other unit was several kilometers away. Overhead flew two Air Force FACs, plus several of our armed choppers. I knew that there was beaucoup Tac-air support available on immediate call, and that our own 105 howitzers were probably even within range.

The main thing I was worried about right then was trying to survive the death march Carl and I had gotten ourselves into by carrying that damn AN/GRC-87. What made the agony we were going through even worse was the knowledge that we couldn't even communicate with it, that the radio was just extra ballast.

On one of our short breaks all of us made the simultaneous discovery that we'd gotten into leech country. They were all over us—under our waistbands, around the tops of our boots, and for some reason, the slimy creatures liked to crawl through your fly and latch on to your genitals. Leeches affect people in different ways. To me they were just one more irritating pest to go along with mosquitoes, gnats, and flies. However, a couple of the guys practically came unglued when they went to take a leak and found their first leech attached to their penises.

About 1600 hours we got ready to move into our defensive position for the night. By this time Carl and I were dragging ass, so we were especially unhappy when we discovered that our assigned position was on the top of the highest, steepest, most overgrown hill in the vicinity. Even the guys carrying only their light combat packs were having trouble getting up it. The only way Carl and I managed it was through pure guts, pride, and determination. We couldn't let those 173rd guys think we were hurting—hell, we were in Special Forces!

After a short rest at the top, Carl and I went through the motions of setting up the radio again and attempting to make contact. This time we got no answer at all. We guessed that the solo operator at the other end had probably given up the experiment in disgust. We put the radio away and didn't bother to mess with it for the rest of the operation.

There had been scattered firefights off and on all day as contacts with small enemy units were made, but so far we'd taken no indirect weapons fire. I'd developed a great respect for VC mortars during my previous tour in Vietnam, however, and the thought of them was never far from my mind. Even so, as we had done on the first operation, we dug only shallow, prone fighting positions for the night.

We had been able to maintain only sporadic radio communication with the other battalion during the day. The PRC-10s just wouldn't hack it, so most of the communicating was done through the FAC. When we went into our defensive positions that night, we had no contact with the other unit at all because the FAC did not fly at night.

Our battalion commander was putting pressure on Sig-Plat to make commo. The radios weren't working, so someone decided to run a landline. Hell, we didn't even know exactly where the other battalion was!

Carl and I watched in amazement as the lieutenant in charge of the wire section briefed the two "volunteers" who had been given the mission of running the line. One of them wore a huge reel of wire on his back that was about the size and weight of a truck tire. It was practically dark when the men were sent out. "The other battalion is in that direction," the lieutenant said, pointing vaguely into the jungle. "We don't know exactly how far away they are, but you should have plenty of wire. Call us on the phone when you get there."

"Airborne-all-the-way, sir!" the two men said in unison, and without hesitation dove into the tangled, darkening jungle, the phone line trailing out behind them.

"I think what we're witnessing is your basic suicide mission," I told Carl.

"Christ, if the NVA don't get 'em, and if they do manage to find the other battalion, they'll get shot by our own guys when they approach their lines. The other battalion doesn't even expect them!"

It got darker and darker. Every few minutes the switchboard operator would try to call the other battalion to see if the wire was hooked up yet. There was no answer. About thirty minutes after it got fully dark, we heard the faint crumps of several grenades and bursts of automatic weapons fire coming from the direction the two men had taken. After that it got real quiet again.

"I suppose this means the landline won't be operational tonight," I told Carl as we lay in our positions, staring out at the ominous jungle.

There were a few occasional shots during the night but no real enemy activity. We still didn't get a whole hell of a lot of sleep, though. At first light we were all up, putting away our ponchos and getting ready to leave.

"Hey, what about those two wire men?" someone asked.

"We ain't got time to go looking for them," one of the officers said. "They're probably over with the other battalion anyway. C'mon, let's move it!"

"What about the wire?" another guy asked. "Don't we want to at least reel it in?"

"Screw it, we got plenty of wire . . . let the fucking Cong have the shit. Let's *move!*"

Stiff, aching, and still hungry, we formed up and slipped, slid, and fell off the steep hill. The officers were pushing us to speed up our march, because we had evidently gotten behind someone's schedule. At about 1100 hours we finally stopped long enough to eat and get a water resupply by chopper.

We were lying there, practically too tired to move, when we heard laughter and loud talking. "Well, look who's here!" someone said in an obviously relieved voice.

It was the lost wire men. In between the jokes, pats on the back, and the congratulations for still being alive, we all got to hear their story. They had walked through the jungle until they came to the end of their wire, they told us, but had still not found the other battalion. They'd decided that the empty reel of wire might be of some use to the enemy, so they destroyed it the best they could with grenades and rifle fire. Then they spent the night in the jungle all alone, and that morning they simply followed the wire back to the battalion bivouac area. When they got there, they discovered that we'd pulled out already.

"Gee, how did you find us, then?" a young PFC asked.

"Are you shitting me?" one of the wire men answered. "You know how big a trail a battalion makes through the jungle? All we had to do was follow the empty candy wrappers, C-rat cans, and the equipment you been throwing away. What's the matter, you pussies getting too tired to carry it?"

The rest of that operation was pretty much just several more days of the same. We made scattered contact with small enemy units, easily overcoming them or forcing them to flee. Eventually we broke out of the jungle one afternoon and discovered we were back in civilization. A road appeared as if by magic. We began seeing houses, the civilians seemed friendly, and pretty soon we came to a convoy of parked trucks that were waiting to take us back home to Bien Hoa.

It was late afternoon by the time we pulled into the bivouac area at Bien Hoa. Captain Goodwin said he'd go get his jeep and give Carl and me a lift back down to the B-team. As we were waiting for him, one of the older platoon sergeants came up to us.

"I just want you to know that me and the other guys think you two did a hell of a good job out there," he told us. "We know how much those fucking rucks weigh. No one else will probably say a damned thing, but I wanted you to know we appreciate it."

Those honest words of praise from the grizzled old SFC meant as much to me as any official award or decoration the Army ever gave me.

These operations with the 173rd were an interesting, different experience for me, and gave me a new perspective. I got to see what the war was like for the average American infantry ground-pounder. On operations with the 173rd, I had no real responsibility other than that of a common grunt. Most of the time I didn't know where we were, where we were going, what was going on, or anything else about the grand scheme of things. On the other hand, during a Special Forces operation, I and the other Americans with me were responsible for everything, from land navigation, to fire support, to commo, to logistics, to tactics.

Chapter 6

When we got back to the B-detachment, Carl and I were happy to hear that we weren't due to start pulling radio shifts again until the end of the week. I had been wanting to visit Saigon again ever since I'd returned to Vietnam and decided this was my chance. Carl said he thought he'd just spend his two free days right there on his cot at the B-team.

"I'll either be in bed or at the mess hall," he told me. By this time Carl, who had a hard time maintaining body weight anyway, had practically melted away to nothing and looked like a refugee from a Nazi death camp.

Bien Hoa was only about twenty miles northeast of Saigon and was connected with a good, paved highway. I found out that this road was supposedly "cleared" and there was even an American military shuttle bus making several runs a day into the city.

Cleared or not, I still felt naked as I stood, weaponless and in civvies, waiting at the bus stop. The big gray vehicle pulled up right on time, and I got on with several other guys. I was walking down the aisle looking for a seat when I heard someone calling my name.

"Hey, Wade, back here!" Who should be on the bus but my good ol' drinking buddy Gunboat!

"Hell, small world, isn't it?" I said, sitting down next to him. "I didn't even know you were here."

Gunboat told me he was stationed out at one of the A-teams but was having blood pressure problems and had to come in to see a doctor. In those days, the Army was still big on giving salt tablets to combat heat prostration, and the excess salt hadn't been doing much good for Gunboat's hypertension.

I told Smitty about the deal Carl and I had gotten ourselves into with the 173rd and explained that I had a couple of days to spend in Saigon.

"Good luck finding a room," Smitty told me. "It ain't like it used to be. Every damned thing is filled up. The place is crawling with Americans now."

"Even the Caravelle?" I said. "I've got lots of money and—"

"They won't even let you in the Caravelle's door these days," Smitty said. "You can't get a room in there anymore unless you're a general, a congressman, or a fucking reporter. They got every room booked up."

Smitty said he'd been in Saigon once already a few weeks before but hadn't enjoyed it much. He told me I should plan on taking the afternoon shuttle back to Bien Hoa with him that day. "At least you got a cot to sleep in at the B-team," he said.

As soon as we came to the outskirts of town I saw what Smitty meant about the place having changed. American troops and vehicles were everywhere. Many of the buildings now had guarded, sandbagged positions out in front, and there was a lot of ugly concertina wire strung about. The town seemed a lot busier and dirtier than before.

Things at the Sporting Bar were about the same as ever, though. The usual bunch of SF rowdies, Navy SEALs, and one or two Australian SAS guys were there telling war stories and lies and bullshitting the bar girls. There hadn't been much of a turnover in girls since I'd last been there either. There was probably a waiting list of applicants to work in the Sporting Bar because Special Forces had a much deserved reputation for throwing away a lot of money. I found out that the Morning Star Bar around the corner had become sort of an annex for the Sporting, taking care of the customer overflow.

I ran into a couple of old pals from the 5th Group who told me all about their rotation to Vietnam. They were all nearing the end of their year tours and only one or two had extended for another one. It was beginning to look like the war might last longer than anyone ever figured, and most of the guys had decided there would be plenty of other opportunities to get shot at.

After a while I left the Sporting to go find a bar girl named Lyn I'd met back in '63. I went down to the last place she'd worked but was told she had moved on to bigger and better things at another bar just up the street. Lyn had advanced from bar girl to bar manager just before I'd gone back to the U.S. the first time, and I found out that she was part owner of the new place. I suppose you could say ol' Lyn was your typical young, upwardly mobile professional, but of course that term wasn't in use yet then.

I spotted her as soon as I walked through the door. She was sitting down at the end of the bar, on the customer side, talking to the female bartender. It was still morning, and there wasn't a lot of business yet. She recognized me as soon as I walked in the door. "Oh, long time no see you!" she said. "When you come back Vietnam?"

I sat down at the bar next to her and ordered a beer. She seemed genuinely happy to see me again and reached out to touch me on the shoulder. Even so small a show of public affection was a much bolder move than she would have made a couple of years earlier. Ever since Madame Nhu had departed the scene, Saigon had gotten more and more Americanized.

Lyn said the beer was on the house, and we talked awhile about where I'd been and what I was doing. "You still in army, Leigh?" she asked. "Last time you tell me you come back as rich civilian," she said, teasing a little. The bar business was booming, she told me, and she not only owned part of the bar we were in, but had an interest in another one in a sleazier part of town.

I finally got around to asking her if I could spend the night with her. She hesitated a moment, then told me that she still had the same apartment as before, and that I could stay there, but she had moved in with a MACV colonel. "He old man," she told me, "have daughter back in States same age me."

She went on to say that she would even furnish me with her best girl. I was a little disappointed that Lyn was otherwise engaged for the time being, but getting the room was actually the most important thing. There were plenty of available women in town; rooms were hard to come by.

Her "best girl" turned out to be the little bartender, and Lyn briefed her in rapid Vietnamese. "I tell her go my place when she get off tonight," Lyn translated for me. I asked Lyn for a key, but she told me she would leave word with her maid to let me in. The maid was the same old woman I'd met before.

We talked a little while longer. I said that her colonel must make a lot of money. Lyn gave a laugh of dismissal. "Now I make more money than him."

I suddenly became aware of the fact that Lyn wasn't wearing a bra. I reached over on impulse and lightly touched one of her breasts through the fabric of her blouse with my index finger. I leered, and she actually blushed. "You no say nothing!" she sputtered. "I forget put on this morning!"

Women's libber, several years ahead of her time.

Pretty soon she looked at her new gold watch and said she had to go conduct some sort of business deal. She asked me how long I was going to be in town, and I told her I had to leave the next morning. She asked when I was coming back, and I said I didn't know. "Old colonel go home two months," she told me.

I wandered back to the Sporting and had a few more drinks with Smitty and the guys, ate a late lunch, and before I knew it the day was almost gone. Smitty went back to Bien Hoa on the shuttle bus, and I went over to Lyn's apartment. Her old crone of a maid was squatting in the downstairs passageway with several other Vietnamese women, and she spotted me as soon as I walked in. She smiled, revealing black, betel nut–stained teeth, and cackled a little. I followed her up the stairs and she let me into Lyn's room. The old woman followed me inside, opened the louvered shutters to let in some air, and turned on the overhead fan.

She seemed to be hanging around for some reason, and I was starting to wonder if I was supposed to give her a tip or something, but then she pulled her deck of cards out of somewhere and asked me if I wanted to play.

The old girl really did remember me from the last time I'd been there, I decided. She'd taken me for twenty dollars' worth of piasters playing cards back then, and now she was giving me my chance to get my money back. I went back down, squatted on the floor, and played Vietnamese six-card with her and a couple of her friends, and by the time I went back up to the room about an hour later, I was down another thirty dollars.

There were a couple of bottles of La Rue beer in Lyn's refrigerator, and I sat in a large wicker chair drinking it and feeling the total exhaustion wash over me. For a few hours I was out of the mud and jungle, away from the war, and about as safe as one ever got in Vietnam. After I finished the beer, I took a shower, then crawled into Lyn's big, ornate bed. The clean sheets felt wonderful. It was just getting dark outside when I zonked out.

When Lyn's pretty little bartender arrived around midnight, I could not even wake up enough for sex. I felt like I'd been drugged. By sunrise, though, I was wide-awake and raring to go. It was the girl's turn to be sleepy, cranky, and groggy, but I woke her up anyway.

A couple of hours later, when we were dressed and getting ready to leave, I tried to give the girl a big wad of piasters—all I had left from the card game—but she didn't want to take it. "Lyn say she take care of," the girl told me. "She say you old friend-her and no take money."

I said I wouldn't tell Lyn if she didn't, and the money quickly disappeared in her pocket. She asked me how long I'd known Lyn, and I told her we'd met about two years before.

"Lyn good boss," the girl told me. "Before she work bar same me, now very rich!"

Lyn did not return to her bar that morning before I had to catch the bus back to Bien Hoa, so I didn't even get a chance to thank her for the hospitality. As usual, I didn't know for sure when or if I'd ever get back to Saigon and see her again.

Chapter 7

True to Colonel Kelly's promise, most of us 1st Group guys were released from our duty with the 173rd at the end of ninety days. A couple of our men had been given important, critical jobs with the 173rd, however, and elected to stay with the unit for an entire year tour. I guess they liked the idea of fighting with a regular American infantry unit better than with our CIDG irregulars.

The 173rd Airborne Brigade, which had originally deployed to Vietnam for "temporary duty," ended up staying over there for more than six years. It was the first major U.S. Army combat unit committed to the war. The unit suffered in excess of ten thousand casualties during this period, which was more than the 187th Airborne in the Korean War, and even greater than the losses of either the 82nd or the 101st Airborne divisions in WWII.

Although my view is probably prejudiced, I've always thought the 173rd was the best conventional Army infantry unit in Vietnam. I've poked a little fun at them here, but I have always been proud of my short tour of duty with the 173rd, and proud of the fact that had I wanted to, I was authorized to wear their combat patch on my right shoulder.

Carl and I both looked like walking skeletons by the time we got back to the 1st Group. Our primary diet of beer, Slim Jims, and crackers just hadn't cut it. I ran into D. J. Taylor in the barracks right after I'd dropped my duffel bag in my room, and noticed he'd been promoted to buck sergeant while I was gone. "Jeez, you look like hell," he told me. "Been sick or something?"

I said Carl and I had been to Vietnam for a few months.

"Oh yeah?" he said. "I thought you'd just figured out the ultimate fuck-off scheme and had moved in permanently over at the Kadena NCO club!"

The war in Vietnam was now taking priority over every other mission the 1st Group had. Even with the entire 5th over there on PCS ("permanent change of station," i.e., assigned there), the 1st was still committed to furnish a lot of TDY teams. I didn't know how much longer Sig-Co could keep Carl and me captive when down at the line companies the A-teams were all hurting for radio operators.

It turned out that the transfer came even quicker than I expected. My leech bites had barely started to fade when I got word to pack my shit and get ready to move down to Company B at Machinato. Carl and several other SF-qualified radio operators moved at the same time.

It was great finally getting away from Signal Company, even though it meant giving up my semiprivate room. At Sig-Co there'd been quite a few PFCs and Sp.4s assigned, so even my lowly rank of buck sergeant had given me some privilege. Down at the line companies, of course, almost all the enlisted men were NCOs, and as a lowly three-striper, I was at the bottom of the pecking order again. In Special Forces units you have to be at least a sergeant major before anyone gives you any respect.

When we processed into the company, I was even more delighted to find out that I was once again assigned to an A-detachment. I was also pleased, but not really surprised, to hear that my new team, A-211, had just been alerted for a six-month TDY mission to Nam.

I walked over to the manning board in the orderly room and looked at it to see if I recognized the names of anyone else on the team. A couple of the slots were still empty, including the other radio operator position. I figured I was going to be the junior operator again, because there were numerous E6 and E7 radiomen in the company.

The position of team sergeant was open too, but I'd heard it was being temporarily filled by Jessie Hollingworth, a man I'd had a few drinks with in the various clubs around the island. The only name I recognized was that of Doc Hardy, the senior medic. Hardy and Gunboat were old friends, and the three of us had raised a little hell in Koza together. SFC Hardy was a lanky, dark-haired guy from Tennessee who constantly carried a big wad of Copenhagen snuff in his bottom lip. I knew that Hardy had already pulled several tours in Vietnam and had the reputation of being one of the best A-team medics in the group.

The next morning at formation I fell in with my new family and got to meet the rest of them.

Captain Durr was the team commander. He was a young, friendly man who had recently married. This would be his first trip to Vietnam, and he was anxious to get over there and show what he could do.

The slot of detachment XO was filled by 1st Lt. George Emert. This would be Emert's second tour with an A-team in Vietnam, so he already knew the ropes. Emert was a good officer, especially for being only a lieutenant, and the men all liked him a lot.

SFC Daniel Dudley was our light weapons man. He was a happy-go-lucky guy who I liked immediately. He was sort of a closet screw-off, although not nearly as bad as I, and I could usually count on him to come have a beer with me at the club after training.

Our intel sergeant was an SFC by the name of Salvatore Rende, another easy-to-get-along-with man who enjoyed bitching at life and the Army about as much as I did. This would also be Rende's second trip to Vietnam on an A-team.

SFC Rufus Warner filled the position of heavy weapons sergeant. Rufus was a black guy with a lean build who usually had a secretly amused look on his face. Rufus had pulled a tour or two in Nam too and knew his stuff with the mortars.

Probably the guy on A-211 with the most prior experience in Vietnam was our senior demolitions/engineer sergeant, James Isley. Although still just staff sergeant (E6), Isley already had numerous tours in Vietnam and, like me, was sort of growing up over there.

Hardy's assistant medic was S. Sgt. James Walters. I quickly discovered that Walt could always be depended on to go to the NCO club too, and we spent many after-duty hours over there solving the world's problems.

M. Sgt. George Ward soon took over as our permanent team sergeant. Ward was a big old boy with an interesting, varied background in the Army. He was easy to work for, had a good sense of humor, and always managed to keep things in perspective. This would be his first trip to Vietnam, and he was looking forward to it.

For a couple of weeks after I was assigned to the team, we still had slots open for another engineer and a second commo man. When the two new men came on board, I was a little surprised because I not only outranked them but was actually older than either one. I'd become used to the idea of always being the "team baby," and now I realized I was moving up to "old hand."

PFC Glenn Moore took the position of junior engineer sergeant. This was Moore's first trip to Vietnam, and I believe it was also his first assignment on an A-team. Moore would be working with the experienced man, Isley, and would be able to learn a lot.

The other new man was also a PFC and was transferred directly from Sig-Co. John Lopinto took the slot of junior radio operator, and I moved up to radio supervisor. I'd known John slightly when we were in the other company, and we got along well. Lopinto was large, strong, and had played a lot of football both in high school and college. He'd just gotten married before shipping out to Okinawa and missed his wife a lot. This six-month tour to Vietnam, his first, was right at the end of his enlistment, and John had already decided to get out and complete his college education when it was over.

By the first week in August, Detachment A-211 was fully manned and ready to start a short premission training cycle. We knew our departure date was September 24, and that gave us only about six weeks. Half the team members had prior experience in Vietnam, and all but a few of us had plenty of experience in Special Forces. The most important thing we had to do during those six weeks was to get to know each other, work together, and make sure there weren't any personality conflicts that could jeopardize team integrity once we were committed to Vietnam and in combat.

We began doing morning runs together on the beach, each day extending the length and duration. Running in sand is a bitch, of course, but for an airborne troop—especially a Special Forces man—dropping out was not an option. We had a couple of health nuts on the team, and for them the runs were a lot of fun. Hell, anyone can run five miles in the sand without a hangover, I used to say. It takes a real man to do it with a throbbing head, your sweat smelling like beer, and having to slow down every mile or so to puke.

We had all been issued the new M-16 rifle—which we were still calling the AR-15—and spent quite a few hours on the range sighting in and getting familiar with it. I'd already carried one in Vietnam while doing my bit with the 173rd and appreciated the weapon's light weight. We were starting to hear horror stories from Vietnam about the M-16 being a "jammer," but I'd never had any trouble with it in this respect and didn't think it could be any worse than the M-1 carbine we'd been carrying over there.

In 1965 the CIDG troops were still armed with the old WWII series weapons such as the M-1 Garand, the M-1 carbine, BAR (Browning automatic rifle), and the Browning .30 machine gun. Our weapons men gave us review classes on assembly and disassembly, functioning and maintenance of these weapons. In addition we spent several days playing with them on the range, burning thousands of rounds of government ammo. It was a gun nut's dream.

We were responsible for our own cross-training, which we performed in a round-robin routine. One day the medics might give the rest of us classes on how to start an IV, the next day the operations and intelligence sergeants might give classes on writing operations orders.

Lopinto and I received training on the new Collins single sideband (SSB) radio and on the PRC-25. Lopinto was much more interested in the new equipment than I was, and I'm afraid I didn't pay as much attention as I should have. My biggest problem with being a radio operator was that radios and electronics always bored the hell out of me. I had a natural aptitude for Morse code and was especially good at receiving messages with low readability, but when the equipment got much more complicated than an AN/GRC-109, I was in over my head.

The PRC-25 was a great improvement over the PRC-10. Not only was it simpler to use, but it was also much more dependable and had a greater range. The radio had preset channels, like a TV set, and required no tuning at all.

On the other hand, the Collins SSB was actually a civilian ham radio and was designed for amateur radio buffs who like nothing better than spending an afternoon tuning their sets. The Collins had vacuum tubes and was never designed for the rigors of combat. It was very susceptible to damage from heat, shock, and moisture. That baby did have power, though, and even on voice mode you could use it to talk with stations from one end of Vietnam to the other.

The Marines were up at the north end of Okinawa, all madly training in counterinsurgency warfare. Our new detachment was ordered to go up and act like guerrillas in one of their war games. Guerrilla war was the thing Special Forces had originally been trained for, of course, so this was the sort of mission we liked. As was practically always the case, we ran the regular Marine units ragged. One night we raided them throwing smoke, tear gas, and artillery simulators. We pulled most of their tents down, then disappeared back into the darkness, all of us giggling like kids.

When we got back from the field we were given a four-day weekend to recuperate, but, to my dismay, I discovered I was scheduled to pull CQ duty that Friday night. There was a typhoon in the area, and the sergeant major told me to keep a close watch on the weather status.

This was to be my first typhoon on Okinawa, and I had been greatly looking forward to it. On Okinawa the weather alert conditions ran from number 4, which meant normal, up to condition 1, which meant that we were in the middle of a tropical storm. When condition 3 was reached, things began to close down, the married men were sent to their homes, and so on. At condition 2 everyone was ordered to stay where they were until the storm was over.

What all of us young, single guys tried to do was make sure we were at a bar or club when condition 2 was announced. That way, we would be "trapped" in the place for the entire length of the storm, which could last for several days! This was where the term "typhoon-fifth" came from, a "typhoon-fifth" being any bottle of booze big enough to last through the storm.

When I took over the duties of Charge of Quarters that Friday night, we had just reached condition 3. At midnight we hit condition 2, and I was screwed. I spent my only typhoon on Okinawa in the Company B orderly room. The storm lasted until Monday morning. My only entertainment during the two days and three nights began at about 0100 Saturday morning when some drunk, crazed American woman started making obscene phone calls every hour or so. I found out later that she had been calling all the CQs, and that no one ever found out who she was.

After finally being relieved of duty that Monday by the company sergeant major, I had to spend the rest of the day listening to all the stories my friends told of the three-day, drunken sex orgies they had just returned from.

I had just enough time left on my eighteen-month tour with the 1st Group to complete this six-month mission, then I knew I would be starting a year tour with the 5th. I decided the best way to take care of getting rid of my car was to go ahead and trade it in on a new one. There were several car dealers on the island where you could purchase a new car at a good, low price, then pick it up anyplace you wanted once you were back in the U.S. Most people elected to pick up their cars in Nevada, because there was no state tax there.

I shopped around a little bit. There was an outfit called International Motors that had a car lot on Kadena AFB and another right next door to the British Motors dealership in Sukiran. I had decided to trade my Healey for another, brand-new one, so I checked with British Motors first. They offered me what was probably a very good deal, but I went next door to International Motors anyway just to see what they could do.

International Motors offered me an unbelievable deal, and I snapped it up. They gave me $1,500 for my '61 Healey, and I handed over $1,500 in cash for the balance. They were to deliver my new Mark III to Las Vegas for me. I said I would check back periodically with them but didn't expect to be picking up my new car for about a year and a half. Then I went happily on my way.

My twenty-third birthday rolled around. I remembered that I had been in Vietnam at Camp Tan Phu when my twenty-first birthday approached, and that I wondered if I'd ever get to celebrate it. On my twenty-third, a couple of experienced NCOs from B Company took me on a tour of the joints in the village of Machinato and the city of Naha. They introduced me to one of the prettiest bar girls on the island, a woman who, for an Okinawan, had a humongous set of breasts.

My pals told me that she had gone to a plastic surgeon in Japan for breast implants, which was still a new procedure then, and the doctor she'd gone to was not particularly reputable. After about a year the implants had hardened, giving the girl huge, shapely breasts that felt like they were made of wood . . . which I found out from firsthand experience.

The team trained hard through the first three weeks of September, then had a one-week stand-down so the married guys could spend some time with their families before we shipped over. Since I had no family to worry about, I spent my week of free time trying to make up for the typhoon bacchanal I'd missed.

Chapter 8

I knew Hardy liked his Copenhagen, but I didn't know how much until we were loading the C-130 for our flight to Vietnam. Doc had an extra footlocker with him, and figuring it was crammed with medical supplies, I asked him what all was in it.

"Copenhagen," he said.

"The whole thing?" I asked, wondering how many cans of snuff it took to fill up a footlocker.

"Yeah," he said, "the whole thing. The PX in Nam doesn't sell Copenhagen. Last tour I ran out in the second month and damned near went crazy. This time I think I got enough to last."

As usual, we had an early morning takeoff time, and it was just getting light as we lugged our bags and footlockers of equipment off the 2½-ton truck and stacked them in the rear of the C-130. We were the only team on the plane, so we had plenty of room during the flight from Kadena to SF headquarters in Nha Trang.

All we really knew so far about the mission was that we were being assigned to a detachment up in II Corps, and that after we processed in at the SFOB, we'd probably be going to the C-team at Pleiku for further briefings and paperwork. I was glad to find out we were going to II Corps, because I'd already been down in III and IV Corps. Most of the Montagnard camps were up in II Corps, and I was looking forward to getting to work with them finally. They had the reputation with Special Forces as being very loyal and good fighters.

Nha Trang still looked as beautiful from the air as I remembered it. After we landed and were taken to our temporary billets, though, I began to see how much the SF headquarters had grown and changed since I'd last been there in '63.

The whole compound had moved farther to the west. There were many new buildings, most of them more substantial than the old screen-and-thatch style we'd used before. More people were running around, there were more vehicles, and much more hustle and bustle. The old, relaxed, laid-back "Terry and the Pirates" attitude was, sadly, gone. It was as if the 5th had brought part of Fort Bragg over with them when they'd moved. I decided I'd liked it much better the way it had been before.

We found out that we'd be at Nha Trang for five days. The usual briefings and administration would take three of the days. On the other two days, we were scheduled to make some parachute jumps with the LLDB (Vietnamese Special Forces). The jumps were mainly for the guys on the team who hadn't yet earned their Vietnam parachute wings.

Lopinto and I went to the commo briefing, and I found out that nothing much had changed. The difference was that in II Corps, I would be communicating directly with the C-team in Pleiku or the SFOB in Nha Trang; our B-detachment was located in Qui Nhon, but was mainly for logistical support. The addition of the Collins radios had solved most of the commo problems A-teams had experienced in the old days. Also, by then all the teams had a primary and an alternate communications bunker. We were told that at some of the camps, the radio operators had discovered they could actually communicate using doublet antennas buried underground. We were urged to experiment with this and other techniques to protect our antennas from incoming fire.

Most of the radio traffic between the detachments was still encrypted and sent via Morse code. The voice capability of the Collins allowed for nontactical administrative traffic also. This meant that at long last a C-team commander could chew out his A-team commanders without having to visit them in person!

For the last few months back on Okinawa, we had been hearing rumors about new types of Special Forces operations being conducted in Vietnam. In fact, our team had originally been slated for one of these special missions, which were part of something called "Leaping Lena" and later went by the designation of Special Project Delta. Exactly what was going on was classified, but we had heard it involved small, six- or seven-man teams infiltrated into VC- and NVA-controlled territory to do such things as bomb-damage assessment of the B-52 strikes that had recently been initiated. Several weeks before our detachment deployed, we were told our mission had been changed back to the regular role in the CIDG program.

Project Delta had its own compound next to the main headquarters in Nha Trang, and, in true SF tradition, already ran their own club. A couple of guys on our detachment knew men in Delta, and one day after we'd finished our parachute jumps, we wandered over to their club for a few beers. I ran into a couple of guys I knew from the 5th Group who had rotated over with the unit. The Delta personnel were wearing tiger-stripe camouflage uniforms complete with the floppy jungle hats that went with them.

"Hell," one of the guys told me, "I worked my ass off to qualify for SF so I could earn a beret, now I end up wearing a flop hat." I could tell he was proud of the uniform, though, and the different, elite status it gave him.

Things were certainly changing, I decided. Before, the cutting edge of combat operations with Special Forces had been out at the A-detachments with the CIDG program. Here, now, was something that seemed even more exciting. I made a mental note to keep my ears open about the goings-on of this new unit and to try to get involved with it when I began my year tour in six months.

That evening after chow, we had a team meeting and Durr and Emert told us what they'd found out so far about our mission and assignment. We would be relieving another Okinawa team, Captain Myers's A-122. That detachment was currently at Camp Tuy Phuoc, which was right on Highway 19. Up until that time, A-122 had been involved with the often bloody project of opening the highway, which ran between the coastal city of Qui Nhon and the central highlands city of Pleiku.

Highway 19, especially the portion that ran through the notorious Mang Yang Pass, had been the site of many fierce battles dating back to the time of the French. Most men in Special Forces had studied the disaster that befell the French Mobile Group 100 when it was ambushed on the highway back in '54. Only seven months before our own arrival that October, the area around the Mang Yang had once again been the scene of bitter fighting between SF-led Montagnard Strikers and main-force VC and NVA troops.

Camp Tuy Phuoc lay east of the Mang Yang, down on flatland closer to the coast, and was in an area that by that summer of '65 was considered "pacified." The 1st Air Cav had recently moved in at An Khe, and elements of the Korean Tiger Division were beginning to arrive at Qui Nhon. Except for occasional harassment ambushes on the highway, the VC and NVA had, for the time being anyway, abandoned their attempt to control the route and had moved farther north, deeper into the mountains and valleys.

Our mission, Captain Durr told us, would be to turn over Camp Tuy Phuoc to the Koreans, then establish a new camp in a hotter location northeast of An Khe. This area was officially known as the Vinh Thanh Valley. Unofficially, it was called "Happy Valley," and had been cynically named this by survivors of a unit from the 1st Brigade, 101st Airborne, who were badly mauled in the vicinity just a few weeks before.

The next day we split the team, half of us flying by helicopter to the B-team at Qui Nhon, the rest of the men taking our equipment and flying via C-130 to the C-team at Pleiku. The people going to Qui Nhon would meet representatives of the departing team, A-122, for briefings at the B-team, then we would all fly by chopper to Pleiku, marry back up with our men and equipment, and proceed by truck to Camp Tuy Phuoc.

I went with the Qui Nhon group so I could sign for some crypto material there. Qui Nhon was another coastal town, and the first time I saw it that summer of '65, it was still fairly quiet, although some signs of the ongoing American buildup were already in evidence. Qui Nhon wasn't as pretty as Nha Trang, but it was still quite picturesque, with a nice beach of white sand.

We met the A-122 representatives, Captain Myers and Master Sergeant Prinn, at the B-team, and they showed us around. The B-det was right on the beach road and was located next door to the MACV headquarters. To get from town to the SF compound, it was necessary to go through the gate, which was controlled by MACV, and this always seemed to be a sore spot.

The MACV people considered themselves to be REMFs, and they liked to pretend that Qui Nhon was a "safe, rear area," and would allow none of their own personnel to enter or leave their area with a weapon. Our B-team, of course, was supporting several A-dets located in some very dangerous areas, and when our guys came to town, they came loaded down with guns, ammo, grenades, bombs, knives, and all of that sort of thing. The American SF personnel were also usually accompanied by a pack of disreputable-looking indigenous troops who were likewise armed. At least once a day, we were told, there was some sort of incident at the MACV gate involving the arrival or departure of our men.

The A-team we were relieving had rented a place near the beach for its members to stay in when they made their runs in and out of the town. Most of the A-teams kept these so-called "safe houses," and it saved a lot of trouble all around. Prinn took us over to their safe house, introduced us to the landlady, and we took over the lease.

The apartment was on the top floor of a two-story building that was surrounded by a fence. The landlady and her family lived in the downstairs part. The building had a flat roof, and a stairway led up there also. There was a small garage where a jeep could be parked to keep it safe from potential booby-trappers. The apartment had two rooms and a bath, and was just the right size to accommodate two or three men at a time.

"There is a woman who will act as a maid when your guys are in town," Prinn told us. "I'd keep an eye on her, though, because we think she's a sneak thief and maybe even a fucking Cong. She's related to the landlady, though, and it would be too much of a hassle to try to replace her."

The A-122 members also introduced us to several NCOs who worked at a logistics unit in town. War souvenirs such as captured VC flags and weapons were a much desired commodity back at the rear echelons and could always be traded for food and cigarettes. "We got a tailor right outside the camp gate who makes the flags for us," Prinn told us, "so you won't ever run out of them. You can get a whole case of steaks for a couple of flags.

"For those of you who are interested," Prinn casually added, "the best whorehouse in town is run by 'Sally,' who I suppose a couple of you have heard of. . . ."

I'd heard of her, all right. She was one of the most famous whores in Vietnam in those days, almost as well known in the Asian theater of operations as the infamous "Tigress of Savannakhet" over in Laos. Sally was reputed to be one of the most beautiful women in Vietnam, supposedly half French, and now very wealthy besides.

"One of our men made a deal with Sally to furnish her with American booze in return for free use of her girls when our guys are in town. I don't know if you want to keep the arrangement going or not. Most of the married guys probably don't mess around, but some of your men might think it's a good deal." Prinn seemed to be looking at me when he added that last part, maybe because I was madly shaking my head in agreement.

We didn't even spend the night in Qui Nhon, but got on choppers that afternoon and flew over to Pleiku for the remainder of our in-processing.

The morning after we arrived at Pleiku, we made another parachute jump, then in the afternoon we attended more briefings. When we got down to details about the Tuy Phuoc CIDG force we would be taking over, I was disappointed to hear that I still would not get to work with Yards, as I had hoped. "The camp is too far east," Myers told us. "The Strike Force is almost one hundred percent Vietnamese."

"Lowland, low-life Vietnamese," I heard Prinn whisper to Sergeant Ward.

We were taken on another tour, first visiting the new Pleiku Mike Force compound, which was across the road from the headquarters. The Pleiku Mike Force was manned by specially recruited Rhade and Jarai Montagnards and had an authorized strength of about 180 men but was still below that level when we visited them. "The best thing is that we got no fucking LLDB to deal with," one of the American Mike Force leaders told us. "We're in control and in command," he added.

Next we were taken to see the "Golf Course," as the 1st Air Cav's base camp was called. With all their air assets, the 1st Cav needed a large LZ, and the one they'd cleared resembled nothing so much as green, rolling links. The 1st Cav Division had only just begun arriving a few weeks before, and things were still in turmoil. From my recent firsthand experience with the 173rd, I knew what the poor bastards were going through.

Our A-211 team members were introduced to several NCOs from the 1st Cav who would act as our unofficial personal contacts with their unit. Using personal contacts was the easiest, quickest way to get anything accomplished during the Vietnam War. Direct, personal contact allowed you to sidestep the slow, inefficient bureaucracy that went along with official military channels.

Chapter 9

The next morning we climbed on deuce-and-a-half trucks and got ready for the ride down Highway 19 to our new camp. The floors of the trucks were sandbagged as protection against mines, and all the canvas and sideboards had been removed. Steel neck-wire catchers had been welded to the front ends. The C-det loaned us a squad of their Montagnard camp security to accompany us on the trip.

We took our positions in the backs of the trucks, weapons pointing out in the standard counterambush attitude, and headed back east toward the Mang Yang. As I mentioned, although the highway was by that time considered "safe," there were still occasional ambushes along the route, and the road had such a long, well-deserved reputation as a death trap that we were not at all relaxed as we started out.

When we passed An Khe and the road started its winding descent through the pass, things got even spookier. This was ambush heaven. Steep, mist-covered jungle hills towered on either side of the road. There were numerous switchbacks and other blind spots where one man with an antitank weapon could hold off an entire motorized column. Occasionally, on either side of the road, we came across old remnants of previous battles, the newest being the wreckage of a C-123 flare ship that had crashed a few months before.

Once out of the pass, the road straightened out and traffic on it increased. We passed many groups of government troops camped at security posts alongside the road, and the local people in the small villages we drove through seemed friendly, although this was partially an illusion.

We'd been told in one of our briefings about a recent incident that had involved an American officer and two NCOs at one of these "friendly" villages. One afternoon a few weeks before, they'd parked their jeep in front of a restaurant along the road while they went in to eat lunch. They came out after about half an hour, jumped in the vehicle, and had gone only a couple of hundred meters down the highway when the jeep blew up in a huge fireball, killing all three men.

"What the VC have been doing," the S-2 officer told us, "is wrapping a piece of tape around the safety lever of a grenade, pulling the pin, then dropping the grenade down in the gas tank of American military vehicles. After a while the gas eats away the adhesive on the tape and the lever is released, allowing the grenade to detonate. Movement of the vehicle speeds up the action of the gasoline on the tape, so usually there is someone driving when it goes off."

To combat this problem, screens were being welded on the gas intakes of all vehicles, but this was taking a while. In the meantime, it was urged that a vehicle never be left unguarded around civilians, no matter how much they smiled and said, "Number-one!"

My first ride down Highway 19 was completed without incident, however, and an hour or so after departing Pleiku, we made a right turn and passed through the front gate of Camp Tuy Phuoc.

Other than introducing us to the LLDB and the CIDG leadership, there wasn't much more we needed to know from the departing team, and they left the next day. In private, Captain Myers and Master Sergeant Simpson had warned us not to expect too much from either the LLDB or the Strikers at Tuy Phuoc, and we learned immediately that this assessment was correct.

In fact, as I look back at it, these were probably the worst bunch of Vietnamese troops I ever had to work with in Vietnam. The LLDB team commander was a young captain named Nam. He had little combat experience, but apparently had "connections" someplace and was very political. The rest of his team was about the same sort. They seemed cynical, uninterested in fighting the war, but very interested in how much they could personally gouge from the situation through graft and corruption.

This attitude had trickled down to the Strike Force. There had been little difficulty finding recruits for Tuy Phuoc, because there was little danger. We were completely up to strength with about four hundred troops, but most of them had little or no combat experience. Tuy Phuoc had not attracted very good recruits to begin with. Because service in our CIDG was a way to fulfill their mandatory military obligation, the Tuy Phuoc Strike Force had become known as a good, easy place to dodge the draft.

Even the few Strikers who originally arrived at Tuy Phuoc

anxious to fight had been corrupted by the others after a year or so of getting fat and lazy. Neither the LLDB team nor our Strikers seemed to have much respect for the American SF team, thinking of us only as rich sugar daddies whom they had to appease just enough so the flow of money would not be cut off.

The reaction we received when we announced that their good life at Tuy Phuoc was over and that we were preparing to move into the VC- and NVA-controlled Vinh Thanh Valley was quite satisfying and amusing. You should have seen the rolling of eyes and heard the muttered whines and moans.

On our second night in camp I made a round of the perimeter while pulling my hour of guard, and discovered more than one of the Strikers asleep at his post. One bastard was so zonked out he didn't wake up even after I stomped my feet, coughed, and spoke to him. I took his carbine with me when I left, and made the Striker and his squad leader go through the degrading process of begging me to give it back to them the next morning.

After a week or two with that bunch, I actually started to miss the crew we'd had at my prior A-team assignment down in Tan Phu. Old Major Phong, our LLDB team commander at Tan Phu, had been a big-time politician too, but at least he'd known his shit. And the bunch of jerk-off Strikers we had at Tuy Phuoc made our Tan Phu Strike Force look like an Airborne Ranger outfit!

The LLDB team sergeant, Dinh, was an old, experienced soldier, and probably their best man. He'd had previous combat experience dating back to duty with the French, but like many old soldiers, he'd developed a long-range, survivor attitude. A couple of the CIDG leaders were pretty good too, but we had a big job ahead of us in trying to make this outfit into any sort of aggressive fighting force.

There were only two Montagnards in our entire Strike Force, and how they got there or why they stayed is beyond me. One of the Yards was an interpreter by the name of Y-Long. He was a brave, dependable man whose loyalty lay strictly with the American team. The other Yard, whose name I can't recall, immediately attached himself to Lieutenant Emert and followed him wherever he went, acting as his bodyguard.

I should also mention a couple of civilians working for us. One of these was our cook, inherited from the prior team. Supposedly, this man had been trained as a master chef in Paris and once worked in several famous restaurants around Saigon. According to the story, an American Special Forces team had lured him away from some gourmet restaurant by offering him about five times more money than he was making there, and he'd been out working at different A-teams ever since. Actually, he really was a pretty good cook, but there was only so much he could do with the raw materials he had to work with, such as water buffalo steak and Spam.

Another civilian employee who I got to know pretty well was a young guy named Minh, who we hired as our camp electrician and generator mechanic. These were both jobs that had been assigned to the A-team radio operators in years past, and I was very glad to no longer have to deal with those chores. Minh didn't know a whole hell of a lot more than I did about being an electrician or fixing generators, but he was anxious to learn, was a hard worker and dependable. It is sad for me to relate that after working with Minh at Vinh Thanh in '65, I would be with him again at another camp, five years later, when he was killed.

We only spent a few weeks at Camp Tuy Phuoc before we moved up into "Happy Valley." Most of our effort during that time period was spent on coordinating the move with the 1st Cav, gathering and stockpiling tools and building material, packing up the supply room, and designing our new camp.

We all had different ideas about how the camp should be laid out. We were given several guidelines from higher headquarters, but the rest of the details were left up to us. Headquarters said to make sure our plan called for an outer as well as an inner perimeter, a well-fortified tactical operations center, a primary and alternate commo bunker, and supply room, dispensary, and quarters in the inner perimeter for the American and the Vietnamese SF teams. Our heavy mortars would also be positioned within the inner perimeter and would be under Special Forces control.

One evening we sat around the dinner table, brainstorming. We decided we wanted a trench line around the perimeter with bunkers positioned at intervals. We knew we wanted to have overhead cover for the machine guns, at the very least, and more if we could get the building material. Those of us who had been on A-detachments in Vietnam in the past knew how much we had to worry about nightly mortar attacks, and we wanted to build well-fortified team quarters, preferably with overhead protection, and to connect these by trenches to the TOC.

Back in '63, at Tan Phu, the barracks for the CIDG had been in the center of our camp along with the LLDB and U.S. Special Forces quarters. When we came under attack, everyone had to run over open ground to get to their positions on the perimeter. At Vinh Thanh we decided to put our Strikers' sleeping quarters right out on the trench line. They would live in squad-size bunkers built into the side of the trench.

This plan called for an awful lot of digging and excavation, of course, and was only possible due to the fact that for the first couple of weeks we were in the valley, we would have help from members of the 1st Cav's 8th Engineer Battalion. They would do most of the excavation with their heavy construction equipment, leaving us the lighter pick and shovel work.

Everyone had different ideas as to what the outline of the perimeter should look like. I was big into the idea of interlocking fields of fire for the machine guns and submitted a star-shaped design. This was wisely deemed too complicated and rejected in favor of a simple rectangular shape.

We were scheduled to make our move into the valley on November 2, and the remaining couple of weeks at Tuy Phuoc went by swiftly. To our surprise, most of our four-hundred-man Strike Force had not deserted after finding out about the upcoming move, and seemed resigned to it.

I wasn't worried at all about the actual movement. A whole infantry battalion of the 1st Cav was going up there with us, and would stay in the area for a couple of days to perform clearing operations before going back to the Golf Course.

A couple of days before we were to make the move, we got the word that several B-52 strikes would also be put in on the foothills of the mountains along either side of the valley. None of us on the team had witnessed one of these spectacular events yet, and we were all standing outside the Tuy Phuoc team house at 1100 hours that morning to watch. Camp Tuy Phuoc was about twenty kilometers from Vinh Thanh Valley, but we spotted the contrails of the three bombers as they made their high-altitude run. Even at that distance we could hear the rumbling roar and feel the ground tremble as the hundreds of 750-pound bombs exploded. "What do you think of that shit, Victor Charlie?" I whispered to myself.

The big moving day arrived, and we were ready to roll. Lieutenant Emert and a couple of our guys were staying back at Tuy Phuoc and would take care of turning over the camp to a Korean unit. The rear party would be rejoining us in about a week. The rest of us boarded trucks the C-detachment had provided for the motorized convoy to our new home.

Chapter 10

When we arrived at the entrance to Vinh Thanh Valley, the 1st Cav's infantry battalion and the engineer unit were there waiting for us. The huge convoy was strung out for a kilometer along the side of Highway 19, and it was quite an impressive sight. On the ground we had trucks, armored personnel carriers, machine gun jeeps, and even a couple of light tanks. Overhead flew swarms of armed choppers, an Air Force FAC, and several Skyraiders.

We pulled our own trucks into position in the middle of this armada, adding an additional four hundred light infantry to the mix. Even when I'd worked with the 173rd I hadn't seen this much concentrated firepower. The column slowly began moving, and turned north onto the practically invisible dirt track that led to our new home.

We went about a kilometer before we hit what was to be the first of several land mines. Blammo! One of our heavier trucks set off an antitank mine with its left front wheel. The driver was killed and several other men in the vehicle were wounded. One of the orbiting dustoff helicopters zipped in and whisked the casualties away. The disabled truck was pushed to the side of the road, and the convoy continued past.

Another kilometer farther on we began taking incoming fire. It was simply harassment, as far as I could tell, maybe a squad of VC with one automatic weapon. They were firing from several hundred meters away, on the other side of the small river that flowed down our right flank.

Like a huge, kilometer-long monster, the column ground to a halt. Every gun and weapon on the convoy swiveled to the right and opened up almost simultaneously. God, what a show! Tracers flew, explosions and dust kicked up along our entire right flank. The helicopter gunships began making strafing and rocket runs,

and the prop-driven Skyraiders started zooming in at likely targets. As a grand finale, a flight of F-100s showed up and saturated
the area with cluster bombs.

I was actually almost embarrassed. Wouldn't it have been
easier to just detach an infantry platoon to go engage the snipers
and continue on up the valley?

Of course on the other hand, we didn't get shot at even one
more time for the remainder of the trip.

The general location for our new camp had been predeter-
mined. It was to be built in the vicinity of a small group of houses
known as Vinh Thanh village. Years before, the French had main-
tained an outpost at the site, and their old cement pillbox still
remained on a little bit of high ground beside the abandoned road.

Our CIDG unit, along with the detachment from the 8th Engineers, separated from the main group and established a defensive
perimeter around the village. The rest of the troops from the 1st
Cav deployed on the valley floor and began running scouting and
reconnaissance operations.

Lopinto had stayed back at Tuy Phuoc with the rear party and
would bring up the fragile Collins SSB radio once we got situated.
I had one of the old AN/GRC-109s with me, and after throwing up
an inverted-L antenna and drafting a couple of Strikers to crank
the generator, I established communications with Pleiku.

Captain Durr, Hardy, and a couple of other guys were on the
hill by the old French emplacement, and I went up there with
them. I reported to Durr that we had commo, and he said he'd
have a message for me to send later. I climbed up on top of the old
bunker and looked over the surrounding terrain.

It actually was a pretty place, and had it not been for the presence of the damn VC, the valley probably would have been
happy. The small river that flowed down from the north was clear
and clean. On the floor of the valley, which was about one kilometer wide, I could see scattered groups of huts, each surrounded
by small areas of cultivation. On either side of us, the tall, jungle-
covered mountains reared ominously.

I have often been asked by members of other units who fought
in Vietnam why Special Forces always situated their camps in
such tactically unsound locations. The answer, of course, is that
our mission was to attempt to control the population in rural areas,
and you can't do that from a firebase that's dug in on the top of a
mountain.

I was already thinking that the old French emplacement might make a good temporary commo bunker. I ducked in through the door to look around and had to use my cigarette lighter to see in the darkness. It smelled dank and was full of cobwebs; the floor was littered with trash, but it appeared to be pretty dry. I put my lighter back in my pocket, and on the way out I reached up to feel for the top of the doorway so I wouldn't bump my head. Something stung my finger and I cursed.

When I came out into the light, Hardy looked at me and said, "Hold it, don't move!" He reached over and flipped something off my collar. "Scorpion," he told me. "Good thing it didn't go down your shirt."

My finger and hand were already starting to swell up. I told him it had stung me, but he reassured me by saying that he probably wouldn't have to amputate my arm unless it turned black and started to rot off.

We walked back down to the little group of huts and established our temporary headquarters there. The villagers we interrogated seemed friendly and glad to see us, but that didn't mean a whole hell of a lot. They told us that, yes, there were many VC operating in the valley, and that in the surrounding mountains there were large units of North Vietnamese soldiers.

That night there was occasional small arms fire, most of it outgoing from the 1st Cav units scattered around the valley floor, but we managed to get a pretty good night's sleep. In the morning we got together with the leaders from the engineer unit and began surveying the perimeter for the new camp.

We decided that the center of camp would be the old French pillbox, because it was built on top of the only high ground in the area. We would use the old bunker as a temporary TOC/commo bunker until construction was complete. This command center would be surrounded by an inner, wire perimeter, anchored by corner machine gun bunkers.

The outer perimeter would consist of the trench with bunkers built in at intervals, protected by three rows of double-apron and concertina barbed wire. The priority of work would be (1) the outer trench, (2) the TOC, and (3) the team quarters. The first sergeant from the engineers was an old, experienced trooper, and he told us they would do as much for us as they could before they had to leave. He said, however, that because all of their earthmoving machinery was airmobile, they didn't have the big, heavy stuff they really needed for this kind of job.

On looking back on it, I suspect that Camp Vinh Thanh was the first Special Forces A-camp built with help from a regular American engineer unit. I don't even know if we could have built the camp the way we did if we hadn't had the engineer support. It might have been possible, but it would have taken years to complete instead of months.

Because by this point in the war the enemy had begun using heavy mortars and 122 rockets, we spent considerable time and effort planning and building our TOC. It was built to American Combat Engineer standards, and was designed to survive a direct hit by a 155 artillery round. We built it completely underground, with poured concrete floor and walls. The roof was supported by twelve-by-twelve-inch beams, and incorporated center support columns. We put on four feet of overhead cover, which was protected from rain by a pitched tin roof.

Each unit in the military has its own specialized traits that make it unique. Combat Engineers are proud of saying that they "all have twenty-inch collars." These boys from the 8th Engineers were living up to this standard and worked like animals, twelve to fourteen hours a day, helping us build that camp. Most of them were young guys, and a lot were draftees. For the first time in the war I was meeting American soldiers who didn't want to be over there.

Up until then, the only U.S. units involved in the conflict had been outfits like Marines, paratroopers, Special Forces, SEALs, Air Commandos, and fighter pilots. The men in these types of units were all professionals—lifers—and most had volunteered to come to Vietnam in the first place.

I was actually a little shocked when I started hearing grumbling and bitching from some of the 1st Cav troops. The old first sergeant from the engineer unit told us that when the outfit had been alerted to go to Vietnam, there had even been cases of desertion. About this same time, I'd begun to read in the American press about "our boys in Vietnam." For some reason this phrase made me shudder, and I've always thought that the use of nonvolunteer draftees marked the beginning of the end of U.S. involvement in the war.

There had been some antiwar sentiment at home even back in '63. This came mostly from small fringe groups, American communist sympathizers, and from some of the civil rights activists who were afraid a war in Vietnam would take public interest away from their own struggle in the United States.

It wasn't until we started sending draftees to Vietnam that the college kids took a sudden interest in peace. Practically all my old friends from high school days were attending college at that time, and they unabashedly told me all about it. One of my buddies wrote me that the campus peace demonstrations were a lot of fun because there was free music, drugs, and plenty of sympathetic chicks.

I couldn't get too pissed off at them for this attitude, because I knew deep down that had I not been voluntarily involved in the war, I probably would have been one of the worst antiwar protesters of them all. What did irritate me about my contemporaries back on campus was their stupidity in not recognizing that this war in Vietnam offered a once-in-a-lifetime chance for great adventure. Hell, I wouldn't have missed it for the world!

The antiwar people back home I really did hate were those in the news media who constantly twisted the reporting of the war to put the communists in the best possible light, while putting us in the worst. Also high on my list of despicables were the self-serving politicians who decided to back the peace freaks only after it became the fashionable stance, and the pack of ignorant entertainers, celebrities, and Hollywood movie stars who did likewise. What a bunch of low-life slime!

I got the old French bunker cleaned out and ran some electricity to it from our 1.5 KW generator. I hooked up some lights, put up a field table, and was in business. I sent a couple of Strikers out to find me the longest piece of bamboo they could, and they came back with a pole about twenty feet long. I put a ground-plane antenna on top of this, erected it next to the bunker, and discovered that it gave the PRC-25 a surprisingly long range. During the day I could usually even reach the 1st Cav base camp at An Khe, which was on the other side of the mountain range.

In about a week Lieutenant Emert turned over our old camp to the Koreans, and the rest of our team moved out to Vinh Thanh with us. Lopinto brought the Collins with him, and we set it up in the bunker as our primary radio, keeping the 109 as our backup. We had excellent commo with all stations, even on voice mode, and even at night. This was a hell of a lot different than it had been in the bad old days, only a couple of years before, when we'd had to depend on the AN/GRC-109s as our only lifeline.

Work on the fortifications was going well, but we didn't have much time. We were anxious to get the outer trench dug and at least one row of wire in place before the 1st Cav infantry battalion finished their operations in the area and left us by ourselves. The engineers were supposed to pull out with the infantry, but had agreed to stay there with us for a couple of extra weeks. They steadily cursed their lightweight equipment, which was slowing down the project even more than they'd expected.

A squad of the engineers had befriended and adopted an old stray bitch dog. She was a scrawny, scared thing when they took her in as their pet, but after a couple of weeks on a C-ration diet, she was fat and feisty. One of the young engineers, a draftee who hated everything he'd seen so far of Vietnam and the war, had become especially attached to the dog. He'd named her Lucy and made her a collar out of an old bandanna; she followed the young guy everywhere.

One day the kid came running into the GP tent we were using as our operations center. He was furious and tears were running down his face.

"Your fucking troops just murdered Lucy!" he screamed at Captain Durr and Master Sergeant Ward, who were huddled over a construction plan with the old engineer top sergeant. I'd just happened to wander in, and at first I thought the kid meant some village woman had been killed.

The first sergeant got the kid settled down enough to get the full story.

"I was workin' on the trench with the backhoe, and Lucy was just playing around like she always does," the kid told us. "A bunch of your slope-head troops were camped next to us, and I saw them offer Lucy some food. She went right over there, wagging her tail, and one of the bastards hit her on the head with a two-by-four!"

Several of us from our A-team agreed to go down to the scene of the crime with the kid and his first sergeant to investigate, although we already suspected what was going on.

We smelled the burning dog hair before we got there. Our boys had a big wood fire going, and old Lucy was cooking on top of it. They hadn't bothered to skin and gut her, and by the time we came walking up, Lucy was burned all black and was smelling like hell.

Ten or twelve of our CIDG troops were gathered around the fire, smiling, joking, and happy as anything. They waved and yelled to us as we approached. "Hey, number-one chop-chop almost finish!"

Dog meat is considered a real delicacy in most of Asia, and our troops thought they'd been real lucky to come across such a plump, tender morsel as Lucy. The kid from the engineers made sort of a screeching noise when he saw what was going on and went staggering over to puke next to a bush.

While the old engineer top sergeant tried to console his young trooper, me and Isley and a couple of other guys from the team joined our men around the fire and got ready for lunch.

Chapter 11

All too soon the day came when the 1st Cav infantry units told us good-bye and were airlifted out of our valley. The engineers had completed digging the trench line around the camp, two double-apron fences were in place, and the TOC only needed the finishing touches, when the engineers too prepared to leave.

Whether or not anyone else appreciated the great job the engineers had done, we sure did. We had a party with them the day before they pulled out, getting as drunk as we dared under the circumstances and vowing undying friendship.

With the large American units gone, things suddenly got a lot quieter and a lot scarier around Happy Valley. Construction work on the camp was still going full bore, and we were using almost all of our Strikers on the project, but now we also had to begin running more ambitious combat operations.

So far there had been little enemy activity. While the 1st Cav had aggressively patrolled the valley floor and surrounding foothills, the VC and NVA had simply followed standard guerrilla tactics and pulled farther back up into the mountains to avoid the superior force. This lack of enemy activity had emboldened our hesitant Strikers, and many of them were anxious to take to the field simply to get away from the daily grind of pick and shovel work they'd been stuck with.

We'd discovered that there was a bubonic plague epidemic in the valley, and we thought we could score some early points with the civilians by running a few medical patrols. In actuality, they were medical-combat-intelligence patrols. These first few operations we ran in Happy Valley were rather small, each consisting of two platoons (about fifty men), one LLDB, and two Americans.

On the first such patrol I accompanied at Vinh Thanh, Hardy was the medic, and the LLDB intelligence sergeant also came along. We were operating on the west side of the valley and had decided not to cross the river, but to push south of camp and check out several small clusters of houses that lay a couple of kilometers from camp. These first few operations were of short duration, and we planned to spend only two days and one night in the field. Besides visiting the small villages and holding sick call for the civilians, we planned to do a recon of several ravines that ran into the large mountain range bordering that side of the valley.

All the farmers in the valley were communist sympathizers, if not actually part-time guerrillas. No government troops had been in the area for years, and anyone loyal to the Saigon regime had long since departed or been killed. The people in the valley all grew rice and vegetables and raised pigs and chickens. They were producing much more than they could possibly be consuming, and no exports left the valley to go to market. It was obvious that the valley's inhabitants were supplying the enemy units with food, and cutting off this supply became one of our top priorities.

All this produce had to be secretly stored in way stations, then picked up and transported to the enemy units in the surrounding mountains. We wanted to find some of the way stations and look over the extensive trail network that connected the valley to the enemy.

Our CIDG at Vinh Thanh were armed with WWII-era small arms, but we had an ample supply of M-1 carbines that they all preferred to the heavier M-1 Garands and .45 caliber submachine guns such as the clunky M-3 "grease gun." Some of them still got stuck carrying the BARs and Browning .30 machine guns, though. For operations, we always converted the MGs to their A-6 configuration, which consisted of the gun with a bipod mount and an attached shoulder stock, but the heavy Brownings were still quite a load for our 115-pound Strikers.

By this stage in the war, all the Americans on the team were carrying M-16s. Regardless of the reports we'd been hearing from some of the other American units, we still weren't having any trouble with the weapon. The main problem we had with carrying all this varied armament was that the ammunition was not interchangeable between weapons. Because of this, when Americans went on operations carrying our unique M-16s, we tended to take a lot of ammo. We still only had the twenty-round magazines in those days, and most of the guys liked to carry at least twenty of these.

Because you couldn't carry enough magazines in the standard-issue carrying pouches, some men carried the old BAR ammo belts, while others went to the local tailor shops and had "bullet vests" made. These vests had numerous pockets for magazines and were a comfortable way to distribute the load. At Vinh Thanh, I was experimenting with carrying the standard web gear, plus a claymore bag slung diagonally across my body. I usually carried a few extra mags in it, plus a couple of grenades and sometimes an extra canteen.

We wore the tiger-stripe uniforms around camp most of the time at Vinh Thanh and always wore them on operations. You have to remember that in '65 the U.S. Army had not yet adopted subdued patches, underwear, or any other such obvious uniform improvements. Plus, of course, when we were on operations with our CIDG, we didn't want to wear anything that would make us stand out and become more obvious targets.

We left camp early in the morning and headed immediately toward the foothills a kilometer or so to the west. Because of the tall mountains to our east, we had an hour or two grace period until the sun started beating down directly on us. Since we'd moved into Vinh Thanh, there had been a steady trickle of government supporters back into the area, and they'd taken up residence in the immediate vicinity of camp. We passed several of these friendly, smiling farmers as we walked along the tops of the paddy dikes on our way to the concealment of the foothills. Of course, we'd all learned that sometimes appearances can be misleading!

The munition known as the cluster bomb unit (CBU) was new at the time, and many of these had been dropped by the B-52s during their preparatory air strikes. A cluster bomb is a large container holding many small bomblets. At a certain distance from the ground the container breaks apart, spreading these bomblets over a wide area. Each bomblet has the approximate killing radius, and power, of an 81mm mortar round.

These CBUs were bright orange and had fins on the top that slowed the bomblets, stabilized them, and helped spread them out in an effective pattern. Once these individual CBUs left the containers, or pods, they became armed. Sometimes, especially when dropped over thick jungle, not all of them would detonate, but would land in the trees or on the ground, waiting for the slightest movement or jar to set them off.

As our patrol started moving into the foothills, we began to run across many of these unexploded CBUs, which hung like strange, ugly, orange fruit in many of the trees and bushes. We halted the patrol and had the LLDB sergeant pass the word to the men not to mess with these lethal objects.

In many ways, our Strikers reminded me of children. Some of them, in fact, were only in their early teens, and often acted like inquisitive youngsters. Telling these guys not to mess with the bright, mysterious CBUs only ensured that sooner or later one of them would. They were drawn to the damn things like kids to Christmas tree ornaments.

We had just taken a short break and then resumed our march up into one of the ravines when there was a loud explosion from our point element. Because the beginning of the foothills also marked the edge of the enemy's territory, we'd all been tensed up and jumpy anyway. At the sound of the explosion, everyone dove for cover, looking out to the flanks in expectation of the ambush we assumed would follow.

There were no shots, but we soon heard someone calling for the *bac-si*. Hardy sighed, then started toward the front of the column. I followed along behind, keeping him in sight. One of the young Strikers lay in agony on the side of the trail, while a couple of his buddies tried to stop the blood squirting from the stump of his right arm.

Apparently, the man had thrown a rock at one of the CBUs hanging in a tree. He was standing too close and lost an arm as a result of his stupidity.

Hardy applied a tourniquet and got an IV started in the man's remaining arm. I got on the radio to tell camp what had happened. They'd heard the explosion, so were waiting for the call. We put together a makeshift stretcher constructed of a poncho and a couple of bamboo poles and sent the wounded man back to camp with a litter party. We thought Walt might be able to save the Striker if he didn't die of shock before he got there.

Things were a little better for our wounded Strikers than they had been several years earlier in the war. Sometimes we could get a dustoff chopper from either the C-detachment at Pleiku or from the 1st Cav at An Khe to fly out and pick up seriously wounded CIDG members, but our wounded still had very low priority. The lucky ones were taken to a Vietnamese hospital at Pleiku, where, we soon discovered, they were also treated like second-class citizens—especially if they happened to be Montagnard or Cambodian. Many of our wounded preferred to stay at camp and be treated by our SF medics rather than sent to the Vietnamese hospital from which many were never heard of again.

Because of the explosion, we'd lost any element of surprise we might have had. The enemy now knew we were at the edge of their sanctuary and could choose either to run or set up some sort of ambush for us. Dealing with the wounded man had delayed us for almost an hour, giving the enemy plenty of time to decide which course of action to take.

After a short conference, we decided not to continue up into the ravine, but to reverse course and follow the edge of the foothills to the south end of our AO. We had concealment by staying in the tree line, although the going was a lot rougher than it would have been down on the flat, open valley floor.

I was walking right behind a skinny little Striker who was toting a BAR when I saw something amusing. The man was carrying the BAR in typical Viet fashion, with the gun over his shoulder, barrel first, and holding on to the muzzle with his right hand. We'd just started going down a steep hill when the heavily burdened gunner tripped on a root, got overbalanced by the gun, and did a complete front flip in the air before landing flat on his butt. I tried not to laugh, but all his buddies weren't so polite. In one of the few times I ever saw one of our Viets really lose composure, he jumped up with an enraged look on his face, cursed, and kicked the hell out of his hated BAR. I knew just how he felt.

We weren't really trying to sneak up on the small group of huts that was our destination, but that's what it amounted to. As it turned out, we got lucky and ended up nailing a couple of bad guys.

I guess what happened is that we arrived at the village from a different direction than they figured we would. The small VC unit we surprised had their security element watching the dirt road that ran alongside the river in the center of the valley. We approached on the trail coming from the wooded mountain, which was the same trail they'd planned to use as their escape route.

We figured after it was all over that there might have been a total of ten enemy soldiers in the village, probably there to pick up supplies, recruit new men, or simply get out of the damn jungle for a few hours. We had no idea they were there, but still managed to walk right up on them before they spotted us. As soon as they did see us, they tried to run.

It was the usual sort of action I was by then pretty used to. Hardy, the LLĐB sergeant, and I were about a third of the way back from the point of the column when there was a yell, several short bursts of fire, followed by more excited yelling and the explosion of a grenade.

The rest of us immediately spread out into a broken skirmish line and ran forward. Our troops were like hunting dogs who would automatically charge mindlessly forward if it appeared the enemy was running away. Frankly, we didn't have a whole hell of a lot of control over our CIDG in times like those, and you ended up having to decide whether to go with them or be left alone in the rear. Many times, of course, the enemy would only pretend to run, attempting to suck us into an ambush—the same tactics I'd learned from watching cowboy-and-Indian movies as a kid. This time, the bad guys really were running away.

When I got up to the edge of the small village, one of the Strikers ran excitedly up to me and the LLDB sergeant and began to jabber and point to one of the nearby huts. Evidently, it was believed that some of the Cong had taken refuge in the house, and the LLDB started yelling for the A-6 machine gun crew. They immediately ran over, threw the gun down, and from a distance of twenty-five meters fired an entire 250-round belt through the flimsy walls of the structure. Christ, it looked like something out of a Sam Peckinpah movie!

All this happened before I was able to stop it, and all I could do was mumble "Oh, shit," and hope that the house wasn't full of women and kids. As a grand finale to this scene of wanton violence, several other Strikers ran to the building as soon as the machine gun stopped firing. After one threw a grenade in the door, they all emptied their carbines through the windows.

I couldn't even bring myself to look inside the pitiful one-room hovel after the shooting finally stopped. The LLDB sergeant walked over to check it out, though, and soon came back with a ho-hum look on his face. "Kill one VC, one pig, two chicken," he reported. Luckily none of the civilian occupants had been present. Amazingly, after all that shooting, the dead VC appeared to have only a single bullet hole in him and was, remarkably, still in one piece. He'd been armed with an American carbine, appeared to be in his early twenties and well fed. As far as we could determine, he was a local VC rather than NVA.

It was time for lunch, and since the chickens and the pig were already dead anyway, we cooked and ate them. We'd killed two other VC during this little shootout, and none of our guys was even wounded. Morale was high as we sat around picking the meat out of our teeth and preparing to conduct sick call.

"Kill 'em one damn minute, cure 'em the next, huh, *bac-si*?" I asked Hardy as he prepared to give shots to some of the confirmed plague cases who were lined up, waiting for treatment. Although there had been no villagers around immediately after the firefight, as soon as word got out that we were holding sick call, about twenty-five of them magically materialized.

There were no young men of military age at the sick call, only women, kids, and a few grandfatherly types. Hardy and I had some piasters with us, and we wanted to pay the owner of the partially demolished house for damages and for the dead pig and chickens. No one would come forward to admit living there, however, so we gave the money to the senior man of the village, apologized for the trouble, and so on. The LLDB sergeant thought we were being stupid to make these efforts. "All people here number-ten," he told us with disdain. "All VC."

As soon as Hardy had finished treating the plague victims, we moved our operation back north, closer to camp. We wanted to bivouac for the night well within range of the camp mortars. From previous experience, Hardy and I both knew that the Cong were very big on giving tit for tat, and we expected them to attack us in revenge for our success at the village.

The location we chose for our overnight defensive position was on the outskirts of another small group of houses, near the dirt road in the center of the open valley. The 1st Cav units had used this spot before leaving, and although they made some attempt to fill in their old fighting positions, we easily shoveled out the loose dirt and thus had instant, well-made foxholes.

We radioed camp and gave them the coordinates of several likely concentrations for them to prelay the mortars on. We also sent out two night-ambush patrols to cover the main trails that approached our position from the enemy-controlled mountains to our west.

Although we knew the main-line NVA units up in the surrounding mountains had some large indirect-fire weapons, we felt pretty secure in our dug-in position. It pretty much takes a direct hit on a hole to kill a well-dug-in infantryman ... unless he happens to have his head sticking up, that is. Anyway, I didn't think they'd try to bring the really big stuff, like their 120 mortars, down off the mountain just to attack our small unit, and it turned out I was right.

The enemy probe that night didn't seem to be well thought out or coordinated. The VC never were good at quickly putting together an impromptu attack, always preferring to do lots of prior planning and practicing beforehand. They attacked from the west—the obvious direction—with automatic-weapons fire and a few rifle grenades. We decided afterward that there had been maybe a platoon of them.

We called in some illumination and HE from the camp mortars as soon as the activities kicked off at a little after midnight, and took no friendly casualties. The enemy unit had bypassed both ambush locations on the way in, but as they retreated they came under fire from our unit, which covered the southern trail. Although the enemy could have easily overrun the six-man ambush, they were not certain how large a unit they faced. The camp mortars also began dropping rounds on their asses within minutes of the contact, and this is quite deadly to troops attacking out in the open.

Although a search of the battle area the next morning did not turn up any enemy dead, we felt like we'd hurt them, and the ambush patrol in particular was certain they'd killed one or two. We returned to camp before noon, feeling good about things. I knew that a lot of our success had been due as much to dumb luck as anything else, however.

While the 1st Cav had operated in our valley, they'd kept the dirt road between camp and the highway open. With them gone, the road became a much more dangerous proposition because we had nowhere near enough men to secure it. We only had one vehicle in camp anyway, an old 2 1/2-ton that belonged to the Vietnamese.

Most of our supplies were delivered either by helicopter or parachute. The drop zone and rifle range were both on the west side of camp, just outside our wire. The 1st Cav had about a zillion choppers, of course, and visited the valley regularly. It was

usually easy to get a ride out of the valley on one of these if
someone had business in Qui Nhon or at Pleiku.

Sometimes we just didn't want to depend on other units for our
travel and went ahead and risked taking the old truck out the road
to the highway. This was very dangerous, because the VC constantly ambushed travelers on the dirt track, especially delighting
in attacking and killing the small groups of loyal civilians attempting to move back into the valley. Getting out of camp was usually
easier than getting back in, because once the Cong saw us leave
with the truck, they knew we would be coming back in a couple
of days.

Our construction efforts were being hampered by our lack of
vehicles. We weren't authorized *any* on our MTO&E (the official
allotment of motor vehicles to the unit), so we took care of the
problem in the usual Special Forces manner: we stole some.

Shortly after the 1st Cav left us alone in the valley, Sergeants
Dudley and Rende caught a hop out of camp on one of the visiting
choppers and flew to Qui Nhon. Besides some items we had on
request from the B-det, they had a large shopping list of commissary and PX supplies to bring back. We'd expected them to come
back by chopper also, so were surprised a couple of days later
when they alerted us by radio that they would instead be returning
the next day by vehicle.

Ten or twelve of our Strikers had gone into town with them,
and we presumed this was a convoy sponsored by the B-team. We
sent an operation down the road, securing the worst part of it, and
at about 1400 hours our two NCOs pulled safely into camp.
Dudley was driving a brand-new jeep, and Rende was behind the
wheel of a weird-looking vehicle we soon discovered was a three-
quarter-ton dump truck. Both men had smug looks on their faces.

They'd "just happened" to be down around the docks where all
the 1st Cav's new equipment was parked, they told us. They
didn't understand how one unit could need so many vehicles,
so they simply walked in, picked out a couple of good ones, and
drove them away from the parking area. Because they were Americans, the Vietnamese guard at the gate waved them through without question.

After painting over all the 1st Cav identification markings, we
immediately put the vehicles to work. They came in very handy,
and after a few days we couldn't figure out how we'd gotten along
without them.

It was about this time that our team had its first casualty, one from illness, not enemy activity, but it cost us a man. SFC Warner, our heavy weapons NCO, came down with chills and fever and didn't respond to any treatment Hardy and Walters gave him. He was showing the classic signs of malaria, although it could have been a number of other things, including the damn plague. Rufus was evacked to Pleiku for observation at the hospital and eventually sent back to Okinawa.

SFC Salvatore Rende took over Warner's job of manning our "heavy artillery," the 4.2-inch mortar we had somehow acquired. This was the biggest weapon I had yet seen down at A-detachment level, and I was surprised we were allowed to keep it once we moved up into Happy Valley. The South Vietnamese military still feared allowing weapons of this size to fall into enemy hands, and because CIDG camps were constantly being overrun, we'd never been allowed to have anything bigger than 81mm mortars before.

The face of the war was changing drastically at that time, however, with both sides upping the ante by pouring more and more troops and bigger and bigger weapons into the fight. Back in '63 about the biggest indirect fire weapon we'd had to fear was the Russian 82mm mortar. By 1965 the enemy was using not only 120mm mortars, but also 122mm rockets, and even a few 140s.

On both sides, the poor infantry had countered by attempting to dig in deeper and build stronger bunkers—just as we were doing at Vinh Thanh. In the "arms race," however, there was never any question about which side was winning. It's a hell of a lot easier to build a bunker to withstand a 122mm rocket than it is to build one that will protect your ass from a B-52 strike.

We were already starting to hear tales from captured NVA and VC about how devastating these B-52 bombardments were. My favorite story came from a young NVA who had given himself up at the first opportunity. When asked how morale was in the NVA units fighting in the South, the young NVA said it was pretty high among the new soldiers, but piss poor among the old ones.

"What's an 'old' soldier?" the interrogator asked the kid.

"It's a soldier who has lived through one B-52 strike," the young man answered.

The only real protection the enemy had against our firepower was to remain spread out and undetected. If we could catch a large group of them concentrated in an area such as a base camp, they were dead meat. The enemy had to mass large units in relatively small areas when attacking or laying siege to our fixed positions in Vietnam, and part of U.S. strategy was to try to sucker them into this sort of situation. The battle of Khe Sanh is a perfect example. Unfortunately for those of us out in the isolated camps, *we* were often the bait.

By the first week of December the construction work on the camp was 95 percent complete. Unlike the earlier days, there was no longer a shortage of building materials such as sandbags, cement, or even perforated steel planking. At night all of us, including our CIDG troops, slept in underground bunkers with enough overhead cover to protect against just about anything the enemy was likely to send our way.

Captain Durr and Master Sergeant Ward put together a roster that we used as a guide for scheduling which team members would accompany the ever increasing number of combat operations. We rotated these duties, with everyone on the team getting plenty of chance either to get his ass shot off or to cover himself in glory. Two or three U.S. Special Forces members accompanied each of our larger operations. I was usually teamed with S. Sgt. James Walters, the junior medic, or with Moore, who had recently been promoted to Spec Four.

We kept one large operation in the field at all times, with only a one- or two-day break between them. A "large" operation at Vinh Thanh was one of at least company size. We also sent out small squad-ambush patrols every night, and continued to run medical patrols of platoon size to some of the nearer groups of houses on the valley floor.

Because we were still training our CIDG troops as we went along, sort of OJT ("on-the-job training"), you might say, at first we ran only short-duration patrols, but eventually began staying out for up to five days at a time. We performed no offensive operations during darkness, however, simply establishing a defensive perimeter and giving the enemy the option of trying to take us out.

In Vinh Thanh Valley we had a curfew. Anyone or anything moving during the hours of darkness was considered enemy, and we blasted them.

Once the NVA figured out that the 1st Cav was gone for good, they became much bolder and began creeping down out of the mountains. Aided by the many communist sympathizers and local guerrilla units in the valley, they had little trouble keeping track of our activities. Because of this, our large operations were usually simply given a certain AO to work in and sent out under the command of the ranking American SF member to roam around the area and engage the enemy as the opportunities arose. By setting no obvious pattern of movement, we hoped to avoid falling into traps or ambushes.

At Camp Vinh Thanh only two or three of the lower-ranking LLDB members ever even went out on operations, and they were always glad to let us run things. Their willingness to let us do so was partly due to their lack of combat training and experience. Mostly it was because the Americans back at camp controlled the 4.2 mortar, other Americans flew the Skyraiders, jet fighter-bombers, and armed helicopters that might be called upon for fire support, and American Special Forces members controlled the PRC-25 radios that were used to communicate with these resources.

By the fall of '65 the U.S. was well on its way to the so-called "Americanization" of the war. "Move over, you lazy, cowardly, unaggressive little gooks," we were saying with our actions, and sometimes even with our words: "Let us show you how to mop up this ragtag bunch of go-rillas that's been givin' you little fellas so much trouble!"

Chapter 12

We were running out of gasoline, and the B-team told us it would be several *weeks* before they could fit us into the air-resupply schedule. The supply officer said he couldn't figure out how we'd run out so quickly seeing as how the only gas-powered equipment we had around camp was the generator. We hadn't bothered to tell him about our recent acquisition of new vehicles. The B-det told us that the fuel was available, if we could figure out how to bring in our empty fifty-five-gallon barrels and pick it up.

Lieutenant Emert and Doc Hardy were scheduled for the next operation, and were thus given the mission of taking the old Vietnamese 2½-ton truck and making the dangerous run to the B-team in Qui Nhon. We loaded all the empty drums in the back of the truck, and, taking a squad of Strikers with them for security, Emert and Hardy set out.

The previous day, we'd sent a small operation on a sweep down the road in an attempt to clear it of ambushes. They'd only been able to "clear" three or four kilometers, however, as we didn't like sending operations beyond mortar range of camp. The part of the road nearest camp was the most dangerous section anyway, and the Koreans had a company camped down on the highway where the dirt road intersected. Besides that, most of the ambushes on the road happened on the return trip, and we planned to run a more aggressive clearing operation for that.

Emert and Hardy both elected to ride in the back of the truck with the empty oil drums and the troops. Our CIDG thought it odd that the Americans would give up their right to the most comfortable seats in front, and two of their ranking members crowded in beside the driver, glad to be making the bumpy trip sitting down.

As always, Emert and Hardy had one of the PRC-25s with them, and by using the tall ground-plane antenna back at camp, I knew I'd be able to maintain voice contact with them all the way to the highway. The truck pulled out about 0800, with the troops all laughing and joking, thrilled at this chance to go into town.

I stayed by the radio as the trip progressed, and Emert made occasional commo checks and progress reports as they advanced down the road, out of the valley. The halfway point was considered the most dangerous part of the trip, because it was the farthest point from possible reinforcement from either end and also just past max range of our 4.2 mortar.

Once the truck passed this danger point, we all breathed a sigh of relief and relaxed a little. They made it to within a few kilometers of the Korean unit's bivouac, and we didn't expect the enemy to be operating that close to the ROK regulars, who had the reputation of being some really bad-ass dudes.

"Base, this is Truck!" came Emert's excited voice over the radio. "We've just been hit. We've got friendly KIA and WIA. Stand by!"

Captain Durr, Sergeant Ward, and several other men who had been working in the TOC came running over to stand around the radio, waiting to see how bad it was. Emert was back on the radio in only a minute or so, but of course it seemed like hours.

"Sitrep," Emert said. "Six CIDG KIA, five CIDG WIA. No American casualties, I say again, no USSF casualties. Enemy casualties unknown."

The lieutenant went on to tell us he was taking the wounded down to the Korean unit at the highway and would ask them for help in returning to the ambush site and sweeping the area. Our group of Strikers on the truck had taken over eighty percent casualties and was no longer an effective fighting force.

In a couple of hours we got another radio message from Emert, telling us that he and Hardy were continuing on to Qui Nhon with the surviving Strikers and the oil drums that weren't shot full of holes, and they would be returning as planned in a couple of days. We would have to wait until then to get the full, first-person account of the ambush.

Before they came back up the road, we ran a large road-clearing operation, but, of course, the enemy had long since pulled back into the mountains. As soon as the LT and Doc climbed down from the truck, all the A-211 team members crowded around to get the details of their experience.

"We'd just passed the halfway point and things seemed okay,"

Emert told us. "We still had our guard up, though, or they'd have probably killed us all."

"They initiated the ambush with some sort of light machine gun, probably an RPD," Hardy said. "A grenade went off too. Whether they threw it or had it rigged on a trip wire, we couldn't tell."

"Yeah," the LT said, "the automatic fire sounded too fast to be a BAR. The first burst took out the two passengers in the cab of the truck. Luckily, the driver didn't get killed. The rest of the ambush was raking us in the back. We were able to return fire and might have done some good. I wish now we'd have taken an MG with us."

Lieutenant Emert took off his web gear and showed us where a round had gone through one of the magazine pouches. "The damned driver froze and almost stalled the truck," he said, "but I yelled at him to get us the fuck out of there, and he did."

"We went tearing ass down to the Korean outfit," Hardy said, "and couldn't get them to help us. They said the ambush site was out of their operational area and they'd only go partway back there with us. We dropped our dead and wounded off at that Vietnamese hospital on the highway."

Later that day, Lieutenant Emert and Hardy were out on the rifle range test-firing their M-16s, and Emert noticed that his weapon was shooting way off to the left. On closer examination he discovered that during the ambush, an enemy round had actually clipped the end of the flash suppressor, bending one of the prongs. After that discovery, both of them decided it was time to drink a little whiskey.

This ambush was the enemy's first real success against us at Vinh Thanh, and it marked an increase in their willingness to fight. I never did figure out if the enemy unit, which we decided was probably NVA, had planned it so the ambush would be out of range of our mortar, but that had been a deciding factor in who won. I'm also not sure if the ambush had even been laid for our truck, or whether they were hoping to catch some unwary Koreans.

The Americans had obviously been very fortunate to come through it without a scratch. This wouldn't be the last time team members would be ambushed on the road, however, and the next time we wouldn't be so lucky.

*   *   *

We had patrols and operations of various kinds constantly going in and coming out at Vinh Thanh. Some of them made no contact with the enemy whatsoever, and were labeled "Walks in the Sun." Many of the operations did make contact, however, and resulted in casualties on both sides. I was starting to get the uncanny feeling that I could tell if any particular departing operation would or would not make enemy contact. The feeling grew stronger when the contact would result in dead or wounded friendly troops.

At that stage in my life I had a completely materialistic view of the world and was naturally skeptical of this sort of hocus-pocus, but at the same time I was very pragmatic, especially in matters related to protecting my ass. I never told anyone on the team about this eerie ability, but tested it often and found that my predictions were correct about 90 percent of the time.

I never looked at my ability as something supernatural, but rather as a latent trait in all humans that only surfaces under conditions such as those encountered in combat. I think this ability is more developed in less civilized populations, and the story of what happened to our Montagnard interpreter, Y-Long, backs up this belief.

Y-Long had begun having premonitions of his death several days before the operation had even been planned. The premonitions apparently came to him in dreams, and he told several people he would soon die and actually made arrangements for the disposition of his personal effects and his body. Y-Long was completely fatalistic about the whole thing, and when notified that he would be accompanying the next large-scale operation with the Americans, he said nothing to get out of it.

The operation made enemy contact on the second day. It was a small enemy unit, and only a few rounds were fired. The only one hit was Y-Long, and he died before we could get him evacuated to the hospital.

Just coincidence, you say? Maybe, maybe not. I don't think it was, and neither did any of our Strike Force. After that I tried even harder to develop my ability to foretell disaster. I got better at it, and I think it eventually saved my life several times.

Chapter 13

Our biggest problem at Vinh Thanh, if you didn't count the enemy threat, was our own CIDG. Besides the fact that for the most part our troops remained inexperienced and poorly trained, we'd been recruiting heavily, and we knew we had a very large percentage of VC in the unit.

The Chieu Hoi program, which was a propaganda campaign to entice VC and NVA soldiers to desert and join the South Vietnamese side, was in full swing. Thousands of leaflets had been air-dropped around the Vinh Thanh area, and just about daily one or two young men in black pajamas showed up at our gate clutching one of the "safe conduct" passes, telling us they wanted to change sides.

We were under orders to accept these suspicious characters in our CIDG, and we did. It was mostly up to the LLDB to screen these men and determine their true loyalty and intentions, but they were incapable of doing this, and unwilling. Some sort of kick-back scheme had been devised whereby each new volunteer had to donate a certain percentage of his pay to the LLDB team for the privilege of joining.

Our original group of four hundred CIDG grew rapidly, and before the Christmas of 1965, we had almost seven hundred men in camp. It was a very unstable, dangerous situation. Lieutenant Emert and Captain Durr sat down one day and determined that out of the whole crew, there were only about three hundred dependable fighters. By that time we figured we actually had more suspected VC in camp than loyal troops.

To combat the constant problem of fraud that occurred each payday, we initiated a program of photographing every one of our CIDG troops. That way we could at least match a name on the pay roster to a face. This ended the popular scam of the same man going through the pay line several times under different names.

Carl Hargus with one of the Montagnards at Plei Lap village.
(Photo courtesy of Carl Hargus)

This was Carl's and my fighting position on the perimeter of the
173rd at the Bien Hoa rubber plantation during the spring of
1965. (Photo courtesy of Carl Hargus)

The author at the Bien Hoa B-team while attached to the 173rd. Notice the old-style fatigues, white name tape, brass belt buckle . . . and two glaring uniform gigs. (Author's collection)

One of the trucks that hit mines as detachment A-211 moved into "Happy Valley" during the late summer of 1965. (Photo courtesy of George Emert)

A typical Striker at Camp Vinh Thanh. We didn't have any minimum age limit. (Photo courtesy of George Emert)

(left) Good photo of Lieutenant Emert, the executive officer of A-211 at Vinh Thanh. (Photo courtesy of George Emert)
(right) The author while at Vinh Thanh. (Photo courtesy of George Emert)

Rende and Lopinto firing the 4.2 mortar. Rende was later wounded during the "Beer Truck Ambush." (Photo courtesy of George Emert)

One of our Vietnamese Special Forces counterparts loading two suspected NVA on a truck for a ride to Pleiku. The other side didn't have any minimum age either. (Photo courtesy of George Emert)

Doc Hardy and "Bobby," our fifteen-year-old combat interpreter. (Photo courtesy of George Emert)

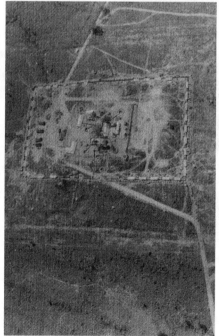

Camp Vinh Thanh from the air. Notice the inner perimeter and the squad living quarters directly on the outer trench line. (Photo courtesy of George Emert)

This is one of the first photos of the MACV Recondo School cadre taken in January 1967. This was shortly after the school became a separate unit, no longer part of Project Delta. Author, front row, second from left. (Author's collection)

(left) Watching an air strike go in at Camp Vinh Thanh. Left to right: Doc Hardy, Captain Durr, author. (Photo courtesy of George Emert)
(right) The Montagnard interpreter, Y-Long, who foresaw his own death. (Photo courtesy of George Emert)

Dudley and Moore posing in front of the jeep we "liberated" from the 1st Cav. (Photo courtesy of George Emert)

The team engineer sergeant, Isley, working on the camp shower system. (Photo courtesy of George Emert)

Staff Sergeant Walters, the junior medic at Vinh Thanh. (Photo courtesy of George Emert)

Our team sergeant at Vinh Thanh, Master Sergeant Ward. (Photo courtesy of George Emert)

It was around this time that we lost our second American from the detachment. The loss wasn't due to a wound or even illness, but for the purpose of stopping a possible mutiny and lynching.

We'd discovered numerous cases of break-ins and pilferage in our supply room and dispensary. Ammunition, weapons, and medical supplies were being stolen—items that obviously were being given or sold to the VC. Sergeant Walters began sleeping in the dispensary as a guard, and Isley, who acted as the team's supply sergeant, took up residence in the supply room. We held a formation of all the troops and told them that if anyone was caught stealing supplies or equipment, they would be considered VC and summarily shot.

They didn't believe us, I guess, because only a few days later Isley was on his cot in the supply room when he heard a thief breaking in. Isley always carried a .38 snub-nose revolver as personal protection, and he accosted the burglar with gun in hand, ordering him to freeze. The thief ran instead, and Isley took a couple of shots at him. The second round nailed the fleeing man, dropping him in his tracks.

Everyone heard the shooting and commotion, of course, and a crowd of CIDG quickly surrounded the wounded thief and Sergeant Isley, who was crouched beside the bleeding man, smoking pistol still in hand. The surrounding mob had already begun muttering unpleasant things by the time Lieutenant Emert and Sergeant Walters arrived on the scene with a stretcher.

"It was a scary situation," the lieutenant told us all later over a beer. "Walters checked the guy over and started to say, 'Hell, this bastard's already dead!' I cut him off before he could say 'dead' and corrected him. 'The man's still alive, Sergeant Walters, get it, still *alive*? Quick, let's put him on the stretcher!' "

Lieutenant Emert, Walters, and Isley quickly carried the dead thief to the dispensary, where Walters and Hardy pretended to work on him. Several of our VC/CIDG rabble-rousers were already circulating, trying to incite some trouble as Emert and Isley casually walked back to our TOC which was within the inner perimeter and guarded by our handpicked security platoon. "Pack your shit, Sergeant Isley, we got to get you the hell out of Dodge!" Sergeant Ward told him.

We notified Pleiku of the situation and they immediately sent out a chopper to take away both the "wounded" thief and Sergeant Isley. We finally got things back under control, and Isley spent the remainder of that tour working at the C-team in Pleiku. It had been a close call, but at least it ended the pilferage.

To further illustrate the problems we had at Vinh Thanh, I'll tell you about a typical operation that Staff Sergeant Walters and I commanded.

Walt and I had known for several days prior to leaving that we would be accompanying the next major patrol. Although Walters had one more stripe than I did, this was his first tour in Vietnam, and he gladly told me I could be in charge of the tactical aspects, which would allow him to concentrate on the many and varied medical chores that would arise.

This particular operation was to involve a reinforced CIDG company, or about 150 men, plus one LLDB team member. The night before we left, Walters, Ward, Rende, Durr, Emert, and I all sat around the big sit-map in the TOC, sketching out the plan.

The operation was scheduled to last five days and four nights. Our AO was southeast of camp, on the opposite side of the river. The area stretched south about four kilometers and east to include the foothills of the mountains. Our western boundary was the river, and we would operate no farther north than the camp. The main idea was to stay within range of our camp 81mm mortars, which, of course, would also keep us in range of the 4.2.

By this time the term "search and destroy mission" was being widely used to describe the kind of thing we would be doing, although "search, capture, and kill" would have been more accurate. We never purposely set out to destroy any of the houses in the valley, because we were still trying to win these civilians back over to our side. When we took fire from any of the small settlements, however, we had no qualms about returning it, and did so often.

Neither the U.S. Air Force nor the armed choppers from the 1st Cav were allowed to hit these targets, though, because of one of those stupid, self-imposed "rules of engagement" all U.S. forces were supposed to abide by. In Special Forces, down at the A-teams, we could get around this rule because we were supposedly under the command and control of the Vietnamese, and they could kill anyone and destroy anything they liked.

We knew at Vinh Thanh that all our troop movements were carefully monitored from the surrounding high ground. There was very little cover and concealment on the valley floor, so it was easy for enemy observers to keep track of our operations. For this reason, we tried to establish no discernible pattern.

"I think what I want to do," I told Walt and the others, "is move out of camp at first light. We'll march right down the road, like we're heading south. When we get to this fording area here," I said, pointing to it on the map, "we'll cross the river. There's some pretty good cover there, and they might not know we're on the other side. We'll keep going south, following that trail along the east bank. Then, when we get down here to these deserted houses, we'll swing around and make a run back the same way we just came, only off to the east of the trail about a hundred meters. We might be able to catch a few of them trying to follow us."

I read off the map coordinates where we would remain overnight (RON), and said that after that we would just play it by ear, roam around the AO in a random pattern and try to pick a fight.

Everyone agreed this sounded like an okay plan, and Rende told me to make sure that sometime during the operation, we checked out two suspicious houses that lay right at the edge of the mountains.

Our operation left the gate the next morning with the usual joking and bravado, but by the time we'd gotten a klick or two down the road, the troops settled down and became more serious. The river was low that time of year, but still moving swiftly, and, even at the fording spot, many of our men lost their footing on the rocky bottom and ended up drenched. On the other side, I sent a squad out ahead of us, parallel to the trail, but fifty meters to our left flank, as security from ambushes. Our right flank was protected by the river.

When we got to the houses at the southern end of our AO, we found they were no longer deserted, but newly occupied by some very hard-eyed, suspicious characters. They were interrogated with exaggerated politeness, then left alone. There wasn't any doubt in my mind they were VC, but there was really nothing we could do about it. We continued our route of march as if we were still heading south, then turned around when we were out of sight of the houses and scooted back the other way.

We had no enemy contact that day, and that night we made our bivouac in and around one of the small groups of huts we considered to be more friendly than some of the others. Walters held a sick call, which was well attended by the villagers, and we passed out a few items, such as transistor radios, which the CA/Psy-Ops people had supplied us with for this purpose. We also collected all the VC flags and propaganda we found, gently scolding the owners of this contraband, but trying to come across as the "good guys" and not getting rough with them.

The next day, while we crouched around the map, I told Walters and the LLDB sergeant of my plan for that morning.

"We'll head southeast again across these open rice paddies, then when we get to the trees along this little stream, we'll split up. Walt, you and Sergeant Troung take the main force and go back north up the steam bed to check out these two houses Rende wants us to look at. Take your time and don't be too sneaky about it. I'll take a platoon, stay in the cover along the other side of the stream, and go lay an ambush along this main trail that leads away from those houses. If you flush out any Cong, they'll make a run for it, and they should come our way."

No one had any better ideas, so we put this one to the test.

Hell, the damned thing actually worked just like I had it figured! As far as I can remember, this was the *only* time any plan I was involved with in Vietnam ever did. I got in position with my platoon on a little high ground just to the west of where the trail crossed the stream. Walt called me on one of our HT-1 radios and said they were approaching the two houses, and just about that time we heard shots and yelling from that direction. A minute or so later, here three of the suckers came, wearing black PJs and running like rabbits.

Our platoon opened up. We were less than fifty meters from the VC, who were running through only sparse cover, exactly parallel to our line. I had twenty-nine men with carbines, and one BAR. They all missed!

So far I hadn't fired a round, being too busy trying to make sure the damn troops were doing their thing. At the last second, as I realized that all three of the enemy were going to get away, I stood up and snapped five fast shots, semiauto, at the last VC just as he disappeared from view. I thought I hit him, but wasn't completely sure.

All the troops were embarrassed at their sorry-ass performance, and in typical fashion they began making fun of me because I'd fired too and apparently missed also. The platoon leader spoke a little English, and I told him I thought I hadn't missed. I bet him a few piasters that we'd find the body when we went down to check out the site, and as it turned out, we did.

The VC was hit in the lower part of the body and once in the upper thigh area. There was a lot of blood, and I suspected the round had cut the femoral artery and he'd bled to death. The man was wearing a pistol belt, but had no weapon of any kind, not even a grenade. Damn! My stomach did a little flip. Even though there was no doubt in anyone's mind that this guy was a Cong, it still gives you a queasy feeling when you zap an unarmed man.

There were no signs indicating that we'd even managed to wound the other two, so we followed the trail back over to where Walt waited for us with the rest of the operation.

On searching the huts, we discovered several large bags of rice, which we destroyed. The occupants had not stuck around for questioning. We found incriminating documents confirming that this was some sort of small VC resupply operation. We didn't stick around the area long, but crossed back over the small stream, moving generally southwest this time.

By noon we were about one kilometer from the ambush site, searching another house that lay on the same small stream. This hut was on the western side of the stream bank, and a well-traveled trail ran past it, crossing the stream at that point and continuing on up into a ravine in the foothills of the mountains.

There was no one home at this dwelling either, and our guard was up. By this time every VC and NVA in the area knew about our ambush that morning and would be trying to figure out a way to hit back. The hut was in a pretty good tactical position, and we decided to stop there for lunch. There was a lot of shade, and it seemed peaceful sitting there near the gurgling brook, eating our fish and rice.

My original plan had been to cross the stream at that point and follow the trail east into the foothills. For some reason, as we were saddling up and preparing to move out again in our order of march, I suddenly changed my mind and told them to go the other way, toward a larger group of houses that stood in the middle of the AO, about a kilometer to the west.

Our LLDB sergeant was up toward the front of the column, I was in the middle, and Walters toward the tail end. Most of the unit had cleared the area and were walking along the trail in the open rice paddy when the attack started.

It sounded like about a platoon of enemy, and they were firing from just on the other side of the stream. In a flash I realized they had been lying in ambush for us there, waiting for us to cross the stream. When they saw we were moving out of their trap, they opened up on the end of our column.

I was right behind the house, out of the line of fire. Walters, unfortunately, was pinned down with a squad of Strikers on the other side. At the first sound of shots, all the rest of my brave unit, led by Sergeant Troung, broke and ran like hell. I was left with my radio bearer and our interpreter, both of whom were looking at me with round, terror-filled eyes.

I could hear Walt working out with his M-16, blasting away on full auto. Some of the Strikers who were pinned down with him were also firing back, but it sounded pretty damn puny.

"Walt! You okay?" I yelled at him.

"I'm not hit, but some of the Strikers are," he yelled back.

I asked him if he could pull back around the house to where I was, and he said he was taking too much fire. Oh shit, I thought, now what? I wanted to see what the situation looked like, so I told the interpreter and radio bearer to wait there a minute.

I ran in a crouch around the back of the house to the other end, and just as I turned the corner into the clear, I almost got greased. The enemy already had that angle covered, and one of them opened up on me with some sort of automatic weapon as soon as I came into view. I had to low-crawl my ass back around the way I'd come.

I dug the handset to the PRC-25 out of the radioman's back-pack and called camp. Lopinto answered immediately, and I gave him the situation as I knew it. I asked for a fire mission from the 4.2, and John told me they were already prelaid in the general direction.

The trouble was, we were pretty close to the enemy, and I didn't want to get hit by mistake. I was just off of the gun-target line, though, and I asked for a round of HE at a coordinate that appeared to be about fifty meters behind the enemy position. I wouldn't be able to see the location of the impact from where I was, but I planned to adjust from the sound of it, walking the rounds back on the enemy position.

You know what they say: sometimes you get the bear, and sometimes he gets you. On this day the gods of war were definitely on my side. That first spotter round landed right on top of the bastards!

"Direct hit!" Walters yelled. "Pour it on the fuckers!"

I called Rende at the mortar pit and told him I wanted three rounds of HE for effect.

"No adjustment?" he asked.

I told him he was dead on target. "Damn, we're good," he said. "Rounds on the way."

After the big 4.2 rounds impacted, the enemy fire slowed down to a trickle. Walt and the squad of Strikers came crawling back to where I was, dragging the dead and wounded with them.

"Where the hell is everyone?" Walt asked, looking around.

I told him they'd run off, but I hoped that they'd stopped at the group of huts a klick away.

Just then I heard a chopper call in on the PRC-25. I thought it was a slick on the weekly milk run coming in with the mail, and I got on the radio, warning him we had a firefight in progress and to stay west of the river.

"Roger that," came the reply. "This is Blackjack Three with a flight of two gunships. Heard all the excitement on the radio, and thought we'd come up and see if you needed a hand. We've got a full load of rockets and 7.62, over."

This was getting better and better! I figured by that time the enemy was withdrawing back up the ravine into the mountains, and after marking my position with smoke, I had the gunships shoot up that area.

I hoped the enemy would think the lucky shot with the mortar and serendipitous arrival of the armed choppers were typical of what they could expect from us in the future.

We had one friendly KIA, three WIA, and Walt had fired all his ammunition. We found the rest of our unit where I thought they'd be, all of them standing around with shamed looks on their faces. I'd lost all faith in them by that time and marched back to camp, terminating the operation.

Chapter 14

"We'll take both the jeep and the truck," Sergeant Ward told me. "Make sure the pedestal mount is in the back of the jeep, and test-fire the MG sometime this afternoon to make sure it's working all right."

"What time do you want to leave?" I asked him.

"Let's try to get out of here as soon as it gets light," he said. "Maybe the Cong will be so tired from sneaking around all night that they'll still be asleep."

This time it was a load of cement we needed to go in and pick up at the B-team, and our team sergeant, Ward, and I had been chosen for the job.

I test-fired the .30 Browning, got it installed in the jeep, and also made sure we had fresh batteries in the PRC-25. I was anxious to get into Qui Nhon for a little rape and rampage (R&R), but was not particularly looking forward to the trip there and back.

Captain Durr told us to give the camp a call on the B-team's single sideband radio when we got there and to call again the day before we were to come back. He promised to send out a good-size road-clearing operation to help us with the return trip. We were depending on the element of surprise to get safely out of the valley.

We put four troops in the jeep, took fifteen of them with us in the back of the deuce-and-a-half truck, and made the scary dash for the highway. Both vehicles had been modified in the usual manner as a precaution against ambush, and the machine gunner in the jeep stood behind his weapon the whole way, hanging on for dear life as we bounced along the rough dirt track.

It was a nice, clear morning, and we made it out to the highway in about two hours without incident. The unit from the Korean Tiger Division was there at the point where our dirt road and the pavement connected, and we waved to them as we pulled out onto the pavement. Once on the safer highway, we hauled ass, and within a couple of hours we were entering the city outskirts.

Qui Nhon had been a fairly quiet place when I'd first seen it not too many months previously, but now it was a real boomtown. The American buildup was in full swing by this time, and troops of various kinds were everywhere. An American MP unit had been assigned to try to keep order.

Our jeep and truck had no markings of any kind, and Ward and I were dressed like our troops in the unmarked camouflage battle dress. We drove down the main drag through all the swarming mob and looked things over. Meanwhile, the MPs looked us over. Special Forces had been in Vietnam for a long time before any other American troops, and we still did pretty much as we pleased. We'd made a truce with the MPs, the deal being that we left them alone and they left us alone.

We checked in at the B-team and sent the radio message that we'd made it okay, then drove over to our rented safe house and set up housekeeping. We stationed several of our troops up on the roof with the machine gun and put a few more down in the yard around the outside of the place with the BAR. They'd pull shifts and still be able to have a little R&R for themselves too.

It was a little after midnight and starting to cool off. A breeze was blowing in off the nearby ocean. Sergeant Ward had run into an old buddy and elected to spend the night at the B-team. I went around and checked with all of our guards, finding them on duty and awake.

I stood up on the flat roof with the machine gun crew for several minutes as they smoked the cigarettes they'd bummed off of me. I looked out over the quiet town. Over on the beach I could see the white foam breakers rolling in and dissolving against the sand. The palm trees rustled and swayed. Briny smells of the ocean, the exotic smells of the Third World town, and the fragrance of tobacco hung in the heavy, tropical air.

Down in my bed, asleep, was the beautiful little waitress I'd met earlier that day. The restaurant was not a place frequented by GIs, and the girl spoke no English. Through our interpreter I'd made her and the *mama-san* a lucrative deal they couldn't refuse, and after she got off work that night, the young woman appeared at my door, silently, like a ghost in her white *au dai*.

I went back downstairs and looked in at her. She lay curled up like a child beneath the white mosquito net, the sheet pulled up under her chin. I walked into the living room and wandered aimlessly over to the table. There was a practically full bottle of scotch whiskey and a couple of dirty, stained glasses. I sat down, poured myself a straight shot, and looked at the various items that littered the table: a submachine gun, seven Army-issue chocolate bars, a *Stars and Stripes*, the whiskey, four or five prophylactics, and a carton of cigarettes. There was also a small, battery-powered radio, and the AFRS rock 'n' roll program from Saigon played quietly in the still night.

I went out to the balcony, stood for a while soaking up the scene, and, like so many times in those early days of the war, thought how glad I was that I'd made the decisions that eventually brought me to that particular point in my life. Although in almost constant fear while in Vietnam, back then I also felt more alive than I ever had before . . . or have since.

I didn't bother to wake the girl when I lay down next to her. She was very young, afraid of American men, and had been unresponsive earlier. Later during the night she murmured in her sleep and cuddled against me, not waking. When we got up the next morning, she was much more willing than she'd been the previous night. Maybe she'd decided that American men were actually no different than Vietnamese, or maybe she was only hoping for a bigger tip. As she was leaving she asked me if she should come back that night, but I lied and said I had to leave town that day.

I met Sergeant Ward back at the B-team for breakfast, and after eating, we took the jeep and made a run over to the warehouses on the dock. For two VC flags and a Russian RPG-7 launcher, we got a whole case of cigarettes. Over in the frozen foods section we traded some tire-tread sandals and a plastic VC helmet for a case of steaks. We also were able to trade for several cases of whiskey and a few cases of beer.

We stored everything except the whiskey over at the B-team, then Ward hooked up with his buddy again and I went back to the safe house with the liquor. After dropping the whiskey at the apartment, I went over to Sally's whorehouse and left word with one of her girls that we had something for her to pick up.

I wandered around town some, hitting a few of the joints. If you've ever seen the movie *Star Wars* and recall the scene in the cantina, you'll have a pretty good idea of what these places were like. Many Korean troops were in town, most of them very drunk, and they were having their own special impact on the locals.

I walked in one place, and the first thing I saw was a big, wasted Korean NCO with a cocked .45 pistol in each hand. He was sitting right there by the door, a terrified Vietnamese whore kneeling between his legs. He had a pistol pressed against each side of the poor woman's head, and he was making her give him a little oral stimulation. Everyone else in the place was trying to ignore them.

I spotted a guy at the bar I knew from my days in the 5th Group and went over to say hello. I ordered a beer, and we watched the Korean and the whore to see how this episode would play out. "You got to hand it to the Koreans," I told my pal. "They really know how to win those ol' hearts and minds, don't they?"

The Korean soldier finally grunted and slumped back in his chair, eyes closed, with a stupid grin on his face. The whore got up, wiping her bruised, swollen mouth, and stormed past us. She had a look of such pure hatred in her eyes that I involuntarily took a step back, bumping against the bar.

As I was leaving that place, heading down the street to another, I heard someone call my name. Two Americans in a jeep screeched to a halt, and I saw that one of them was my old buddy Sidney Cross, who had been my radio supervisor a couple of years before at Camp Tan Phu. He was busy doing something else, and I got to talk to him only a short while. Sidney said he was no longer with the Special Forces, but had transferred to the 101st and just recently returned to Vietnam with them.

I went back to our apartment that afternoon, and while I was there, Sally stopped by with her driver to pick up the whiskey. Sally was in her early thirties, I guess, and was one of the most beautiful Vietnamese women I'd ever seen. She never whored anymore herself, was very wealthy, and only occasionally bestowed her famed lovemaking abilities on a lucky few of her old, established former clients and friends.

Sally saw that I was there in the apartment alone and told her man to carry out the cases of booze and wait for her in the car.

At the age of twenty-three, I still looked about fourteen years old, and I probably appealed to Sally for the same reason my young waitress of the previous night had appealed to me. Sally started giving me sultry "Mrs. Robinson" looks from lovely eyes that held all the ancient knowledge of the pyramids, and I was completely cowed. She hung around a long time making small

talk, and I knew she was mine for the asking, but I was too intimidated by her to make any advances. Finally she gave a little laugh,
patted me on the cheek, and said something like, "You're a nice
young boy." I knew I'd blown my one chance for real fame and
glory in Special Forces circles, but what can I say?

That night I went back to Sally's den of ill repute. I took the
jeep and several of our CIDG thugs along for bodyguards. No
American vehicles were allowed in town after dark, but our jeep
had no markings identifying it as U.S., and our detachment members paid no attention to this new MP rule. The whorehouse was
posted OFF LIMITS too, but that was another rule we ignored.

I was the only American in Sally's that night, practically the
only customer, and the girls were glad to see me. Since the MPs
had arrived in Qui Nhon, they told me, things had been a real drag.
I ordered drinks on the house for everyone and asked if there was
someone we could send out to get us some food.

One of the girls yelled out the door, and a Vietnamese boy of
about fifteen came in, walked over to my table, and asked me in
almost perfect English what I wanted to order. When he came
back with everything, I told him to keep the change and asked him
to sit down and talk to me. We introduced ourselves, and he told
me his name was Bobby. He readily accepted the beer I offered,
and I got his story.

Bobby was an orphan and was being raised there in Sally's by
the girls. He called Sally his mother, but they really weren't
related. Bobby was obviously Eurasian, and sported a dusting of
freckles across the bridge of his nose. He said he thought his father
had been in the French army, but he didn't know for sure.

Just as sort of a joke, I told him he spoke better English than any
of our interpreters out at camp, and asked him if he wanted to
come out and work for us. To my surprise, he immediately answered that he would like that very much. We actually did have an
opening for another interpreter, because of losing Y-Long, so I
told him I would check it out with my boss, Sergeant Ward, and
get back with him the next day.

Ward and I returned to Sally's the next day and talked to the
beautiful madam about the possibility of hiring Bobby as a
combat interpreter. Sally said that Bobby was all fired up and
ready to go, and that she had no real authority to stop him from
leaving. "If you no take him, in couple of years ARVN get him

anyway," she told us. We told the excited boy to have his bags packed and to be ready to leave at 0800 the next morning.

He was standing by the curb the next day with all his worldly possessions wrapped in one pitifully small bundle. He wanted to ride in the jeep with the machine gunner, but we made him get in the back of the truck with us where it was safer. We gave him a carbine, showed him how it worked, and he rode the whole way back to camp anxiously looking for someone to kill. As luck would have it, however, we didn't get shot at one time on the return trip.

In the following months, Bobby went to work with gusto. He was very loyal to the U.S. team members, hated the communists, showed utter disdain for the LLDB, and was absolutely fearless on combat operations. Several years later Bobby became one of the best-known and best-liked combat interpreters in MACV SOG.

Chapter 15

Before we knew it, the holiday season was upon us. The C-team delivered a frozen turkey with all the trimmings for Thanksgiving, and our "gourmet" cook prepared the meal without ruining anything. He even baked some pies.

One morning in early December, I noticed the LLDB were all wearing their best camouflage uniforms, and we found out that their II Corps commander, a Colonel Phong, was coming to visit our camp. I didn't know if this was the same Phong I knew from Camp Tan Phu or not, but when he got off his helicopter accompanied by his entourage, I recognized him immediately.

Both teams lined up to meet him, and as he was introduced to me, he gave his usual thin, faint smile. "Ah yes, I know Sergeant Wade from before."

After Phong had been formally briefed on everything, he came over to where I sat on top of a bunker and we talked about the days at Camp Tan Phu. He told me that there were confirmed intelligence reports that Rowe and Pitzer—two of my teammates who'd been captured at an ambush—were still alive and being held as POWs,* but that there had been no word about the missing LLDB sergeant we called Pee Hole. Phong told me his daughters were both in France going to school, but that his wife still lived in Saigon. He asked me about our old team, rather pointedly leaving out any mention of Captain Leites, our original detachment commander at Tan Phu, who Phong had caused to be relieved of command unjustly.

After Phong left, I noticed that I was treated with a little more

---

*See my *Tan Phu: Special Forces Team A-23 in Combat* (Ivy, 1997), and Rowe's own *Five Years to Freedom* (Ballantine, 1984). James "Nick" Rowe eventually escaped from imprisonment, but was later assassinated while on duty in the Philippines.

respect by the LLDB and even by some of the Strikers. The fact that I was obviously buddy-buddy with their boss put some new spin on my ball.

As Christmas Day approached there was a discernible slacking off of combat operations both by us and the enemy. The U.S. declared a unilateral cease-fire to include a bombing halt, and it appeared that the Cong in our area went along with it. Of course, during these bombing halts the enemy used the respite to funnel huge quantities of men and material down the Ho Chi Minh Trail, so in the months following these "truces," things always picked up dramatically.

We put on a big Christmas celebration at Vinh Thanh, and as I think back, it must have been confusing to most of the locals. About the only Christians in the area were us Americans and several of the LLDB. Everyone else in the valley was Buddhist or animist. The CA/Psy-Ops people played it up real big, though, sending out a few local dignitaries, several very beautiful Vietnamese women from the USO, and a ton of presents, which we passed out to anyone who showed up for the event.

The truce held through the first of the year, and we brought in 1966 by having a small party with the LLDB. At the stroke of midnight several Strikers and a few of us from the team fired all-tracer bursts into the air as a fireworks display. Several of us drank too much, and one of the guys, I don't remember who, went staggering outside in the pitch-black night to piss and fell in a trench. The idiot landed upside down, became stuck somehow, and others had to grab him by the feet to pull him out. Hell, now that I think about it, that idiot was *me*!

On January 2 both sides of the conflict gave a huge sigh of relief and went back to the normal routine of killing each other.

The holiday season had drastically drained our beer supply around camp, making another trip to Qui Nhon necessary. Rende, Doc Hardy, and a replacement who had been sent to us from the C-team were given this critical mission.

As usual, they made it out of the valley with no problem. They purchased an entire pallet load of Black Label beer, which we hoped would be enough to last us the rest of our tour of duty. When loading the many cases of beer in the back of the truck for the return trip, the three NCOs built themselves a little fort to stand in. This probably saved all their lives.

At the junction where our dirt road intersected the highway, the truck stopped to give a lift to a couple of civilian merchants who were bravely making their way into the valley. One of them was a bread salesman who dauntlessly made the trip on his bicycle once a week, loaded down with at least fifty loaves each time. The civilians gladly accepted the offer of a ride, hopped in, and sat at the end of the truck bed with their legs hanging over the tailgate.

At the usual trouble spot, the truck was ambushed. By this time the enemy had figured out that the Americans always rode in the back of the vehicle, not the cab, so they concentrated their fire on that area.

Leading by example, with M-16s on full auto, the three Americans in the beer fort immediately returned a blistering volume of fire. The truck driver was untouched and drove them through the hail of bullets. Once safely out of the kill zone, our NCOs were able to determine the damage.

Rende had taken a slug through the arm, but the other two Americans were not wounded. Most of the Strikers in the truck were either dead or wounded, however, and both the poor civilians had been killed. The bread salesman, sprawled atop his bloody loaves, had been shot several times in the chest.

The truck continued on to camp, carrying the dead and wounded. Beer and blood poured out of the truck bed as we unloaded the unfortunates. Rende was immediately evacked by chopper and, after a short stay at the local field hospital, returned to Okinawa.

This operation was henceforth known around camp as the Famous Beer Truck Ambush. We took pictures of the riddled cases of beer before unloading them from the truck. The plan was to send them to the Black Label brewery with the caption: "Black Label beer saved my life!" But no one ever got around to doing it.

Toward the end of January I began picking up bits and pieces of radio transmissions I knew were coming from one of Project Delta's operations. They were working out of Camp Bong Son, in a hot area called the An Lao Valley, and I could tell they were in a lot of trouble.

It took several weeks for the full story of this disaster, named Operation Masher, to filter down to us at Vinh Thanh. Evidently, the recon teams were inserted in their AOs hastily, without the usual thorough preplanning and preparation. The weather conditions—critical for operations such as these, which depended on air insertion, extraction, and fire support—were quite marginal.

At that time, Delta was using five- and six-man teams composed entirely of seasoned, experienced Special Forces NCOs. These senior NCOs were some of the cream of our unit, yet during Operation Masher, the recon teams took eighty and ninety percent casualties. "Chargin' Charlie" Beckwith, the commander of Delta at the time, was himself wounded while flying with the recovery missions. After the smoke cleared and the full extent of Delta's losses in the An Lao were tabulated, it was decided that from then on each recon team would only consist of two American members and several indigenous. This way we wouldn't be putting all our eggs in one basket, so to speak.

As weird as it may seem, hearing about Delta's bloody reversal during Masher only made me more interested in becoming involved with those types of operations. It was still pretty hard to get accepted into Project Delta, and I didn't know if I was qualified, but it sounded like new vacancies were opening up all the time.

We always had a lot of visitors dropping in for inspection tours, dog-and-pony shows and so forth, at Vinh Thanh. One day we got a message from an informant at higher HQ that a CID team was on the way.

Apparently, one of the tourists had seen us using the three-quarter-ton dump truck, and the sniveling snitch had wasted no time ratting us out to the 1st Cav. Since the 1st Cav was the only unit in the U.S. Army that had these small, airmobile dump trucks, it was a no-brainer to figure out that we hadn't acquired ours through normal supply channels.

We called one of our contacts with the 1st Cav's engineer unit and advised him of our problem. He arranged for a Sky Crane chopper to come right out and pick up the evidence, but it was still a close call. The big Sky Crane had no sooner disappeared over the mountain with the sling-loaded truck than I got a message on the PRC-25 that the chopper carrying the CID pukes was entering the mouth of the valley.

"Dump truck? What dump truck?" Captain Durr asked innocently as the three criminal investigators glared at him suspiciously. "Hell, if you don't believe us, take a look around. I don't have time to escort you because we just got word there's a large unit of NVA headed this way, but one of our Vietnamese can take you—by the way, have you guys down there in Saigon been shot at with the Russian 120 mortars yet? It's quite an experience! If you hear incoming, try to get to one of our bunkers. . . ."

The cops left, and we never heard anything more about it. We never did give the 1st Cav back their jeep.

Vinh Thanh was also a popular place to test some of the "secret weapons" the Army seemed constantly to be dreaming up. One day a huge spotlight was airlifted in, accompanied by its three-man crew. Along with them came several guys from an electronic warfare unit who brought a new ground surveillance radar set. The idea was that the radar team would try to pick up enemy troop movement in the valley at night. The spotlight would then be shined on the surprised Cong, and we would blast them with our camp mortars.

It turned out that this spotlight outfit was part of some Army Reserve antiaircraft unit, one of the few Reserve units to serve in the Vietnam War. The unit was armed with track-mounted twin 40mm automatic cannons—called pom-pom guns in WWII. We called them dusters in Vietnam, and they were a pretty useful weapon against ground troops. But what to do with the damn spotlights?

To make a long story short, the ground surveillance radar set never did work very well. We turned on the spotlight a few times and played with it, but didn't like to use it because its self-contained generator made too much noise and the spotlight gave the enemy something to aim at in the dark. We would have liked one of the dusters out there at Vinh Thanh, but higher head-quarters was afraid it might fall into enemy hands. A couple of weeks later these guys and their equipment were airlifted out again and went back to wherever they came from.

Chapter 16

During the first part of February, Emert and Lopinto left on what was to be our detachment's most successful combat operation. Their AO was once again across the river, to the east of camp. We'd received many recent intel reports of enemy activity in low foothills on that side of the valley.

On one particular hill over there, we had sometimes actually observed smoke from campfires drifting up through the jungle canopy. We didn't know if the smoke came from enemy cook fires or simply from a few local farmers, maybe even women and kids. For this reason, we hadn't placed any mortar fire on the hill, even though it was well within range of not only the big 4.2, but also our camp's two 81s.

The lieutenant's operation left early one morning, immediately crossed the river at one of the fording areas near camp, and spent that first day visiting a couple of the more friendly small communities on the valley floor.

"We set up a perimeter around that one large group of houses where we've had so many plague cases," Emert told us later. "We decided to spend the night there, but it wasn't until a rat crawled over me and woke me up about 0200 that I remembered about the stupid epidemic. I spent the rest of the night worrying about the plague fleas on those damned rats . . . didn't get a whole hell of a lot of sleep after that."

The operation pulled out real early, when it was just barely light enough to see. "There was a lot of ground fog—as you remember—and that helped hide our move," the LT continued. "We marched straight over to that hill and started up the side of it, not taking the trail, but moving through the bush."

"We smelled the bastards first," Lopinto said, picking up the story. "It was foggy, real quiet, and spooky as hell when we came to the military crest of the hill. We started smelling human shit, and realized we were walking through some sort of latrine area."

"That's when we called in the first time," Emert said, "and gave you warning that we might be needing some fire support. We formed a skirmish line and moved up to the top of the hill, and were already right in the middle of their camp before we realized it. *Very* good camouflage."

"It's actually lucky the place was already empty," Lopinto added. "You know how our troops are. They were scared shitless just knowing how close we were to the bad guys."

"Then we established a perimeter, occupying the enemy positions," Emert continued, "and set up a five-man ambush party on the trail that runs from the top of the hill, off the back side, then heads up that ravine into the mountain."

Emert paused a moment, and I asked him if that was when he'd called in the second time.

"Yeah," he said. "That's when I told you we thought the enemy had left, and had you guys lay in the mortars on the trail just in case. Anyway, it looked like the camp hadn't been completely abandoned, and I suspected they planned to come back and use it again, maybe that night."

"Just about that time, this squad of VC come diddy-bopping right back up the trail," Lopinto said. "They were bullshitting and playing grab-ass, not expecting a thing. We had a couple of our best Strikers down there manning the ambush—that old BAR man who supposedly was at Dien Bien Phu was one of them—and we greased the fuckers good!"

"Then we started taking fire from down the hill, and we figured out we'd just hit the point element of a bigger force," Emert said, concluding the story. "That's when I called for the mortars to blast the trail and that ravine."

One of the enemy killed in the ambush turned out to be a Viet Cong VIP. From documents discovered on his body, it was suspected he was an important character, so his body was lugged back to camp, where it was photographed and fingerprinted. We forwarded these pictures and prints to higher headquarters at Pleiku, and the intel people confirmed we'd managed to knock off a pretty notorious man.

We also found out later through our own local intel sources that our mortar fire on the trail and ravine had caught an NVA company flat-footed, and had accounted for at least forty KIA. The first group we'd ambushed were local VC, and had been acting as guides for the North Vietnamese regulars. It shows how little respect they had for us that they would be walking on the trails in the daytime and bivouacking within sight of our camp at night.

The only downside of that whole action was that Emert's body-guard, the tall Montagnard who followed him everywhere on operations, was shot and killed. Lieutenant Emert said he felt pretty bad about it, and suspected that the Yard had taken a slug meant for him. He was the last Montagnard we had in camp, and from then on our Strike Force was just about one hundred percent lowland Vietnamese.

At Vinh Thanh we had the usual, almost nightly probes and harassment attacks that just about all the A-camps had to deal with in those days. The enemy lobbed in mortars and an occasional rocket. Because we were so well dug-in and fortified, though, these attacks didn't mean as much as they had a couple of years earlier. We were constantly aware, however, that there were some very large NVA units in the surrounding hills. If the enemy wanted to pay the price, we knew they could probably overrun the camp in a matter of hours.

By early '66, however, there were plenty of large American combat units that could be counted on to come to our aid. Also, the Pleiku Mike Force was by then fully up to strength, trained, and anxious to kick ass. The U.S. had enough helicopters in the country to airlift large units of reinforcements, which eliminated the need to fight through enemy ambushes with an armed convoy.

The Air Force had at least one AC-47 gunship on call for each of the four corps areas, along with C-123 flareships. These AC-47s, nicknamed "Puff," from the song "Puff the Magic Dragon," were one of the most successful innovations of the war. The original versions carried three rapid-fire 7.62 Gatling guns that stuck out the side of the aircraft. Each of these guns spewed six thousand rounds a minute, or a hundred rounds a second!

Later versions used the old C-119 Flying Boxcars for a gun platform. These AC-119s usually mounted a 40mm automatic cannon that hung out the tailgate, and that version soon became known as "Stinger." The final stage of this development was the AC-130 gunship, which carried a variety of weapons, including everything from 7.62 miniguns to Vulcan 20mm Gatling guns and

105 howitzers. These bad muthas were painted flat black and went by such call signs as Specter and Blind Bat.

Special Forces camps in Vietnam, which were normally isolated and outside the range of friendly artillery support, depended on and used these Air Force gunships more than other units. Almost all serious enemy attacks on our camps took place at night, and during the hours of darkness these gunships were the only Tac-air allowed to fly. All the friendly ground units in Vietnam loved the gunships, however, and the enemy feared them greatly.

As suspected, the tempo of combat increased after the Christmas cease-fire. We held our own in Vinh Thanh, giving the enemy as much grief as he was giving us. We'd accomplished our primary mission—completing construction of the camp—several months ahead of schedule, and many of our design innovations, such as our connected, underground TOC and sleeping quarters, and our trench line with the fortified squad bunkers built in at intervals, later became SOP for SF A-camps. (These were all ideas that had been around since WWI, of course, but the military seems constantly to reinvent the wheel.)

Our six-month tour was nearing completion when I decoded a high-priority message one day that concerned me personally. Sergeant Wade was ordered to return to Okinawa immediately, it said, because he was due to start a year tour with the 5th Group in two weeks and needed to clear his old unit before he could sign in to his new one.

I packed my bags, said hurried farewells to all the A-211 team members, and a couple of days later I was back in Nha Trang trying to catch a hop to Okinawa.

Chapter 17

There was an awful lot of excitement in the air at 5th Group headquarters in early '66. Many new units, such as the Mike Forces, were being raised, new techniques and tactics were constantly being developed, and because of the recent, large commitment of U.S. ground forces, it looked like the war might last awhile. Special Forces always thrived in that sort of creative, flexible, turbulent atmosphere.

I heard that Colonel Kelly, who had been my group commander on Okinawa, had recently arrived to take command of the 5th. I decided he must be following me around for some reason.

I spent a couple of days at the headquarters, sniffing around, trying to set myself up with an interesting assignment for the coming year. I happened to run into a guy I knew who had also just transferred over from the 1st Group for a PCS tour, and he told me about a new classified unit he was with. From what little he could tell me about the outfit, which was going under the name of C-5, it sounded like just the kind of thing I was looking for.

"It's going to be pretty high-risk, and the commander is looking for volunteers who are unmarried and who don't have families," my buddy told me. "If you don't have a Top Secret security clearance yet, you'll have to get the paperwork in for it. You can work with an interim clearance in the meantime. They're especially interested in getting some men with at least a year of Vietnam A-team experience."

I told my friend that I was very interested in joining the unit and that I would be back in about a week to begin a new tour. He told me he would put in a good word for me with his boss, a Major Terry, and that someone would get in touch with me when I came back to process into the 5th.

* * *

The next day I got a ride on a C-130 and flew to Okinawa. The escalating war in Vietnam was affecting not only the 1st Group but the entire island. The barracks down in Machinato were practically deserted. Just about everyone was off-island somewhere, with most of the teams being deployed on TDY missions to Vietnam. Hargus was deployed someplace, and my drinking buddy Gunboat was stationed way up in the north training area at Camp Hardy. It was all pretty dreary.

In the meantime, down in the local dives things were too crowded and inflation had sent the prices of all-important commodities, such as drinks and short-times, soaring. The island was jammed with newbies heading for the war, and the locals were gouging them for all they were worth.

I didn't waste any time clearing the 1st Group. I turned down the offer of a thirty-day, predeployment furlough back to the U.S. because I was afraid it would screw up my chances to get into that mysterious new unit, C-5. Besides, I'd already heard how returning Vietnam veterans were being treated by some of the American "peace and love" bunch, and I was in no mood to go through any of that BS.

I did go over to International Motors and check with them to make sure everything was still all right with my new car deal. "No problem at all, Mr. Wade," the smiling manager told me. "Just drop us a letter a month or so before you are due to return to the States, and we'll have your new Healey ready for you to pick up in Las Vegas." The manager promised to be sending me copies of the paperwork in a few weeks. My old Healey, the one I'd traded in, had already been resold to some Air Force major who had promptly demolished it while playing boy-racer up in the north part of the island, which was like hearing that one of my family had been murdered.

Eight days after I'd processed out of Nha Trang, I was there again, processing back in. It confused the personnel types to no end. I was told I'd be there at headquarters for a couple of days again while they decided where to send me. No one mentioned anything about my assignment to C-5, and I figured that, as usual, everything had gotten screwed up.

I didn't have anything to do for the rest of the afternoon so I bummed a ride with some guys in a jeep and went to town. Nha Trang city was also much changed, and as expected, all the changes were for the worse. Several new REMF units were located in the downtown area, including an MP outfit. The old Nautique bar and restaurant was still in operation and was still a popular place for SF to hang out, but it was crowded. Martha Raye, the singer and entertainer, who was in and out of the country all the time visiting her adopted Special Forces, was putting on a free show there.

The next morning, still bleary from a night of excess, I got word to report to the Puzzle Palace and to see Major Terry about my assignment.

"I won't tell you the details of what we're up to until you are a member of our unit," Terry told me. "I will tell you that we will be performing some dangerous, classified missions. Some of them are similar to what Project Delta is doing. Still interested?"

I said I was.

"One thing you will probably be glad to hear, since I know you've had some experience down at the A-teams already, is that our unit has no LLDB in it. Americans have complete command and control of the project. I will tell you that we'll be having a lot of fun, and that the work will involve all the standard SF operations such as raids, prisoner snatches, assassination of high-ranking NVA officers, sneak-and-peek recon, and even a pure guerrilla warfare mission. Like every other SF unit in the country, we need good radio operators. This is strictly a voluntary assignment, though, so what do you think?"

I said I definitely wanted to join.

Terry gave me the address of their safe house down in Saigon, the name of the person to report to there, and said he'd probably be seeing me again soon. The next morning I got a ride on a C-123, flew down to Tan Son Nhut, and took a cab to the address I'd been given.

The driver let me off in front a large, beautiful, walled villa. A Vietnamese guard let me through the gate after checking my military ID card, and I entered the biggest of several buildings on the compound. A pretty Vietnamese receptionist directed me to the officer to whom I'd been told to report.

The personnel officer greeted me and said they'd been told to expect me. I went through a short, painless round of paperwork, and received another short briefing.

"It's too late in the day to do anything else," I was told. "Take a look around and meet some of the guys. You probably know some of them already. For OPSEC, the duty uniform here is civvies. Make sure you wear this ID badge on your right pocket all the time you're in the compound. We aren't the only outfit in here."

He asked me if I'd ever been in Saigon before, and I told him I had.

"Guess you know the ropes then," he concluded. "I'll probably be seeing you again tomorrow."

After dumping my bags by my cot and changing into civilian clothes, I wandered around the compound, looking for the dining area and the club. By this time, of course, I was thinking that I'd definitely gotten involved with a good unit.

The club at the safe house was much more like some sort of senior officer's mess than the kind of SF hangout I was used to. It resembled one of those high-class sportsmen's clubs from the old colonial days. At any time I expected some guy to walk in carrying a polo mallet. Most of the club patrons were in civilian clothes, but some were in uniform. As the personnel guy had warned me, our unit wasn't the only one working in there, and just about all the other bar patrons were garrison-trooper types. I didn't see anyone under the rank of major. There were even a few round-eyed women in the place—the first ones I'd ever seen in Vietnam, nurses from some hospital unit. I soon discovered that they weren't interested in making the acquaintance of anyone under the rank of O-5 (lieutenant colonel).

After about thirty minutes of that stuffy place, I was ready to head down to Tu Do.

Saigon was also very crowded with troops, and there seemed to be Americans every damn place. A couple of hotels had been turned into living quarters for the swarm of rear-echelon pukes. Many more of the old colonial villas now had ugly sandbag and barbed-wire emplacements out front. It was difficult to get a cab, and when I did, I found out the fare had gone sky high.

The bars on Tu Do were booming, and there was standing room only at most of them. Things were better at the Sporting Bar, however. Occasionally some "outsider" who hadn't gotten the word stumbled by accident into the Sporting, but he got the same reception that a straight male might get in a dyke biker joint.

By this time the Morning Star Bar was just about as popular with our people as the Sporting, so there was always elbow room at one of the two places. I cruised back and forth between the two establishments, meeting many old friends, and eventually I went over to Lyn's bar to say hello.

That place was jammed, and I didn't see her or the girl bartender I knew. A shifty-eyed man was serving drinks, and he pretended not to know who I was talking about when I asked for Lyn by name. Some Navy guy and a Marine got in a fight about then, knocking over a table and rolling around on the floor, so I decided it was time to leave.

I caught a cab an hour or so before curfew so as to beat the rush, and went back to the safe house. I was tired from all the traveling I'd been doing, and turned in early.

The next morning I received a couple more briefings, and discovered I'd be leaving the very next morning to travel to Dalat. I'd arrived at the unit just in time to take part in one of their first operations and would be working out of the mission support site (MSS).

So far all my briefings had been of a rather general nature, and I'd been given no specifics concerning our exact mission. I was beginning to understand that the unit was very compartmentalized, and that there were more things going on than met the eye. The intelligence officer who briefed me in Saigon promised I'd be told more about what was happening when I got up to Dalat.

That afternoon I met a couple of other communicators, Frank Hillman and Wes Kamalu, who were testing some radios in the temporary communications center located in an upstairs room of the villa.

The original members of C-5 seemed to have been recruited primarily from either old, experienced guys who had served many years in the 10th Group or from men recently transferred from the 1st Group. Hillman was one of those old 10th Group members who could function in just about any position on a Special Forces A-detachment. I discovered he'd been raised in the same part of the U.S. I had, in southern Arizona, and I liked Frank immediately. Hillman had a very dry sense of humor and was quite amusing to go drinking with. Kamalu was one of our Hawaiian SF members who I'd had the pleasure to work and party with a little on several earlier occasions.

Bright and early the next morning I put my uniform on and flew up to the beautiful mountain city of Dalat. That was the first time I'd ever been there, and I was struck by how different it looked from other places in Vietnam. In the central highlands, Dalat sat nestled in a small mountain valley, and resembled an alpine village more than anything else. The weather was quite cool up there year-round, and the town was a popular resort area for Vietnam's rich, powerful, and famous.

Hillman, I, and several other guys from the unit I didn't know had flown up together. Before long a Vietnamese in civilian clothes arrived in an unmarked Land Rover and took us from the airfield to yet another safe house. At this location too the duty uniform was civilian clothes, and we were warned to keep a low profile. There were very few other American soldiers in the area, and we had a very thin cover story about being part of a civilian relief agency.

The day after I got up there, I was finally given a more thorough briefing about just what the hell I'd got myself into.

We had a "third country" mission, I was told. Specifically, our area of interest was Cambodia. Since Cambodia was still supposedly a neutral country, this had to be kept a clandestine operation. The unit had several things going on at once, the intel officer told me, but each section was kept separate from the others for security reasons, and I would only be working with the "ground operations" part of it.

The general plan was to establish a network of agents in Cambodia who would attempt to make contact with some of the anticommunist groups in that country. Once contact was established, small teams, each consisting of two or three Americans and several Cambodians, would be inserted to work with these partisans on a long-term basis to conduct guerrilla operations against the Ho Chi Minh Trail.

Each of these small teams had to have a qualified radio operator, and that's what I would eventually be doing. Final approval for this mission had to come from some very high level in the U.S. government, and so far this approval had not been forthcoming. In the meantime, the unit was putting together and training the teams.

This was just the sort of unconventional warfare mission that Special Forces had originally been developed and trained for. In particular, this plan sounded remarkably like the way the old OSS had operated in Europe and Asia during WWII. I was convinced I'd gotten myself into something really exciting.

Until the go-ahead was received from Washington, or wherever, the teams would be conducting LRP (long-range patrol) missions similar to Delta's. This would give the unit a cover story, and give everyone some good training. My briefer told me that just then the unit had only two operational teams of two Americans and four indigenous each. None of the four American team members was a Morse code operator, so they would be using the PRC-25s, an air-relay, and other communications techniques already developed by Project Delta.

Like all the other Special Forces units in country, C-5 was very shorthanded when it came to radio operators. Only two were assigned to Dalat, and they were working twelve-hour shifts. I was shown around their commo room and introduced to a couple of new radios I'd never seen before.

One of these was a medium-size unit known as an AN/GRC-74, a nice little set that operated single sideband, could be used on voice mode over short distances, and could be used with dry cell batteries or plugged into a DC power supply. The 74 was transistorized, had been specifically developed for hard, military use, and was quite rugged. It was easy to tune, practically idiot proof—which endeared it to me right from the start—and made a perfect backup unit for the Collins radio.

The other new radio, known as a PRC-64—a small unit about the size of a loaf of bread—had been recently developed specifically for use by LRP units. This radio ran off a small dry cell and had an operating range of about three hundred miles on Morse or thirty miles on voice. It had a small built-in telegrapher key, and even had a "whisper mode" for its miniature mike.

I spent only a day or two in Dalat, then, along with the two recon teams and the rest of the mission support team, we flew to our forward launch site, which was one of our border A-camps, Du Co, if I remember right.

To show you what a small operation we were running in those early days, the whole mission support team was about seven people. There was one other radio operator besides me, a guy named Jones, I think. We had a couple of officers and several senior operations NCOs, and that's it. Our air assets consisted of three slicks, one or two gunships, and a bird dog, which would act as both FAC and air relay.

The A-team loaned us a GP tent for our TOC and an empty machine gun bunker for our communications center. Our commo setup consisted of an AN/GRC-74 and a PRC-25. I have to admit that we had the 25 hooked up to a two-niner-two antenna, though, and this gave us some semblance of being high-tech. We used the 74 radio to communicate with our unit in Dalat, and the 25 to talk with the aircraft.

To keep out the A-team's nosy CIDG troops, our small MSS was surrounded by a roll of concertina wire. I wasn't invited to the mission briefing or the team's brief-back, but I was told that the two teams would both be inserted in their AOs by helicopter in a standard, last-light infiltration. The two teams would have voice commo with the FAC, who would relay the messages to us at the MSS. Our communications with Dalat were all encoded Morse.

We had good weather for the infiltration, but the timing was a bit off, and it was just a little too dark when the insertion choppers hit their LZs. One team got in without incident, but the other chopper hit a tree stump they were unable to see in the dim light, and they crashed.

No one was killed, but several were badly injured. The mission was compromised, of course, and it then became a case of getting all the team and downed aircrew pulled out before the enemy found them and wiped them out. The small group spent a scary night in a tight perimeter around the tiny LZ, but there was no enemy contact. At first light they were exfiltrated by rope ladder, and the downed chopper was destroyed by an air strike.

The second team was able to remain in its AO and continue the mission. On the third day, however, they were spotted by some woodcutters and requested exfiltration. The exfiltration went off smoothly with no enemy contact, and after they were returned to the MSS and debriefed, we closed up shop, got on the choppers, and flew back to Dalat.

After a night of postmission revelry that left us all sick, hung-over, and exhausted, those of us who had come up from Saigon went out to the airfield the next morning to meet the aircraft that was to pick us up. We sat around in the sun for a couple of hours, then got word that our C-123 had been diverted and we would have to get back to Tan Son Nhut the best way we could.

We managed this with typical Special Forces flair. Vietnam's flamboyant new prime minister, Nguyen Cao Ky, was in Dalat that day for a briefing. He and his entourage always flew around the country in two specially outfitted C-47s, one of which was simply a spare. For security reasons, Ky would make the decision as to which he would actually fly in at the last minute.

While we were sitting there on the runway trying to catch a hop back to Saigon, Ky and his party arrived, preparing to fly back there themselves. One of the senior NCOs in our bunch of guys was an old Vietnam hand who knew Ky, and he walked up to the prime minister and asked him if he'd give us a ride back down south. Ky was a cool dude, basically just an Air Force fighter pilot who had been thrust into politics, and he didn't bat an eye at our request. "Sure," he said, "take my spare plane." So that's how we traveled back to Saigon—on Vietnam's equivalent of Air Force One.

Chapter 18

A Vietnamese driver in a three-quarter came out to meet us at Tan Son Nhut, and this time we were delivered to a different place, not too far from the airfield. This new safe house was a nondescript, two-story building tucked away on a side street. It had a wall around it, like most buildings in Saigon, and a Nung guard at the gate. There was no sign out front.

The bottom floor consisted of a kitchen, bath, living room, and one large bedroom, and upstairs there was another bath and several more bedrooms. The building's flat roof was accessible from inside. Manned by one lone operator, a radio was in operation in one of the upstairs bedrooms. Except for two or three Nung security guards, there were no other indigenous personnel.

Only a few men were permanently assigned there. The radio operator, whose name I've forgotten, lived upstairs, and SFC Beatty, who was another of the old 10th Group guys, lived in the downstairs bedroom. People drifted in and out, most of them in civilian clothes. A couple of these guys were connected with military intelligence units, and some were actually with civilian agencies, but most of them were SF men in mufti.

I was informed that several new recon/guerrilla teams were being recruited, and that I would be given a slot on one as soon as possible. The unit was also in the process of trying to find a suitable location for a training camp. In the meantime, I was told, I didn't have a real job yet, so I should just stay out of trouble, check in a couple of times a day, and so on. My kind of assignment!

The radio operator upstairs turned down my offer of help. He knew he had a cushy assignment and was guarding his one-man empire jealously. That was fine with me because I didn't want to get stuck with a rear-echelon job like his anyway. Beatty was pretty much in charge of the Nung security and general day-to-day household operations, and he needed no help either. Every few days I had to pull CQ all night, but that was no problem because I could sleep all I wanted the next day.

I began spending a lot of time down on Tu Do, and discovered what it was like to be a Saigon garret troop. I finally got in touch with Lyn, after several visits to her bar, and found out she hadn't been working there lately. She constantly had other secret business deals cooking, and the bar had become sort of a sideline. I always wondered if she was actually involved with the Viet Cong, but she was such a rabid capitalist that I never worried too much about it. Lyn was involved in the black market up to her elbows, of course, but so was just about everyone else in Saigon.

On several occasions during this period she took me to her apartment near Tu Do for lunch. Sometimes we made love, sometimes we simply ate, talked, and played cards.

"Now I have Vietnamese boyfriend," she casually told me one quiet afternoon.

"What happened to the MACV colonel?"

"He go home three months ago," she said. "He write me letter all time, say he love me, want leave his wife and bring me live with him in States."

I asked her why she didn't jump on the chance, and she told me she didn't want to leave her old mother all alone.

"Well," I told her, "I can't believe that you've sunk so low that you're now sleeping with a damn slopehead."

"Sometimes you number-hucking-'wenty, you know that?" Lyn said, throwing the cards at me. But I finally got her to see the joke and smile.

She said the Vietnamese boyfriend was also one of her business partners. "He play 'round other girl all time. Try cheat me for money. Probably not stay boyfriend too long."

One afternoon while hanging around the Sporting Bar, I ran into Lee, the Navy SEAL I'd briefly met back in '63. After carefully talking around the subject of what we were each up to, we figured out that we were probably both in the same outfit. I never did actually work with Lee, however, and it would be another couple of years before I'd run into him again.

I was having a great time with my fling at being a Saigon REMF. I almost managed to do it without getting into any trouble, but then my luck ran out.

One night I sat drinking in the Sporting right up to the curfew hour, and when I finally closed the bar down, there were no available taxicabs. Curfew had been in effect for about thirty minutes already when I flagged down a Viet on a motor scooter and offered him a fistful of P's to take me back out to the safe house. We were cruising along, me enjoying the night air, when an American MP jeep roared up alongside and ordered us to pull over.

I guess I looked like a very suspicious character. It was past curfew, I was in civilian clothes, riding on the back of a Vietnamese motor scooter, and drunk as a lord. They checked my ID card with obvious suspicion and asked me where I was stationed. When I told them the address of the safe house, they didn't recognize it as any of the usual authorized living quarters for U.S. personnel. They started asking me questions about what unit I was with and so forth, and I told them it was none of their fucking business.

They frisked me, handcuffed me, threw me in the back of the jeep, and took me to their station house. I sat around there for about an hour until their shift commander finally arrived.

He was a little brighter than the pair who'd arrested me, and he told them to take me to the address I'd given them. "Take Sergeant Wade in to his commanding officer or his CQ, or whatever. Make sure his story checks. Make sure his unit knows he was out after curfew, was riding on unauthorized transportation, refused to furnish requested information to the arresting officers, and recommend that he gets a delinquency report. Then get your asses back on patrol."

The MPs parked their jeep in front of the safe-house gate. The old Nung gate guard jumped to attention and jacked a round in his carbine. I was walking several feet in front of the two cops, and the Nung guard recognized me and let me through. When the two MPs tried to follow me in, however, the tough little Nung snapped his carbine to port arms and stepped in front of them, blocking their path.

I turned around to look at the two fuming MPs. "See you around, dickheads! Thanks for the fucking ride." Then I went in and went to bed. The MPs finally gave up trying to talk their way past our guard and drove away cursing.

It wasn't too long after this escapade that I was told to report to Major Terry. I don't know if word of my brush with the MPs had actually filtered down or if someone had simply decided that I seemed to be having way too much fun.

"Have you ever heard of Con Son Island?" Terry asked.

"It's a prison island, isn't it, sir? Sort of Vietnam's version of Devil's Island?"

"That's right, Sergeant. Only half of the island is actually being used as a penal colony, however. Look at this map."

Con Son was a small, hourglass-shaped island about thirty miles off the east coast. The waist of the island was flat and just about at sea level. The map indicated a runway. On the two ends of the island the ground rose.

"The prison camp is all on this side of the runway," Terry said. "No one is occupying this other side, and we want to move there and set up our training site. The trouble is, there's a Navy unit also interested in using this same area for some sort of communications base. We want to get there first. Possession is ninety percent of the law and all of that. We're going to send you and a couple of other guys there to homestead until we firm up the deal and move the rest of the operation out. You'll set up a radio here on this hill," he told me, pointing it out on the map. "There's an abandoned villa up there that's still in good shape, so you should be pretty comfortable."

The rest of the details would be worked out once we got there. A chopper was already laid on to take me and the other two guys to the island that afternoon, so I threw some stuff in my ruck, picked up one of the PRC-64 radios and some batteries, and was ready to go.

Once we got to Con Son, we discovered that we weren't the only Americans out there after all. A civilian construction crew was building a facility of some sort. They turned out to be a good bunch and were glad to see some other Americans.

The two guys with me—I think they were Hillman and an NCO named Wilson—put up poncho hooches near the RMK site. Before returning to Saigon, the helicopter took me, my radios, and a couple of cases of C-rats up to the top of the nearby hill and dropped me off.

I took a look around at my new home. As the major had promised, the old villa was in good shape. It had concrete walls, a tile roof, and a deep water cistern that had been designed to catch rainwater. The cistern was full, and the water tasted good. At one time the inhabitants had planted a small orchard, and the fruit trees still grew out back, although the area was overgrown by weeds. I had a beautiful sea view from the covered veranda, and I strung up my jungle hammock out there.

I'd taken a PRC-25 to talk to Hillman and Wilson down on the isthmus, and after throwing up a doublet antenna for the 64, I made contact with the safe house back in Saigon. The radio operator there and I had worked out a contact schedule that required me to make only one radio check a day. In case of emergency I would be able to contact the main guard net back at Group Headquarters in Nha Trang.

The first evening approached and I sat on my front porch watching the beautiful sunset. Hell, I thought, this was the life! No Cong, plenty to eat, and nothing to do. I'd been smart enough to bring a couple of John D. MacDonald books up there with me in my ruck, so I figured I wouldn't get too bored. As the first purple shades of evening crept over my hill, however, so did the rats!

These were huge, slimy things. They were so big that at first I thought they were rabbits. The buggers weren't afraid of me at all, acted tame as pets, and would only run off a short distance when I threw rocks or tried to chase them. I was glad I had my hammock with its built-in mosquito net to keep the horrid creatures off me while I slept. Rats were known to try to eat exposed body parts while you were sleeping, and in Vietnam a rat bite meant an automatic series of rabies shots.

The next morning, mostly to give me something to do, I launched my War Against the Rats. I'd noticed some old, home-made box traps around the villa earlier, but hadn't realized what they were for. I overhauled a couple of these, baited them, and put them out; then I built some snares, deadfalls, and other experimental traps of my own. By that second evening I was ready for the invasion. Soon the night air was filled not only with the squeaks of captured rodents but the thumps of my club as I made the rounds of the traps, beating the POWs to a pulp.

It was hot and muggy up there on the hill, and I soon adopted my own duty uniform: jungle boots, PT shorts, and bush hat. The C-rations started tasting like hell before the first week was out, and I began eating only the crackers and fruit. I spent a couple of hours a day sunbathing, and soon became as dark and lean as a Montagnard.

I'd finished my reading material in two days. Time dragged on. The first week I was there, just for something to do, I made the long hike down my hill to visit the other guys and go swimming in the ocean. The sea around the island was swarming with jelly-fish, though, so it wasn't the greatest place to bathe. The trip was hot and tiring, not worth the effort, I decided, so after that I just stayed up at the villa by myself.

I picked up a couple of long, colorful bird feathers and tied them to my hat so that they hung down off the back in redskin style. I also started wearing a necklace made of hand-carved wood, berries, and a few of the bleached, dried rat skulls.

At first I treated with iodine tablets all the drinking water I drew from the cistern. The rainwater tasted very good and pure, however, and after a while I stopped bothering with the treatment. One day, after drinking it straight from the cistern for at least a week, I pulled up a bucket and discovered a decomposed rat floating in it. After that I went back to using the iodine.

I'd been up there on the hill for about three weeks when I heard choppers approaching the island. They landed down on the isthmus. I called Hillman on the PRC-25 and found out it was only touring big shots from somewhere—State Department, CIA, MACV, or maybe even the U.S. Congress. After they'd been there for about an hour, one of the helicopters flew up and landed in my front yard.

The pilot cut the engine, and a couple of MACV colonels in clean, freshly pressed fatigues climbed down. They were accompanied by some nerd in civvies. I hadn't bothered to change clothes myself, because I hadn't expected company. I skittered out to meet them wearing my usual duty uniform of shorts, feathered bush hat, and skull necklace. I snapped what I thought was a sharp salute.

"Sergeant Wade reporting, sir!" I said. I hadn't had anyone to talk to in a while, and my voice came out sounding like a cackle.

I gave them a guided tour, showing them my miniature radio, my rat traps, the orchards out back, my hammock, the water cistern, and all the other points of interest.

"What's *that*, Sergeant?" the nerd in civvies said, pointing distastefully at one of my rat-drying racks.

I was overjoyed at his interest in my new hobby and went into great detail explaining how I killed the rats at night, then hung them up in the sun so the bugs and birds could strip the flesh. "I tried boiling the meat off first, but that was too much trouble. Now I just let it sort of rot off. I'm collecting the skulls, see?" I said, proudly showing him my C-ration box full of bones. "I'm going to make more necklaces like this one I'm wearing and sell them!"

They left right after that. The next day another helicopter came out and brought Wes Kamalu to relieve me on the hill. "Someone thinks you've been up here too long," he told me.

A little sadly, I changed back into jungle fatigues, packed my ruck, picked up my M-16, and trudged back down the hill to civilization.

Chapter 19

A short time later the rest of the unit began moving out to Con Son. Some new men had come on board while I'd been in exile up at the Rat Villa, and one of these was Carl Hargus.

"Wow, this is almost as good as the Bien Hoa rubber plantation," Carl said, looking around at the small tent city we'd hastily erected in the sand next to the runway. "Which way is town?"

Carl had arrived with a couple of other new radio operators, and they'd brought out a Collins SSB along with one of the new 500-watt linear amplifiers. Carl and several other guys in the signal section were old ham radio buffs, and a couple of them had worked at MARS stations. It only took them about a week to get in trouble.

"What do you think of our new antenna?" Carl asked me one morning.

"What the hell is it, a cubical quad?" I said, looking up at the rickety contraption that resembled a giant box kite on a thirty-foot pole.

"Yeah," Carl said, "or call it a parasitic array . . . or whatever."

"I had five-by-five commo with the mainland using that little PRC-64 and a doublet," I told him. "What do you need an antenna like that for when you've got 500 watts?"

"We're talking to the mainland too," Carl said, "but it's mainland USA!"

Carl told me they had established a bootleg net directly with America. They were using fake MARS station call signs and posing as a ship at sea. "Commo's usually pretty good in the evening," he told me. "If you want to call home, come over and we'll do a phone patch with this ham operator we've been talking to in Oregon."

It only took the Army Security Agency boys a couple of weeks to become real interested in this mysterious, unauthorized radio signal. Luckily, we were tipped off that the jig was up and that a team of ASA investigators was on the way out to bust our operation. By the time their plane landed, the quad antenna had been taken down and disassembled.

The ASA spooks checked out our other, unsuspicious, doublet antennas, and once they determined that none of these were cut to the meter range that matched their mystery signal, they flew back to Saigon. Of course, they knew we were the guilty party, and we knew that they knew. The USS *Con Son* never fired up its radios again, much to the regret of several married men who had enjoyed talking with their families back at home each night.

In the meantime, some new recon team personnel had been recruited, and I joined the small group to begin training in the specialized LRP techniques we would soon be using. There were still only a few of us, not even enough to make up four full teams. The original guys out there were Allan Goad, Walt Miller, Bill Menkins, Curtis Brown, and Arthur Wilbur.

Along with a couple of senior NCOs who had previous experience with Project Delta, and about sixteen specially recruited indigenous personnel, we were lifted by helicopter around to the far end of the island. We were given an engineer tool kit and told to build ourselves a camp and to start training.

The first thing we had to do was clear out an area for a decent-size LZ. It immediately became apparent that the best man with an ax was Sergeant Miller, who'd been a lumberjack before joining the Army and could cut down a tree with about two swipes. It took us almost a week of brutal physical labor to get the training camp built, and without Miller (a.k.a. Paul Bunyan) it probably would have taken twice as long.

Goad was the ranking NCO. He already had a lot of military service behind him when he joined C-5. He was another of those ex-Marines (excuse me, *former* Marines) who had seen the light and switched services. Goad was very pleasant, and easy to work for and with.

Curtis Brown was an experienced man, and also a qualified radio operator. We decided we knew each other from someplace, either on Okinawa or Vietnam, but never did figure out where. I didn't know Wilbur or Menkins yet, but soon we were one jolly little family in our jungle hideaway.

Our training started with a review of basic combat patrolling, then we launched into the new techniques that Delta had developed by trial and error during the past couple of years. We had one interpreter out there with us, and everything we Americans learned had to subsequently be taught to our indigenous troops.

The patrolling methods and tactics then in use on recon teams were a conglomeration of techniques, some of them dating back to the French and Indian War, some stolen from the British SAS in Malaya, and some recently invented in Vietnam by Project Delta.

The whole concept of small-unit recon was stealth. A perfect reconnaissance mission would be one in which a team was infiltrated, gathered the required information, and was then exfiltrated without the enemy ever knowing about it. Staying undetected was the main thing that kept these small units alive, and once a six-man recon team was compromised, the mission turned into an escape-and-evasion problem.

Stealth techniques that seem obvious today were considered innovative back then. As previously mentioned, in the early days of the war the regular Army was still wearing starched fatigues, white T-shirts, white name tapes, and large, yellow chevrons. Our recon teams, on the other hand, wore the tiger-stripe fatigues, floppy bush hats, and full-face and hand cammo.

Green duct tape was actually a new item back then and quickly became very popular. It was wrapped around weapons to break up the outline, wrapped around any shiny metal such as the brass belt buckles we still wore, wrapped around straps and buckles, and wrapped around trouser legs to keep out the leeches.

Slings were removed from weapons. This was done not only to reduce noise, but also to remove any temptation to sling the weapon over the shoulder while on the march. A short piece of parachute suspension line was carried by each man in case an improvised rifle sling was required for something like climbing a rope ladder.

The teams used the basic file formation for movement. The point man was the team's most experienced indigenous member. Another indige was next in line, followed by the U.S. team leader, then the U.S. radio operator, and the other two indigenous. The position of "tail gunner" was also critical, and was also given to one of the most experienced indigenous. If the team ran into the enemy while moving, the first people the enemy saw at either end of the file would be Oriental, not American. If the recon team did not start shooting, often the enemy would not know who we were.

Trying to move at night without giving away the team location had proved too difficult. The usual tactic was to begin moving as soon as it got light enough to see, and to continue moving right up to full darkness. At night the teams holed up in a very tight perimeter—within arm's reach of one another. At least one team member was awake at all times, and in fact no one got a whole hell of a lot of sleep.

Noise discipline was extremely important, of course, and once inserted in the recon zone, all talking was in whispers. Many hand and arm signals were used, some of these the standard Army signals, but others newly developed for these specialized missions. There were signals for "freeze," for "enemy sighted," and for "enemy coming this way, establish hasty ambush."

We learned and practiced several immediate-action drills, one of the most important of which was for breaking contact with the enemy. There were different versions of this "break-contact" drill, with each team adding or deleting parts as they saw fit.

The basic drill started with the team point man either shooting at the enemy or being shot at. The other team members would step off to either side of the route of march and immediately return covering fire up either flank. The point element would then turn and run straight back the way they'd just come, with team members peeling off and following as they were passed. The last man to run would be the tail gunner, who would throw a grenade of some sort, either frag or CN tear gas, before he took off.

On our practice LRP missions we carried PRC-25 radios as the primary means of communications and HT-1s as alternates. Brown and I were still the only qualified radio operators in the recon section, and would also experiment with the PRC-64. We learned the use of air-to-ground signaling devices such as panels, mirrors, pen flares, and smoke. Smoke and pen flare were only used after a team was compromised, of course, because those methods also told the enemy where we were.

Much of our personal equipment, such as the rucks, binoculars, compasses, and so forth, had been purchased in Japan and thus had no U.S. markings. I was told that a "sterile" clandestine radio would probably take the place of the PRC-64. We had a small assortment of special weapons to play with too. These included some brand-new Swedish-Ks, a couple of silenced Sten guns, silenced .22 pistols, and a couple of sniper rifles.

The .22s had already been used a few times by Delta personnel in combat, and we were warned that although they were in fact very silent, they also had little killing power.

"One of the guys in Delta was lying alongside a trail and shot an NVA right in the middle of the chest with one of these pistols," our trainer told us. "He actually saw dust fly off the bastard's uniform. The NVA yelled, *'Choi yoi!'* and ran away."

We were advised that when shooting someone with one of the silenced guns, either the .22s or the submachine guns, we should aim for the head and always fire two or three rounds. Several other suppressed pistols were in development. One was a .45, and the other, a 9mm version, was being made by Smith & Wesson.

The idea was kicking around that maybe we should carry the same weapons the enemy used, and we had a couple of AKs and RPDs to train with. Carrying enemy weapons made a lot of sense for several reasons. For one thing, we would be able to use captured ammo. Probably the best reason, however, was that if the enemy spotted our point or tail elements carrying AKs, they would be more inclined to think we were friendly. And once a firefight broke out, it would be harder for them to pinpoint our location from the sound of our weapons. The only bad part was that it would also be harder for our own friendly forces, particularly air, to identify us.

We were given a brand-new "Starlight" night vision scope to field-test and evaluate. This was still a classified item of equipment in those days, and we all marveled at how well it worked. Unfortunately, the original version was too big, heavy, and fragile to take on our type of operation, although we later used it for camp defense. We were told that there was a lot of other neat new stuff in the pipeline, and that, within reason, we could get about anything we asked for.

The primary means of infiltration and exfiltration was helicopter. We were told there was a possibility that our indigenous troops would later be put through parachute training, however, and that when and if we were inserted for our "real," long-term mission, we might be going in by parachute.

We received classes on the newly developed emergency exfiltration techniques then in use. One of these methods had been developed by a Special Forces NCO by the name of McGuire, and was simply a long rope with a sling seat at the end that was dropped from a hovering helicopter. The man on the ground sat in the sling, put his wrist in a safety loop, and the chopper pulled him out. Usually, two of these slings were used at one time, one rope from each side of the UH-IB. The men would link arms and spread-eagle to stop the spinning that occurred with only one rope.

Each man on the team carried a snap link and a six-foot piece of rope. These were used to fashion Swiss seats, which could be used either for rappelling out of a chopper into the AO or, more likely, to snap onto the rungs of a rope ladder for exfiltration.

In the rope ladder exfiltration, the chopper would lower the ladder to the waiting team. While two team members held the bottom of the ladder as tight and steady as possible, the first man would climb up the ladder about ten feet, then snap in. The other team members would then climb up beneath, and when the last man hooked in, he gave the signal to take off.

Today's STABO extraction rig was eventually developed from these early experiments.

Out there on Con Son we had neither the aircraft nor the required open area to do much hands-on training with the helicopters, but we were able to practice the other new patrolling tactics and techniques. After training for several weeks at the jungle base, we went back to the main camp and prepared for a full-dress practice run.

We divided into four training teams, were given a mission briefing, worked out our recon plans, gave brief-backs, and then, one team at a time, we were inserted by chopper at the end of the island. The mission was a standard five-day recon, and each team had four or five targets to check out. We had the entire north end of the island as an AO. The terrain was all straight up and down, covered with extremely thick vegetation, and there was no groundwater.

This turned out to be a real ball-buster of a training exercise, with some of the members falling off cliffs, others dropping of heat exhaustion, and all of us requiring frequent water resupply by air. Although all the team members were in excellent physical condition and well acclimatized, I believe most of us were surprised at just how physically demanding that kind of patrolling was—and out there on Con Son, we had no enemy to worry about!

As I recall, none of the teams lasted the entire five days. The team I was on made it to day three, then had to be pulled out due to illnesses suffered by our indigenous members. After a thorough debriefing and a training critique, we were released and told to take a couple of days' rest. This was good timing because a U.S. Coast Guard cutter had just anchored offshore and a big party with their crew was planned for that night.

Most people don't even know that the Coast Guard was also involved with the war in Vietnam, and I have to admit that this was the only Coast Guard bunch I ever ran into over there. These guys had been at sea for a while when they stopped by the island to visit us, and were ready for some serious drinking.

They'd come to the right place for that, as the headquarters element had recently turned one of the GP tents into a club and had managed to have a couple of hundred cases of beer flown in from the Saigon commissary.

That evening we made the Coast Guard ship's captain, who was an O-5 (commander, equivalent to a lieutenant colonel), into an honorary Green Beret. This involved much drinking, exchanging of hats, drinking out of hats, pissing in hats, and stomping on hats—not necessarily in that order. Unfortunately, I was too exhausted from the recent training to do more than watch all the festivities in a mild stupor. The two cans of beer I drank that night were the first I'd had in over a month, and they knocked me on my ass.

Chapter 20

While we were all out training on the island, the wheels of progress had been grinding away back on the mainland. Detachment C-5 took possession of an old A-team camp that lay on the highway midway between Saigon and Bien Hoa. Camp Ho Ngoc Tao was in a supposedly pacified area, and was next door to Vietnam's new military academy, Tu Duc. It seemed a perfect location for us, being near two major airfields and right on the main road.

Shortly after we finished initial training on the island, the recon section, accompanied by the operations and intelligence personnel, moved to our new home. The headquarters section, commanded by Lieutenant Colonel Reish, was already in place. There was still some construction of new barracks and of a new cement TOC taking place, but basically all we had to do was move in.

The operations section, on the north end of camp, was separated from the rest of the complex by a concertina-wire inner fence. In this isolation area were the recon section, the newly recruited commando company, which would be our quick-reaction force, and the O&I crew. The other end of camp, nearest the highway, contained the headquarters, the TOC, the dining facility, and of course the most important thing—the club. Camp security was handled by a company of Nungs who were under the able command of M. Sgt. (E8) Paul Vukovich.

The unit was growing quickly. One day I met a couple of new men, M. Sgt. Wally Sergant and Sgt. Boyd Anderson, who had just transferred over together from one of the A-team camps. I already knew Wally Sergant by reputation, as he had been a Black Hat (instructor) at the jump school in Benning for several years, and I'd heard many stories from recent graduates about the infamous "Sergeant Sergant." Wally went to work in the air operations section, and Andy volunteered for duty with recon.

164

Rumors were flying that we would soon be committed to our first combat operation. At that time we still had not been able to practice the extraction techniques. Luckily, we were assigned a few air assets not long after we arrived at Ho Ngoc Tao, and were able to finish up our training. We spent an entire week training with the helicopters at a large open area to the west of camp. We began with the simpler tasks of learning how to board and dismount the birds. Once again we used the same techniques that Project Delta had developed.

During infil and exfil, the seats were removed from the HU-1Bs. On infiltration, the teams sat on the floor of the choppers, three men facing each door. One American was on either side, nearest the pilots. The pilots were trained to swoop into the LZ quickly and hover four or five feet off the ground, thus avoiding hidden obstacles or mines. The decision to insert ("go" or "no go") was up to the recon team leader. If he un-assed the chopper, everyone else did also, all at the same time, from both doors. This took only a second or two, and the pilot then roared off again.

The teams also practiced boarding from both sides at once. When it came time to get the hell out of an area, the recon team lay in an open V formation, three men to a side, with the panel man at the apex. The chopper flew into the open end of the formation, touched lightly down, and the team members ran and dove into the open doors. As soon as the pilot got the thumbs-up from the recon team leader, signaling that all his people were accounted for, the pilot threw the coals to the engine and they took off.

Besides practicing with the McGuire rigs and rope ladders, we also learned how to rappel from the choppers. Although all of the U.S. Special Forces members knew how to rappel from towers and in mountain terrain, most of us had not yet rappelled from a helicopter. After reviewing what we already knew by teaching it to our indigenous team members, we advanced to trying it from the choppers. I was never sold on this means of infiltrating an AO, as it seemed to take too long and put the hovering helicopter in too much danger of being blasted out of the sky.

During the helicopter training, we had been joined by a young lieutenant named Deacon, who went by the nickname of "Ack-ack." I discovered he would be my team leader on our upcoming operation. Ack-ack was typical of the kind of junior officer we had in SF in those days, meaning he was a pretty wild son of a bitch.

* * *

I believe it was toward the end of May that we got our warning order. After a brief flurry of activity in the operations hooch, during which plans were received, maps assembled, and so on, we prepared for movement to the mission support site. This, we were told, was 150 miles north of us, up in the central highlands, near Ban Me Thuot.

Our advance party, taking all the heavy equipment such as the tents, base radio gear, and other supplies, left a couple of days before the rest of us. They trucked to Bien Hoa airfield and flew from there to Ban Me Thuot by C-123. The recon section flew up on our choppers, departing directly from Ho Ngoc Tao.

Members of our B-detachment met us on the runway with a couple of trucks and took us to their compound to spend the first night. We had a pleasant evening in their club and I ran into several old pals. The next day the B-team took us out to the small tent city the advance party had already established in some trees down off one end of the runway.

That first afternoon we were given a general briefing of the situation. We were part of a large-scale operation being conducted by one of the recently arrived American infantry units. Delta was just completing a series of reconnaissance missions for this same operation. There were still several areas that Delta had not had time to check out, however, and we would be working those.

We only had four operational recon teams for this operation. I was going in with Ack-ack, Goad and Miller were on another team, and I've forgotten who was paired with who on the other two teams. On D minus 3 we were given our mission briefings.

So far, we were told, the infantry had been making moderate contact with the enemy. The operation still had a few weeks left to run, and they were hoping to find a lucrative area to exploit. The Delta teams had successfully completed all their assigned missions, and hadn't reported much enemy activity. Although several large NVA units had been identified in the area, they appeared to be widely spread out. Our teams from C-5 would be working in the final unexplored corner of the infantry's AO. Each of our teams had a four-square-kilometer area to recon. The missions were to be of five days' duration.

The lieutenant and I studied the maps of our AO. There were plenty of possible locations for infiltration and exfiltration LZs.

"This whole southern edge of the AO looks pretty flat and open," Deacon said. It was unlikely that we would find any enemy in that area, and we decided we should simply stay out of that section due to lack of concealment. The northern side of the AO was all steep hills and jungle, however.

"I wonder if there's any water in these," I asked, pointing out the two small streams. I was thinking that if there was, we might find the enemy camped nearby. I was also wondering what our own water situation would be like, remembering how thirsty I'd gotten during the training out at Con Son.

"We're scheduled to do a flyover tomorrow," the lieutenant said. "That's one thing we'll need to look at."

We made a tentative plan, but decided to wait until we got an actual look at the terrain before we firmed anything up.

"Looked dry as a bone to me," I said as soon as we'd walked far enough away from the chopper's engine noise to be able to talk without yelling. It was the next morning, and we'd just concluded our air recon.

"We won't be able to tell for sure until we get in on the ground," Deacon said. "But we'll try to round up a few extra canteens and maybe a couple of those two-quart, collapsible jobs. Let's go look at that map again."

For infiltration we selected an open area in the southeast corner of the AO, just at the base of a large hill. One of the stream beds wound around the back side of this hill, and if there was any enemy, we thought this might be a good place to find them. Unfortunately, the high ground afforded a great view of the flat, low land we would be using for our infil and exfil LZs, but there was no other way to do it.

The basic plan was to move into the jungle at the base of the hill, spend the night there, then continue on at first light up to the top of that hill and down the back side toward the stream. We would continue to check out the AO by moving in a zigzag pattern and staying in the hilly, jungle-covered northern half. If all went well, we would move back down to the flat, open area on the evening of the fourth day and exfiltrate from an LZ in the southwest corner of our AO.

We were still worried about the water situation. It was simply impossible to carry enough to last five days, and if we were resupplied by air, we risked alerting the enemy to our presence. We decided that if we were going to need a water drop, we'd work our way down to the clear area and pick it up there. That way, if we were compromised, we would be near some good LZs to use for our getaway.

We brought the four indigenous team members in next and, through an interpreter, briefed them on the plan. These were hand-picked men, and each one had proved himself many times in combat situations. They seemed pretty cool and confident, but just like the lieutenant and me, this was the first time any of them had been on this sort of patrol.

"Do you think they're scared?" the LT asked me when they'd gone.

"About as scared as me," I told him.

"Is the commo all squared away?"

I told him that the main commo would be through the FAC using the PRC-25. "I'm also carrying the PRC-64," I told him. "There'll be a guy monitoring the code frequency back here on a twenty-four-hour basis. If we get a chance, I'm supposed to try to make a couple of commo checks on it, and we can use it for a backup if we have to. Frankly," I added, "I don't think we'll be able to use the 64 much on this kind of operation."

The lieutenant asked why not, and I explained it to him. "The PRC-64 operates off of a doublet antenna, sir. For the low AM frequency it uses, the antenna has to be fairly long. It needs to be pretty high off the ground too, and should be in a clear area. The radio doesn't have much power, and if you string the antenna low, down in that triple canopy we'll be in, the vegetation just sucks up all the RF waves. It would probably work okay in a real guerrilla warfare situation, where we'd be operating from a fairly safe area, but on these recon missions we're right in the middle of the enemy, and I won't be able to climb trees and all of that shit to hang the damn antenna."

Because of the need to carry as much water as possible, we repacked our rucks and web gear, leaving behind the claymore mine and some of the extra grenades and ammo we'd originally planned to take in. Since this AO was not in a so-called denied area, there was no need to get too sneaky with sterile equipment, and our team had decided to carry M-2 carbines. The indigenous had still not been issued the M-16s at that time, and the lieutenant and I figured it best if everyone on the team was carrying the same kind of weapon.

Although our indigenous really liked the Swedish-K sub-machine gun, I didn't think this was such a hot weapon, especially for recon. The Swedish-K was one of the best built, most accurate, and most respected submachine guns back in the early sixties. Like all weapons of its type, however, there were inherent problems.

The long magazine that fed from the bottom of the weapon made it hard to fire in the prone position. The 9mm pistol cartridge it was chambered for really wasn't powerful enough for shooting through brush. But the biggest problem, as far as I was concerned, was that it fired from the open bolt position. If the weapon was carried cocked/bolt back, a sudden jar, a twig, or an accidental squeeze of the trigger would cause it to fire. If the weapon was carried with the bolt to the rear and locked in the safety notch, it took too long to get it into action.

With the stock folded, the Swedish-K was a handy weapon to carry in a vehicle. It was different, and looked way cool too, so many men, especially the rear-area crowd, liked to get their pictures taken while brandishing one of these "exotic" guns.

Each team was issued one of the silenced High Standard pistols, and the lieutenant elected to carry ours. We thought this weapon might come in very handy when we were in our night defensive position. If an enemy soldier happened to stumble onto us as we lay in the dark jungle, we hoped to be able to kill him without giving away our position. Besides the silenced pistol, each man on the team carried a knife.

There has been much nonsense and just pure bullshit written about the knives Special Forces personnel carried in Vietnam. Actually, there was never any one particular knife issued as the "official" SF knife. One very popular knife that actually was issued by the 5th SF for a while in the early days was the K-Bar. Project Delta's mess association also gave away a knife to its members that they'd had manufactured in Japan. This was what is now known as the "SOG knife." In the fifties and early sixties, many Special Forces men purchased handmade knives from Bo Randall in Florida, and later from makers such as Cooper, Hibbens, and Draper.

What kind of knife a guy carried depended on what kind of mission he was performing. For a long-term guerrilla warfare mission, which would involve living in the woods for months at a time, general utility knives such as the Air Force survival knife were popular. For our recon missions, however, no field craft was done. There *was* a good possibility you might actually need to kill someone with a knife, though, so most recon men kept this in mind when selecting a blade. I carried a Buck Folding Hunter in my pocket for general chores. I also taped an M-3 trench knife to my left web gear suspender in case things got bloody.

The early recon teams usually carried the same dried "indigenous rations" that were standard issue for the CIDG troops. These consisted of a bag of instant rice and a few small packets of dried fish, vegetables, and seasoning. I always rehydrated one bag of this before starting a patrol, and usually still had some left over when we got back.

Each man also had a four-foot-by-six-foot plastic ground sheet. This wasn't so much to keep a person dry, which was an impossibility, but to wrap up in at night to keep from getting chilled.

The two American team members kept tight control of the radios on these recon missions, and this meant that we also carried the damn things. Once you added the weight of a PRC-25, HT-1, and extra batteries to the weight of the ammo, weapons, and water, you had quite a load. On those early missions with C-5, I was also lugging around the PRC-64.

We were pretty lucky on that first operation. The weather, always a critical element, was perfect. The sky remained cloudless, with practically no fog in the morning to worry about. We only had enough helicopters assigned to insert two teams at a time, and on the evening of D-1, our team and Goad's were put in on adjacent AOs without incident. At least, that's how it probably reads in the after-action report.

Down there on the ground, in the dark, in the middle of enemy-controlled territory, it seemed like there were endless incidents. To start off with, we misjudged how high the chopper was, and jumped out when we were still about ten feet off the ground. A couple of the indigenous were shaken up when we hit, but we decided we could continue the mission.

We moved off the LZ as soon as our eyes and ears became accustomed to the jungle sounds and rapidly decreasing light. It was almost full dark once we entered the triple-layer jungle canopy, and we were only able to move about four hundred meters before it became too dark to move without making a racket.

The lieutenant gave the hand signal to make night bivouac, and we all silently formed a circle and sat down, each man facing out, with our rifles in our laps. We loosened the straps on our rucks a little, but kept them around our shoulders. It became pitch-dark. We all sat, trying to relax, but straining our ears for the sounds of searching enemy soldiers.

There are an amazing variety of night sounds in a jungle. Bugs sing, frogs croak, night birds flap through the overhead branches. When you're as keyed up as we were, an animal as small as a rabbit seems to make as much noise as a man as it moves through the underbrush. I probably didn't sleep a whole hour the entire night. It seemed like every time I'd start to drift off, one of the men next to me would squeeze my arm to alert me to possible danger.

It finally started getting light. At first I was glad the night was finally over . . . until I realized that meant the enemy could now also see us. We quietly stood, trying to stretch our cold, stiff muscles. I got on the radio and made our scheduled first-light contact with the orbiting FAC. Commo was good, and I sent a message saying we were continuing the mission as planned. Deacon gave the signal to move out, and the point man started slowly picking his way up to the top of the first hill. We hadn't gone very far when we ran into the first trail.

It ran in the same direction we were going, and it looked as if it hadn't been used in some time. Still, we didn't take it, nor did we even risk crossing it and thus leaving tracks, but continued on through the tangled underbrush toward the summit.

Suddenly, the lieutenant, who was directly in front of me, gave me the signal to freeze, and I relayed it to the man behind me. The point man motioned to Deacon and me to move up to where he crouched. We squatted on either side of the man and looked up where he pointed. There in a tree, only ten meters away, was an observation platform.

The position was empty, but it was so well camouflaged that we'd gotten practically underneath it before our point man had spotted it. We showed the observation post to the rest of our men and continued on. Now we tried to watch not only the ground around us, but also up in the trees. We spotted several more of these platforms, all empty, before we came to the top of the hill.

We were actually in the middle of the damn base camp before we realized it. The abandoned NVA fighting positions around the camp perimeter were so well camouflaged that we walked past them without seeing them. The first things we did see were several hooches, and an old campfire.

We poked around the empty campsite, searching for enemy caches. We either couldn't find them or there were none. Each recon team carried a miniature 35mm camera, and we used ours to photograph a few of the fighting positions, the hooches, and the trails leading to and from the location.

As we were taking a break on top of the hill, we heard shooting from Goad and Miller's AO. I listened on the radio to find out what was going on. Apparently they had made contact with an enemy unit of unknown size. They were being pursued, and requested an emergency exfil.

We stayed put on top of our hill until the other team was safely pulled out. We didn't want to risk running into trouble ourselves until our limited air assets were once again uncommitted and free to come to our aid if needed. Once their extraction was complete, we moved out, heading downhill toward the stream bed.

The stream was dry, and we found no enemy. We took another break and tried to eat a little. We checked on the physical condition of our indigenous, and found out that one had a sore, swollen ankle from hitting the ground too hard on the insertion, and our tail gunner was complaining of stomach pains. I made another radio contact, giving our current location, and said we were continuing mission.

We headed back to the south, around the base of the hill we'd just come over. By the evening of the first day we'd run across more old emplacements, but had seen no live enemy nor signs indicating they had recently been in our area. We had discovered no source of groundwater. The man with the bad ankle was starting to limp badly, and the one with the stomach problems now appeared to be in real pain. We decided to make our night bivouac near the clear, flat area in the southern half of the AO, and if the two men weren't any better by morning, to terminate the mission.

We spent another sleepless night, this time not only alert for sounds of enemy movement, but also listening to the muffled moans of agony from our tail gunner. As soon as it got light enough to see, we knew we had to get out of there immediately. The man with the stomach pains was chalky white, covered with sweat, and could no longer even stand.

I called the FAC and advised him of the situation. I was able to signal him with my mirror so he could get a fix on our exact location. He directed us to the nearest LZ, which was only about five hundred meters distant from us.

It was still a real bitch getting there, as we had to carry the sick man, and the guy with the ankle problem could barely hobble along. By the time we got to the clearing, the extraction chopper and the covering gunships had been orbiting the area for about ten minutes. We encountered no enemy at the LZ, the chopper zipped in and picked us up just like we'd practiced it, and half an hour later we were back at the MSS being debriefed. The indigenous with the stomach problems apparently had appendicitis, the medics told me, and probably would have died before the day was out had we stayed in the AO.

Chapter 21

Although all four of our recon teams ended up requesting exfiltration before completing the scheduled five-day missions, we suffered no casualties. Two teams had made enemy contact, but there didn't appear to be any large NVA or VC concentrations in the AO. We were thoroughly debriefed, turned in our cameras and other special equipment, then folded our tents and headed back to Ho Ngoc Tao.

Recon personnel were given a four-day stand-down, which most of us spent in the usual search for max debauchery. I headed immediately for Tu Do Street, where I divided my time between the Sporting Bar, the Morning Star Bar, and Lyn's apartment.

I was discovering what men have known for several thousand years. There seems to be some innate drive in humans that makes us want to mate immediately after being in dangerous, life-and-death situations. This desire to reproduce after a brush with death probably has something to do with survival of the species and is one hell of an aphrodisiac.

Not only sex, but everything else in life suddenly takes on a glorious new meaning when you're able look around and realize you've come through it all again. You tend to begin living each moment to the fullest, devouring each new second of life as it comes along. The only problem is that these "fixes" don't last long enough. It is very easy to become addicted to the highs of survival. Then you start going back again and again for more stimulation, until the old luck finally runs out.

And as all combat soldiers know, luck is very important when it comes to survival. Most new soldiers figure this out after their very first taste of combat. One guy does everything exactly as he was trained, is very careful, takes no unnecessary chances, and gets blown away. Another runs around in the open, charges a machine gun single-handedly, and doesn't get a scratch. A bullet misses your head by an inch . . . pretty lucky you'd just leaned the other way, huh? The man next to you gets shot five times, and you're unwounded.

Although a statistician would probably tell you that your odds of surviving each encounter are always exactly fifty-fifty, the combat soldier begins to believe his odds of surviving get worse with time. That's how I was beginning to feel by that summer of '66. By then I'd lived through almost two years of pretty hazardous assignments and had survived some very close calls. I was over the halfway mark of my year tour, and was starting to get short-timer pains.

One day, several weeks after we'd returned from Ban Me Thuot, I realized there was something mysterious going on around camp. There were many secretive meetings and whispered conversations taking place. Word finally leaked out to those of us not directly involved that our "real" mission was getting ready to begin. C-5 was preparing to infiltrate several of our intelligence operatives that night, and were only waiting for final approval from higher up to go ahead with this first phase of our plan.

The spy teams were brought to Ho Ngoc Tao from Saigon, where they had been kept under wraps in one of our many safe houses. The actual insertion was to be by helicopter, and they would launch from Tu Duc Military Academy. The tension increased as the afternoon progressed and no official go-ahead had yet been received. At dusk the agents and their handlers were standing by the choppers, waiting to board, when we got word that the mission was a big no-go.

The next day there was a feeling of dejection in the air. What was going on? Apparently our whole operation was out the window. Would all of our training and preparation turn out to be wasted? Would the unit be disbanded? Wild rumors flew.

We were all being transferred to Nha Trang to build a new demonstration area, like the one at Fort Bragg, which would be used to impress visiting politicians. No, that wasn't right, another man said. The real plan was to divide us up and attach us to "leg" infantry units for the remainder of our tours. The infantry units would use us for suicide missions so the draftees wouldn't get killed. Naw, that wasn't right, said someone else. We were all going to the Mike Force.

* * *

With everything in confusion and my immediate future in doubt, I did the smart thing: I went on R&R back to Okinawa. Actually, it wasn't just a pleasure trip. I'd written several letters to International Motors back on the island inquiring about my new car deal, and receiving no reply, was beginning to get worried. I took four days of furlough, caught a ride on a C-130 at Bien Hoa, and that afternoon I landed at Kadena.

I checked into one of the small hotels near Koza, and early the next morning took a cab to the car dealership. You can probably imagine how I felt when we pulled up in front of the address and found out that International Motors was no longer there.

I went next door to the British Motors dealer and talked to an assistant manager I knew. Seems that the owner/manager of International Motors had been in some sort of monetary difficulties and one day simply disappeared. He'd taken all the books and records with him, plus all the company assets. It was thought he was living in Hong Kong, but no one knew for sure.

"I guess you're just screwed," the guy at British Motors told me. "You should have dealt with us!"

I checked around a little more and discovered I wasn't the only one who'd gotten the shaft. Some Air Force pilot at Kadena had paid for a Mercedes he never received. When I went to the local Bank of America branch to get a copy of the $1,500 check I'd used for my final payment, one of the bank managers came out to talk with me. "If you find that bastard, let us know," he said. "He owes us over $50,000."

This, I decided, was your basic case of live-and-learn. I never did recover any of my $3,000 loss, and as far as I know, neither did anyone else. My only hope is that the crooked SOB who ripped off so many people eventually died in a horrible, painful manner.

I spent the remaining three days of my leave drowning my sorrows in some of my old haunts down on Gate Two Street. All the girls there were glad to see me and my money again, and they even let me pay the old, preinflation prices for services rendered.

When I got back to Ho Ngoc Tao, all the decisions had been made concerning our futures. C-5 was being reorganized. We were being divided into three new special projects: Sigma, Omega, and Gamma. Sigma and Omega would be performing missions similar to Delta's. Project Sigma would stay at Ho Ngoc Tao. Omega would operate out of Nha Trang. The third unit, Project Gamma, would be more involved with agent handling and would be working primarily from Du Co.

I found out that I'd be staying with the Sigma element at Ho Ngoc Tao. My buddy Hargus went with Gamma. Within a few weeks of the reorganization, many new people had arrived at camp and many of the old ones had departed. There was excitement in the air as we prepared for our new mission.

One day a bunch of us were sitting around the club arguing the merits of different military small arms. The discussion had gotten around to the .30 caliber carbine. I and several others were stating our opinion that the weapon tended to malfunction and that the cartridge it was chambered for had little killing power.

A newly assigned major, a little bantam rooster of a guy, was sitting at another table. He'd been listening to our discussion and now decided to put in his own two cents' worth. "I never had any trouble with the carbine," he said.

I looked over at him, wondering what this new guy could possibly know about guns and combat. "One night in Korea I killed a hundred and fifty gooks with one," the major added.

He went on to tell us that back in the Korean War, when he'd still been an NCO, he and another man were the only survivors after their unit was overrun by communists. "We were in this bunker," he told us. "We had several carbines and plenty of ammo. The guy with me was wounded, but he could still load magazines. I just kept shooting the fuckers all night, and when our guys counterattacked the next morning, there was a big pile of bodies around the bunker."

This new major was Ola Mize, and I later found out that he'd been awarded the Medal of Honor for that particular action in Korea.

The recon section was expanded from four teams to six. I was promoted to staff sergeant and given my own team. This was the second promotion I'd received while serving in Vietnam, the first one having been to buck sergeant three years before, when I'd been at Camp Tan Phu. My birthday also rolled around again, and I was pleased to realize that I'd survived to my twenty-fourth year.

Sergeant Anderson finished his first phases of recon training and joined me as number-two man on the team. Boyd was a big, gung-ho kind of guy, and we had a lot of stuff in common. We'd both been raised in the Southwest, he in New Mexico, and I in

Arizona. Both of us had grown up with guns and shooting. Boyd enjoyed varmint hunting, he told me, and out on the rifle range I discovered that he was indeed a crack shot.

We began team training in the area around Ho Ngoc Tao, working on our patrolling techniques, hand signals, immediate-action drills, and so on. At night we'd leave the camp perimeter and practice doing it all in the dark. Since there were numerous VC and NVA squads also moving around the area at night, this training got to be quite realistic at times.

Several choppers had been assigned to Sigma on a more or less permanent basis. Us "old recon hands" trained Boyd and the other new men on the specialized extraction and insertion methods. It was also around this time that an Air Force FAC pilot, Gammons, was assigned to Sigma. He was a young, courageous captain to whom many of us would owe our lives before it was all over with.

While training with Andy and the team, one glitch had come to light. We found out about it when we began working out the problem of how to move while carrying a dead or wounded team member. Because Anderson was so damn big and strong, he could easily carry me or anyone else on the team by himself, but it took several of us to lug him around. This actually was a critical consideration, especially from Boyd's perspective. Not being able to trust the indigenous when it came right down to it, the two American team members depended almost completely on each other.

"Don't worry, Boyd," I told him. "If you get wounded and I have to leave your big ass, I'll make sure you have plenty of ammo and dried rations. Of course, I'll have to take your weapon and the radio with me so they won't fall into enemy hands!"

With our change of mission, Sigma's recon teams stopped messing around with the PRC-64 radio. We used Project Delta's commo methods, including our own versions of their signal operating instructions (SOI). The number-two man on all the recon teams still acted as the "radio operator"—although anyone on the team was capable of using the PRC-25—and I was happy to pass on the chore of lugging the heavy thing to Anderson. Since I now carried our alternate radio, the HT-1, plus the silenced pistol and the claymore, I probably didn't really get off any lighter.

It was early September. The rainy season was starting there in Vietnam. Back in the good old USA it was fall. The college kids were beginning a new year of football games, frat parties, and antiwar love-ins. "Everybody must get stoned!" Bob Dylan was singing in his ugly, nasal voice. More and more celebrities, U.S. politicians, and members of the news media were jumping on the antiwar bandwagon all the time. It was obviously the "in" position, the one to take.

The protests were becoming uglier all the time, and tales of returning Vietnam veterans being spit on and having human shit thrown at them were widely circulated in the news. Some antiwar celebrity woman told college girls that they should withhold sexual favors from males who didn't support the antiwar movement—that would teach the dirty-capitalistic-warmongering pigs! The United States flag was being burned in the streets of America, and mobs of drunk, drugged longhairs ran around waving VC flags and swearing their undying support for Uncle Ho.

"Don't knock it if you haven't tried it," was a popular hippie slogan. Those of us in the Special Forces community just looked at each other and grinned—that was our feeling exactly. After all, in Vietnam we were simply "doing our thing."

On September 7, 1966, we got our warning order for Operation Golf. "MISSION: To infiltrate and conduct ground reconnaissance and surveillance in the assigned reconnaissance zones (RZs) within area of operations (AOs)."

We would be operating out of an A-team camp named Dong Xoai on that mission, and the advance party departed Ho Ngoc Tao on September 11 at 0800. The shit was getting ready to hit the fan.

Chapter 22

The infiltration had been timed perfectly, and as the sun fell below the horizon, our UH-1B dipped briefly to the small LZ and I jumped to the ground. I ran several steps straight ahead toward the edge of the jungle clearing, then fell into the prone position. Within seconds I was joined by Andy and the rest of the team.

As soon as the sound of the departing chopper died away, we all became aware of a new noise. Mixed with the buzzing and chirping of the insects was a steady, rapid drumming. It sounded like someone hitting two pieces of bamboo together. The sound was picked up and repeated by other drummers farther away.

The point man was lying next to me, and he reached over and grabbed my arm to get my attention. I looked at him, and he gave the hand signal for "enemy is near." His eyes were wide and fearful, so I tried to look unconcerned.

I had to make a very quick decision. Immediately upon insertion, each team leader was required to send his initial entry report. This report was basically either an "All okay, continuing mission," or a "We're in shit, *help!*" The way the last-light infiltrations were timed, there was a very short "window of opportunity" to request and receive any required assistance before all the aircraft departed the area for the night. Within two or three minutes of insertion it became too dark for the chopper to get back in to pull you out. I took the PRC-25 handset that Andy was already offering me and made our report. "Team Five, in with no enemy contact," I whispered into the mouthpiece. "Continuing mission, out." I shrugged to Andy and the rest of the frightened team members, tried to smile, and motioned for the point man to lead us off deeper into the jungle.

Light was fading quickly, and I wanted to get as far away from our insertion point as we could. It was obvious that our infiltration LZ had been under observation and that the enemy guard was signaling our arrival. We moved as quickly as we possibly could without making noise or compromising march security. I occasionally glanced at my compass to check our direction of movement, and kept track of the distance we'd traveled by counting my steps. By the time it was almost pitch-dark we'd gotten about five hundred meters from our LZ. I spotted an extra-thick patch of underbrush, and we wormed our way into the center of it.

The six of us formed our small, back-to-back perimeter and sat down. I didn't have to tell anyone to be quiet or to remain alert. As we'd been moving away from the LZ, we heard sounds that indicated enemy search parties. No one on the team even attempted to take out a ground sheet for fear of making excess noise.

I eased my small, indigenous ruck around in front of me, pulled out the silenced pistol and put it in my lap alongside the M-16, then slid the pack straps over my shoulders once again. It had been raining a lot, and the jungle floor and all the vegetation were wet. My uniform was completely soaked through, and within half an hour I was chilled. I knew the indigenous, due to their extreme leanness, were probably suffering worse than I, and occasionally I could even hear teeth chattering.

I peeled back the piece of green tape that covered the glow of my watch and checked the time. It was 2010 hours, which meant we'd been on the ground for a little over an hour. In the distance I heard the barking of dogs. Oh, fuck! I wondered if the enemy was using them to search for us or if they were only used as watchdogs around their campsites. I let one hand rest on the pistol in my lap and tried to prepare myself for a very long night of deadly hide-and-seek.

There were different theories about how to handle the type of situation we were in, a common one for recon teams. Some thought it wise to change bivouac locations at least once during the night, especially if it was suspected that the enemy had a pretty good idea where you were. I believed this was unwise.

It would be a matter of dumb luck for a search party to stumble on our small group as we sat motionless there in the dark jungle. Movement at night would only increase the chances of making contact with the enemy, and I much preferred to have this happen during daylight, when we'd be able to call in some help. If contact was made during movement at night, this also greatly increased the chances of becoming split up. As long as we were all together in one bunch, we knew that everyone else out there were bad guys, so we could freely blaze away without fear of killing each other. This would give us a slight edge over the enemy.

Shortly after 2000 hours we heard several shouted commands in Vietnamese. It sounded like it came from the vicinity of our infiltration LZ. I wondered if they were good enough to track us at night through the jungle. We'd been very careful, of course, to leave as little evidence of our passing as we could. But they would undoubtedly be able to find where we'd landed in the soft, grassy clearing and probably be able to determine the general direction we'd taken when we left. Dogs could find us for sure.

The night dragged on. Every so often, thinking it must be almost dawn, I checked my watch, to discover that only thirty or forty minutes had passed. There were fireflies in the jungle, and they had a hypnotic effect on me as they danced and flitted through the tangled vines and leaves. I was almost ready to doze off as I watched one particularly big and sluggish bug moving close to the ground, maybe twenty meters from our position.

I felt Andy suddenly tense up and squeeze my arm. I immediately snapped back to full alertness and understood what he was trying to tell me. That wasn't any damn firefly I'd been watching, but a man carrying a miniature light. He was moving very slowly and holding the small bulb close to the ground, looking for our tracks. God, I thought, what a bunch of slick sonsabitches! If I could barely tell his little light from a bug at twenty meters, it would certainly be impossible to spot it from the air.

No one on my team dared to even breathe as the light man, followed by another soldier, continued past our hideout. I knew then we were in some serious, deep shit, but hoped the search had now moved past us and that we'd be able to make it until dawn.

Another hour or two passed, and we hadn't heard or seen any other enemy. Thump-crash! There was a distinctive rattle as someone's AK-47 bounced against a log. We heard the unlucky soldier grunt as he tripped over something and hit the ground. Another NVA several meters away from the first murmured a question in Vietnamese, obviously inquiring if everything was okay. The first one whispered an irritated reply, and they continued their movement. I could empathize so well with the poor bastard who'd fallen that it was actually hard to keep from laughing. What made the situation less than funny was that it sounded like the two of them were coming directly toward our location.

Next to me, I heard the whisper of steel against leather as Andy removed his K-Bar from its sheath. I already had the .22 in my hand. We'd planned and practiced for just such a situation as this one, and now it looked like we might get to see how it worked for real. It wasn't a very complicated plan.

It was so dark in the jungle that an enemy soldier could actually bump right into us before he knew we were there. We would try to take him out silently. The plan was for me to empty the .22 into the man's head and face while Andy attempted to cut the bastard's throat. Our main problem was that there were at least two of them in the immediate vicinity. I wished we'd brought one of the silenced Stens.

The general rule we used on my team was not to shoot unless shot at first. As the sounds of the approaching enemy grew nearer, I knew that each one of our indige had his submachine gun off safety and his hand on the trigger. Don't fire, damn it, please don't fire, I thought wildly as I eased the pistol off safety.

I could just see the dark shadows of the two enemy soldiers as they approached our position. As I'd hoped, when they reached the thicket we were in, they went around it. They walked slowly past, not more than five feet from where the six of us lay holding our breaths and not so much as batting an eyelash. The two NVA once again dissolved into the black jungle, neither having any inkling of how close they'd just come to sudden and violent death.

Several more hours went by. Around 0300 hours we heard the sounds of a gasoline engine. Now what the hell? I thought. It didn't sound big enough to be a truck or car, but might have been a generator or maybe a motor scooter. I had a sudden vision of an NVA zipping along a jungle path, lights out, on a damn Vespa. Hell, they seemed so damn sure of themselves, maybe he had the lights on!

By 0400 hours we hadn't heard or seen any more searchers. I had the gnawing suspicion that they'd probably formed into a large, loose perimeter around the general area and were waiting for us to begin moving when it got light. Trying to travel the trails would be suicidal, but if we stayed off the beaten track, we had a good chance of slipping through their lines. It was an awful big jungle out there, and six men made a small target.

It grew gradually lighter, and a thin, patchy layer of ground fog hung over and around us. We remained motionless for a time, quietly surveying the immediate surroundings. We saw and heard nothing except a few birds and animals out making their morning hunting rounds. As we'd practiced, the team began eating and drinking in shifts. Half ate while the other three kept watch. Several men had to piss, and accomplished this by rocking up on their knees, but not fully standing. This was leech season again, and one of the indige whispered a curse as he squirted insect repellent on his dick.

Overhead, some distance away, I heard the drone of the FAC. Captain Gammons was on duty. My morale suddenly improved, as it always did when there was a friendly aircraft overhead. Gammons, or someone else, would be up there all day acting both as radio relay and as the forward air controller if we needed to call in Tac-air. Checking my watch, I saw it was almost time for the morning radio contact.

I took the handset from Andy, gave the FAC a call, and was immediately answered. My message, in a simple transposition cipher, gave our present coordinates, said the enemy knew we were in the area and had been looking for us, but that we would attempt to evade them and continue the mission. The next scheduled contact was at noon, but Gammons would be on standby for emergencies.

I'd had plenty of time during the night to think about our situation and to develop a plan. I laid my map on the ground as the team members crouched around me, and in a whisper I briefed them. I said I suspected that the enemy had cordoned off the area we were in, but that we would try to infiltrate through them. We would move due west, then drop straight south toward our alternate LZ. I hoped that the enemy would be concentrating his attention in the vicinity of our infiltration LZ, and that the other clearing, which was several kilometers distant, would be clear.

"If we get split up, this will be our first rally point," I told them, pointing it out on the map. "We'll stop here for the night," I concluded, indicating a location about halfway to the exfiltration LZ. There was no way we could cover the entire distance before it got dark.

We were careful to sterilize our bivouac area. Then I shot an azimuth for our new heading, and showed it to our compass man. Silently we filed out of our thicket and began slowly moving through the wet, fog-shrouded jungle.

The fog turned the meager morning sunlight into an eerie shade of gray. It also affected sounds, dulling them, making me feel like I had cotton in my ears. We moved very slowly and carefully, trying to watch all directions at once. Within thirty minutes we came to a large, well-traveled trail. There were many fresh footprints and tire marks in the soft earth. The tire tracks were narrow and had probably been made by bicycles or some sort of pushcart.

I didn't want to stop long enough to photograph the trail, as I was anxious to put some distance between us and our night's bivouac area. We walked parallel to the trail, staying in the jungle until we came to a bend. After listening and watching for a few minutes, we crossed the trail by jumping over it as one would a small stream. We attempted to hide any tracks we'd made near our crossing site, then pressed on, following the 270-degree heading.

Behind us, some distance away, we heard two rifle shots fired in rapid succession. I turned, glanced back at Andy, and saw him mouth the word "Fuck!" The point man had frozen and was looking back at me with big, worried eyes. I motioned him to continue on. It sounded like someone had picked up our tracks.

The terrain we were moving through was gently rolling and covered with vegetation that ranged from very thick to fairly open. We were in one of those open areas, and our file had spread out with about fifteen meters between men. The two indige in front of me suddenly froze, and I immediately followed suit. Without even turning my head, I tried to peer through the bushes and trees to see what had alerted the point man.

Four enemy soldiers, two in black and two in khaki, moved into my field of vision. Each carried an AK-47. They were walking in file on a course perpendicular to our own, and they passed not more than twenty-five meters in front of our point man. One of them seemed to look directly at me, gave no indication of having spotted us, and walked on past. The last NVA in line reached absently back to scratch his ass as they disappeared once again from view.

We found some nearby cover and had a hurried team conference. The indige were obviously rattled. Andy was excited but not particularly worried. I was scared absolutely shitless but tried to keep up appearances. As far as we could tell, we'd gone undetected. The enemy who'd looked our way might have been faking it, though, correctly believing that if he made a wrong move he'd die.

I didn't want to cross directly over the enemy route of march, fearing that others would come that way and find our tracks. I didn't want to go in the same direction the enemy patrol had taken, and I sure as hell didn't want to go back the way we'd come. I told the point man to turn right, parallel to the route the enemy had come from. This was taking us due north, in the opposite direction of our extraction LZ, but it was the safest direction we had to choose from. I planned to turn back to the south after we'd covered a few hundred meters.

Besides heading farther and farther away from our exfiltration point, we were also moving toward a small river. I suspected that due to all the rain we'd been getting, it would be running high, and river crossings were a very hazardous proposition anyway, especially if you had to use a known fording point.

Behind us, we heard shouted commands in Vietnamese. They came from the area where we'd seen the enemy patrol. I hoped they wouldn't be able to tell that we'd changed directions. We covered another hundred meters or so and I was just about to give the point man the signal to return to our original heading when we heard more signaling shots from the south.

Great, just fucking great, I thought. Now they were not only tracking us, but between us and the exfil point. There was no other direction to go but straight ahead. By my estimate, it wouldn't be long before we hit the damn river. Ten minutes later we were there.

Andy and I crawled up beside the point man, who lay on the river's edge and looked the situation over. The water, as I'd suspected, was high and moving swiftly. With Andy holding on to my harness, I gingerly lowered myself in to check out the depth. I went up to my neck before I found the bottom and was almost swept away by the force of the current.

Andy and the point man hauled me out again. I shook my head. I had to make another damn decision. We either had to find a better place to cross or go back the way we'd come. As I lay there trying to decide what to do, an enemy soldier began beating one of those bamboo signaling devices. It sounded like he was only two or three hundred meters behind us, and that made up my mind. I motioned the point man to move to our left, down the side of the river.

This was easier said than done, of course, because the growth along the riverbank was much thicker than it had been out under the rain forest canopy. Another half hour of painfully slow movement brought us to a well-used trail and fording point. Once again Andy and I wormed our way up next to the point. The trail had been used often and recently. It was wide enough to drive a jeep on and completely hidden from air recon by the overhanging trees. I became aware of a strangely familiar odor that at first I couldn't quite place. Then memory clicked. It was the smell of a zoo or a circus, the one that's strongest around the elephants.

Were the enemy using them for pack animals, I wondered, or were they wild? I had a sudden vision of being trampled to death by an enraged elephant herd. As if we didn't have enough to worry about already! We lay motionless for as long as I dared, observing the trail and the bank on the opposite side. We heard and saw nothing that indicated enemy. Was there an ambush waiting for us on the other side?

I gave the point man the signal to cross. Poor bastard, I thought. Of course, if the enemy were really over there someplace and had their shit together, they'd probably wait for the rest of us anyway. Our team had practiced for this situation numerous times, and each man knew what to do. As the point man cautiously made his way through the knee-deep water, the rest of us covered the opposite bank with our weapons. He made it across without incident and disappeared into the bush on the other side. In a minute or two he reappeared and gave the signal for "all clear." Either there were no enemy or he just hadn't found the waiting ambush.

The rest of us crossed over in a group, as quickly as we could. As I climbed the muddy bank on the other side, I saw an elephant footprint. So, it hadn't been my imagination. Our patrol also left numerous footprints in the soft, muddy ground, and we had no time to erase them. Once again we heard shouted commands from behind us.

The thought came to me that maybe we should set up our own ambush here at the crossing point and grease the bastards who were following us. I quickly discarded this idea, though. We had no idea who or what might be moving toward us on the trail from the opposite direction. We didn't even know how large a force was after us, plus there was at least one other enemy unit already on our flank.

Everyone on the team was looking at me, waiting for me to make a decision. It was nearing time for the noon contact. "To hell with it," I whispered, "let's get the fuck out of here and go home!" There was a collective sigh of relief from the whole team.

I called Gammons in the FAC and said we needed an emergency exfiltration. He relayed this to the MSS and came right back on the radio to say that "The cavalry is on the way!" This meant that the gunships and exfiltration slicks had been scrambled, and that he'd notified the Air Force's Tac-air group to send us something too.

I gave Gammons the coordinates of our general location, which was all I knew at that time. It got him close enough so that I was able to flash him with the mirror, and a few moments later he read me our exact location. Gammons had already been looking around for the nearest possible clearing, and he gave me the direction and distance to it. "It's not big enough to land in, so you'll have to come out by McGuire rig," he advised us.

We began moving toward the extraction point, and as luck would have it, immediately entered the thickest tangle of vines, bamboo patches, and underbrush I'd ever been in. We were going as fast as we could, but making hardly any headway. It was like one of those nightmares where you're trying to walk through a field of glue. When the gunships and slicks arrived overhead, we still had several hundred meters to traverse.

We were leaving a back trail that even a child could follow, and occasionally we heard indications that the bunch behind us were quickly gaining. Just then we unexpectedly broke out of the thicket onto yet another large enemy trail. Hell, it might have been the same one we'd been on back at the river!

This trail, which looked like a freeway after the shit we'd been slogging through, ran straight as a string in the general direction of the exfiltration point. There was a trick we'd learned from Project Delta for just such a situation as we were now in. We even had a brevity code worked out for it, and I called Gammons on the radio again and told him what we were up to.

What I had in mind was risky, but no more so than continuing the way we had been. I popped a green smoke, tossed it off to one side, then we moved onto the trail and ran like hell in the direction of the LZ.

Every second we were on the open, enemy-controlled trail we were in mortal danger, of course. We might run into an ambush or an NVA unit coming along the trail toward us at any moment. We ran for about two hundred meters, as long as I dared, then cut off, heading toward the exfil clearing, which by then was only another hundred meters away. At the point we changed directions and exited the trail, I dropped a yellow smoke.

The gunships knew what to do next. Behind us I heard them strafing and rocketing the trail between the two smoke grenades. If the bunch trailing us were in the area, they were history!

Another ten minutes of tough travel took us to the clearing. As promised, it was small, but we could see daylight up through the towering trees. The clearing was also a depression in the ground. This put the center of it even farther away from the surrounding treetops. Leaving Andy with the rest of the team to watch the back trail, I went out into the open area and flashed my panel at Gammons as he flew over. He waved the plane's wings to tell me I'd been spotted.

All right, I thought, maybe we'll make it out of this shit alive after all! Now all we had to do was pull off a McGuire rig extraction. I told Gammons we were ready to go. There was a pause before he answered.

"We, uh, will have a slight delay," Gammons told me. "The extraction slicks had to go refuel. Estimated time of return, fifteen minutes, over."

My heart sank and my stomach knotted up again. The indige saw the look on my face, so they were already prepared for bad news when I relayed the situation to them. We remained on the edge of the clearing, watching our back trail, hoping the gunships had taken care of our pursuers.

Maybe five minutes went by. Once again we heard the enemy coming through the brush, following our trail. They were making no attempt at stealth. Maybe they didn't know we were that near, or perhaps they'd seen the slicks flying off and thought we'd already been pulled out. From the southern flank of our position came two signal shots.

I whispered into the PRC-25 handset, telling Gammons we were surrounded on two sides and needed some help. The unit on our flank concerned me the most because they were so close we could hear them talking. "They're twenty-five meters from the south edge of the clearing," I told him.

I always suspected that Gammons was a frustrated fighter pilot. Now here he came in the little unarmed FAC, flying about thirty mph at treetop level. As he passed over the enemy location, Gammons dropped a white phosphorous grenade out the window to mark the target. The startled NVA only managed to get off a couple of shots at him before he was gone.

Three gunships came in right behind Gammons, the first one letting off a salvo of rockets, the next two cutting loose with their four side-mounted 7.62 MGs. After the gunships made their run, we could plainly hear the enemy's screams of pain, confusion, and fear. Andy and the indige were smiling widely. "Number-hucking-*mot*" ("number one," that is, excellent), the point man whispered, giving the thumbs-up sign.

Gammons told me the slicks were back and ready to start the exfiltration. I left Andy at the edge of the LZ to guard, and took the four indige down to the center of the clearing. As soon as we got there, the first UH-1B flew over, hovered, and dropped a rope from each door. But the damn trees were so tall, and we were so far down in the depression, that the ropes did not reach the ground. I frantically waved at the pilot to come lower, and the chopper pilot began to descend slowly, the tips of his rotors actually clipping the leaves of the surrounding trees. All of this was taking too much time, of course, giving the enemy a great opportunity.

They didn't miss out on it. There were gunshots from three sides of the clearing, and the door gunners on the slick opened up. The sling ends of the McGuire rigs finally reached us, and the first two indige quickly sat in place and secured the wrist loops. I gave the hovering chopper the signal, and he took off in a rush. The pilot misjudged just a little, dragging the two indige through the top branches of a tree on the way out.

The next slick moved into place overhead, and we had to go through the same slow, dangerous process. There was even more ground fire this time, as the enemy figured out what was going on. The second chopper had just flown off with its two extractees dangling from the rigs when Andy opened up at the edge of the clearing, his M-16 on full auto.

He came moving backward in my direction at a crouch, still firing. I looked over to the left in time to see four NVA standing in the brush, trying to get a shot at him. They didn't see me at all. I had my own rifle on semi and emptied the entire magazine into them as fast as I could pull the trigger.

I hit at least three of them before they dropped out of sight. I released the empty magazine, let it fall, slammed in another, and fired another eighteen rounds into the same area. This time I shot slower, methodically spacing my shots. These were the first rounds Andy and I had fired, and I was swept with a feeling of wild elation at finally being free to personally kill a few of the assholes who'd been terrorizing us since we'd gotten off the chopper.

Andy got to where I was and we knelt side by side. Neither of us was wounded. Evidently, the enemy didn't realize we were in a depression, because all their fire at us was going over our heads.

I grabbed the handset to the radio and relayed the information that we were now surrounded on three sides. I told Gammons to stand by.

I showed Andy where I'd just seen the four NVA. "Can you throw one of those fucking WPs that far?" I asked him. The white phosphorous grenades we had were bigger and heavier than a frag, and I knew I couldn't throw one that distance. Andy said he could, and I told the FAC we were marking the target.

Andy tossed the grenade like you'd throw a football, in a perfect bullet pass, and it sailed directly into the enemy location.

"I identify WP," Gammons said over the PRC-25.

"Let 'er rip!" I said, and the gunships came back in, blasting the hell out of the enemy again, this time within about twenty-five meters of our position.

The enemy fire slacked off, and the pilot of the last extraction chopper told us he was coming in to get Andy and me. Then there was another one of those scary pauses on the radio, and when the pilot came back on, he told us there was another small problem.

"Someone screwed up," he said. "We only have one McGuire rig on board!"

Well, I thought, that's the fucking end of it. I suddenly became completely calm, resigned to my fate. "They only got one rig left," I told Andy. "Get ready to go."

Of course he refused to leave me by myself.

I told the extraction aircraft that Andy and I would stay where we were, try to fight off the enemy, and wait for one of the other two choppers to come back for us after they'd dropped off the indige.

Andy and I crouched there together, listening while the NVA moved around to close off the last open area of the encirclement. Their wounded were still crying and moaning, and their leaders were yelling encouragement. "I'll bet they're some pissed-off muthas," I whispered to Andy.

The pilot of the extraction chopper suddenly came back on the air. They had an idea, he told us. Although there was only the one McGuire rig, they had another length of rope on board. This other rope was only about fifteen feet long. The pilot said they would try to drop down far enough for one of us to catch the end of this second rope and try to climb it into the chopper.

Some plan, I thought, but probably the only chance we had. I knew Andy, who weighed much more than I, would never be able to climb the damn rope, but I thought I had a chance at it. The chopper appeared back overhead, door guns blazing. It dropped the two ropes and slowly began inching down toward us. The clearance between the trees became even more narrow toward the ground, and the damn rotors were knocking off leaves and branches.

The gunships were buzzing around the clearing in a circle, their MGs firing almost nonstop. There was still a lot of enemy ground fire, though. When the McGuire rig loop reached us, Andy got in it and secured his wrist. I used my snap link to secure my heavy ruck to the bottom of the rig, and slung my M-16 across my back.

Down, down came the chopper. Finally I was able to jump up and catch the end of the second, shorter rope, and begin making my way up it, hand over hand. I'd gotten less than halfway when I realized I could go no farther. Even spurred on by the knowledge that if I dropped off it would mean sure death, I simply could not climb another foot. Enemy rounds were cracking all around, and I was preparing to turn loose when I felt the rope begin to rise.

Suddenly, the chopper's skid was in front of my face, and I swung up and hooked a knee over it. Someone grabbed me and dragged me into the chopper. I lay there on the floor, too exhausted even to sit up, and felt the bird quickly gain altitude then fly away.

Abruptly, it seemed very silent, and I realized the door gunners had stopped firing. Someone was pounding me on the shoulder, and I looked up into the ugly, smiling face of Wally Sergant. He went into a double-biceps pose, and I knew he was the one who had pulled me up to safety.

I remembered Andy and crawled over to look out the door. He was down there, hanging from the lone rig, spinning slowly around in circles.

We had to fly for ten or fifteen minutes before we got to an area that was safe enough to land. As soon as we were down, I jumped out and ran back to where Andy was still disentangling himself from the rig. He was unwounded but had injured his elbow on extraction.

"We did it, goddamn it!" I yelled at him. "We outfoxed the bastards!" I was so happy I wanted to kiss him, but he was just too damn sweaty, nasty, and dirty.

Chapter 23

"I was lying up there on the edge of the clearing," Boyd told me as the medic put his arm in a sling. "The second exfil chopper had just taken off, when these two Cong stood up right in front of me. Couldn't have been more than ten feet away. They were trying to get a shot at the chopper, and they never even knew I was there." The medic finished with Boyd and we walked over to the debriefing tent. "I got 'em both with the same burst," Andy said. "They were standing almost shoulder-to-shoulder and I stitched them right across their chests."

During the debriefing, Andy and I added up a total of five enemy that we'd personally killed and a couple of probables. The helicopter gunships had killed many more, plus, within minutes of our exfiltration, Air Force F-100s had also worked over the entire area with napalm, CBUs, and 20mm. We had no idea of total enemy casualties but knew that we'd waxed the bastards good.

On the friendly side, we had two indige with minor cuts and bruises, and Andy had dislocated his right elbow. "When the chopper took off," Andy told us, "it jerked me right out of the sling seat. The only thing that saved me was the wrist loop, but I felt the elbow joint go." Andy had made the entire exfil flight hanging from one arm.

I recommended that the helicopter aircrew, especially those who had pulled Andy and me out, be awarded medals. I also said that I probably owed my life to Wally Sergant. I doubt if any decorations were given, however. The attitude was that everyone had simply been doing their jobs . . . which, of course, was true.

Operation Golf, Sigma's first official combat operation, was considered a success. Five of the seven teams were compromised and came out under enemy fire as Andy and I had, but a lot of information had been gathered. An enemy base camp and an ammo cache were reported, along with seven major trails. Another team also reported that elephants were in the area and that they were being used as enemy pack animals. Total friendly losses for the operation were two U.S. and four indige WIA, versus fifteen enemy KIA and three WIA. Again, this doesn't count the unknown number killed and wounded by the aircraft.

Back at Ho Ngoc Tao the recon section was given another four-day stand-down. Planning for the next operation was already under way, however, and we were warned not to get too relaxed.

I was in the usual state of survivor euphoria when I hit Tu Do Street. Saigon was becoming my adopted hometown by then, and I made my rounds of the bars in a postcombat high. I didn't notice the dirt, sleaze, and corruption. For the first couple of days I was even able to ignore the presence of the fifty million other American GIs who were crowding all my old, familiar haunts.

I drank and caroused all day, and after curfew I crashed at Lyn's apartment. The last two nights I was in town, Lyn showed up to sleep with me.

"No have boyfriend now," she told me. "No have partner either," she said. It was the morning of my last day in town. I was sitting at the table nursing a bad hangover. I had to return to camp that night, and by then my survivor high had faded, leaving the realization that I'd soon be back in the barrel again.

"He steal too much money, then run away. Go Qui Nhon," Lyn said.

"That's what you get for dealing with an Oriental," I told her. She ignored me and went on.

"My brother get shot, almost die," Lyn said. It was the first I'd heard of her younger brother, an officer in the ARVN, in several years. "Mama very worry."

"What rank's your brother now?" I asked, trying to change the subject. "He must be a major, huh?"

"Never see brother," Lyn said. "He embarrassed have sister work bar."

"He's probably just jealous because you make more money than he does," I told her.

"Lyn tired of make money. Lyn sick of fucking war," she told me. Lyn hardly ever used the F-word.

"Why don't you just leave Vietnam and go live somewhere else?" I asked her. "You have plenty of money. Go to America or to France. . . ."

"Mama no want go with me," she said, "and I no leave Mama here alone."

"The war's about over," I lied. "We're killing the commies quicker than they can breed, so it can't last much longer. When it's over, we'll both move to Dalat like we planned once, remember?"

"War never end," Lyn said gloomily. "Communist never quit."

Later that day as I was strolling down crowded Tu Do, heading for a couple of final beers at the Sporting, there was a loud explosion several blocks away. It shook the glass in the store windows. You could tell the combat troops from the rear-echelon types by their reactions—the combat troops all automatically dropped for cover, while the REMFs looked around and said, "What was that?" When I realized it was probably just an isolated terrorist bombing, I got up from the gutter I'd thrown myself into and shakily brushed off the crud.

When I got to the Sporting and tried to drink the beer I'd ordered, I realized how bad my nerves were getting. My hand kept shaking so badly that I spilled more down my shirtfront than I got in my mouth.

A man I knew from the 1st Group, sitting next to me, appeared to be about as stressed out as I was. He told me he'd volunteered for one of the new Mobile Guerrilla Forces that the 5th SF had begun to experiment with. It was like the Mike Force, he said, but they went to the field for extended periods of time. They were kind of a cross between Merrill's Marauders of WWII, a Ranger unit, and guerrillas. Each Mobile Guerrilla unit consisted of twelve to fifteen Americans and about 150 Montagnards.

He told me he'd just gotten back from one of their first operations, where he'd been in the field for several weeks, roving around deep in NVA-controlled territory. The last time I'd seen him, he'd been a plump, jolly sort of fellow, and now he was skinny, haggard, and morose.

"It was a real bitch," he said.

The recon section stayed up late that night, drinking in Sigma's newly remodeled club room. It wasn't very well stocked yet and soon ran out of booze. Everyone except Andy and me had given up and gone to bed, but I'd found a dusty half bottle of vermouth, and we sat slouched over a table, finishing it off.

I'd been wondering if I should tell Andy about the troubling premonitions I'd been having lately. For the last couple of days a real feeling of gloom and doom had settled over me, and I thought I knew what the message was. If I hadn't been drunk, I probably would never have told Andy what was on my mind.

"I think I'm going to get killed soon," I said.

He knew I was serious and didn't make light of this statement. "If I felt that way, I'd get the hell out of this recon shit fast," he told me. "You know you can quit any time with no questions asked by anyone. How much time you got in-country now, anyway?"

I had to stop and add it all up. "Almost twenty-four months," I told him. "Most of it at hot A-camps, and here, doing this shit. I feel like I'm really pressing my luck. Plus, I've just got this bad feeling lately. . . ."

"Tell 'em you want to transfer to the commando company," Andy advised. "Shit, you're a radio operator, tell 'em you want to transfer to the commo section. There's a bigger shortage of good radio operators than there is of people stupid enough to volunteer for this crap."

We finished the bottle of wine and went to bed. The next morning we were alerted to be ready for a new operation that would depart in two days.

Chapter 24

Before the upcoming operation, several of the recon teams were reorganized and people were shuffled around. Because Andy and two of the indigenous from Team 5 were still on medical hold due to their injuries, I took over Team 4. An NCO named Derby was going in as my number-two man. This was Staff Sergeant Derby's first recon operation, and although he had more time in grade than I, he let me be in command.

We received the operations order on the morning of September 22. We found out that this operation, code-named Tazewell, would stage out of Phuoc Vinh, which was smack-dab in the middle of War Zone D. In fact, our AO for Tazewell was only about twenty miles from Dong Xoai, where we'd just been.

The recon teams had a dual mission this time. Besides conducting reconnaissance of the area, we were also to capture some prisoners.

The next morning, September 23, we all trucked to nearby Bien Hoa airfield and got on C-130s for the ride up to Phuoc Vinh. By that afternoon the mission support site was operational and we were ready to get down to business. Teams 3 and 6 were being inserted first, and they received their order at 1430 hours. Their infiltration was scheduled for last light of the next day.

Things went along smoothly right up until their scheduled takeoff time, then the weather closed in. The two teams were put on a twenty-four-hour weather delay, the first of many such delays we would suffer through. It seemed to me that from then on Operation Tazewell went pretty much to hell.

On our previous two operations we'd been lucky. Now the luck was starting to run against us. Actually, we had two major problems during Tazewell that turned the operation into a minor cluster-fuck. The first problem was that we were right in the middle of the rainy season. During the wet season, the storms always started in the late afternoon and evening—the time we liked to perform our infiltrations.

The second and most serious problem was that the enemy knew we were operating in their area. They had apparently also figured out *how* we operated. There were very few LZs in the Tazewell AO, and we soon discovered that the enemy had these covered.

The suspense increased as we sat out that first twenty-four-hour delay. The stress on Teams 3 and 6 must have been hell. As the afternoon of the next day approached, so did the rain clouds. Two minutes before the rescheduled takeoff time, the mission was again scrubbed due to weather. This time the mission was laid on for the next morning at first light.

First-light insertions had their good and bad points. The good part was that you had commo and air support for the first ten or twelve hours of the patrol instead of being totally on your own. The bad part, of course, was that you gave away a good deal of stealth. As I now look back on Operation Tazewell, I can see that things would have been better had we simply given up on last-light infiltrations completely and switched to going in during the morning.

The weather was clear on the morning of September 26, and both teams made it into their AOs by 0630 hours. Team 3, led by an SFC named Webb, made its infiltration without incident and began moving east. This was the beginning of a very successful patrol for Webb and his team—the most successful of the entire operation.

Team 6 didn't have it so good. For some reason, the pilots were unable to find the primary LZ, and the team was inserted into a clearing five kilometers from their intended AO. Team 6 had two very good NCOs in charge, SFC Menkins and my buddy, Sergeant Curtis Brown. After they figured out how far they were from their AO, the team began moving north toward it.

At 0800 that same morning my team and Team 1 received our operation orders. We would be inserted that same night, we discovered, so we didn't have a lot of time. After a hurried map study, we made our air reconnaissance of the AO at 1000 hours and began working out our plan of action. The brief-backs were scheduled for 1500 hours that afternoon.

My team's recon zone was six square kilometers of mostly heavy jungle. There were two possible LZs. One fairly large clearing, which appeared from the air to be covered with elephant grass, was just about in the center of the AO. The other possibility was an abandoned dirt road that ran along the entire southern boundary.

I decided to use the clearing in the middle of the AO for the primary LZ, then work south to gather information on the area. I planned to hide in the vicinity of the road for a day or two in hopes of taking a prisoner. I thought we might be able to catch a courier running the road at night. If we did manage to capture one, at first light we could simply tell the exfil chopper to pick us up right there on the road.

It was just after lunch when we heard that Team 6 was in trouble, and we all ran over to the commo tent to monitor events. We learned that the team had made contact with an enemy unit of unknown size. A short firefight had ensued, and before the team could break contact and run, SFC Menkins had been wounded. The team was trying to retreat to an exfiltration point while carrying the wounded man. They were still being pursued by the enemy, but two F-100s were already on station, and the FAC was directing them in.

We listened to the garbled radio transmissions as the team fought its way to the small clearing and the choppers began pulling the team out, by twos, on McGuire rigs. Sergeant Brown put the wounded Menkins and one indigenous out on the first lift, the second two indigenous came out next, and Brown exfiltrated with the last indigenous soldier at 1400 hours.

The exfil choppers began arriving back at the MSS, the team members still dangling from the rigs. An ambulance was waiting, and several of us helped load Menkins on a stretcher. He was conscious, and not in a lot of pain yet because Brown had administered a shot of morphine. Menkins had taken an AK round through the pelvis and lost a lot of blood, but was still able to smile and tried to joke with us as we loaded him in the ambulance.

As soon as Sergeant Brown got out of the debriefing, he told us the full story.

"Things were fucked up from the word go," Curtis said. "It had been three days since we made the damn air recon of the AO. There was some ground fog, and that made identifying the LZ even harder. Anyway, we got off the chopper and landed in this friggin' grass that's over our heads.

"We took an azimuth and started off in the direction we'd planned. Nothing looked right. We started hitting all these damn rivers and streams that weren't supposed to be there. There were enemy positions and footprints everywhere. We come to this one big bastard of a river and it's got one of those vine suspension bridges built over it—just like in a goddamn Tarzan movie!" Curtis took a big swig of the beer someone handed him, then went on with the story.

"We knew for sure we were lost then and called the FAC to give us a fix. That's when we finally found out that we'd gone in on the wrong LZ, and that we ain't even in the fucking right AO. We were five thousand meters away from where we were supposed to be—so far out that we didn't even have that location on our maps.

"The FAC told us we needed to move due north, so we started heading that way. It's really thick shit out there, the worst I've seen yet. We could hardly get through it. We'd gone maybe five hundred meters when we heard voices. It sounded like we were right in the middle of a bunch of them, so we laid low and listened. We called in and reported what was going on, and they said to continue the mission." Brown finished the first beer and started on a second one.

"We didn't see anyone, and after about half an hour of that shit, it sounded like the bastards moved off to the west of us. We started heading north again, trying to get back in our AO. We hadn't gone too much farther when we came to a trail.

"Menkins and the point man crawled up to check it out. I was with the rest of the guys about thirty meters behind them. I'm watching Menkins when all of a sudden he starts signaling us to move back. I hear this fucking VC shout something, then he started firing. We all opened up too and began to fall back. We'd only made it about thirty meters when Menkins got shot.

"The bastards were trying to flank us, but the tail gunner shot one of them and we managed to break contact. Menkins couldn't walk, and we had to carry him—he's heavy, let me tell you! When we got a little way from the trail, we stopped and I put a bandage on him and gave him morphine. Then I get on the radio, call the FAC, and guess what? No fucking answer!"

"Another nightmare come true," I put in.

"Yeah, no shit," Brown continued. "I put up the long antenna and finally got through. I asked for extraction, and Gammons had some jets there real quick. The jets are dropping CBUs and nape, and we're steadily trying to get to a fucking place clear enough for the McGuire rigs. It's taking me and all the rest of the team to carry Menkins, and it seemed like it took forever. We're almost to the clearing, and I think we got it made, when more damned VC get behind us and start shooting. The gunships came in and greased 'em, and we finally got pulled out."

We talked awhile longer, then I told Brown I had to leave to attend my brief-back. "Be careful out there, Wade," Curtis told me. "This fucking AO is definitely crawling with Cong."

There were no surprises during the brief-back. The weather was the uppermost concern, and we were advised that it would be monitored closely. Derby and I walked back to our tent, inspected the indigenous and their equipment one last time, then sat back, nervously watching the sky for dark clouds. About 1630 Team 3 made their scheduled radio contact, reporting negative enemy contact, and said they planned to begin moving west.

Our infiltration was planned for 1850 hours, but as the takeoff time neared, the weather steadily deteriorated. A rain squall passed over the MSS, and for thirty minutes or so it looked for sure like the mission would be delayed. By 1730 hours the storm had blown through, however, and the FAC was reporting from the AO that it was starting to look pretty good. Some large, ominous clouds were building in the west, though, and it was decided to set the infiltration time forward twenty minutes. As it turned out, this decision probably saved our lives.

I shook hands with SFC Quimby, the leader of Team 1, and wished him luck. Then our two teams walked out to the waiting choppers, boarded, and took off. Andy, Brown, and the detachment CO were all there to wave us good-bye.

It wasn't a long ride. Once we got airborne I saw huge thunderheads to the west of us. They blotted out the sun, making the jungle beneath us seem darker and more foreboding than normal. I kept an especially sharp lookout during the flight, identifying landmarks and checking them off with the pilot. None of us wanted a repeat of what had happened with Team 6.

The pilot had given us the one-minute warning, and we'd begun our descent when I noticed the smoke from several small fires drifting up through the jungle canopy. We were just coming into the LZ when one of the indige grabbed my arm and pointed to the smoke. "Wee Cee!" he yelled, his eyes wide. I had about five seconds in which to abort the mission.

It's got to be woodcutters or farmers, I thought. The NVA

surely aren't stupid enough to have such obvious fires burning. The chopper flared out and I jumped, the rest of my team following obediently behind me.

Hell, everyone deserves an occasional mistake!

As suspected, the LZ was covered with elephant grass, but it turned out to be only chest high. We lay still for a moment or two, waiting for the sound of the chopper to fade away. As soon as it did, we heard the familiar noise of enemy signaling devices on one side of the clearing, answered by yells from another.

No shots had been fired yet, and I thought we still had a good chance if we could get off the LZ and into the rapidly darkening jungle.

I motioned for the point man to lead us off in a direction away from the enemy sounds. It was maybe thirty meters to the edge of the clearing, and the tall grass and shadows hid our movement somewhat. Ten feet from the edge of the jungle, the point man froze. I looked past his shoulder and spotted the VC halfway up a tree, staring back at us with a surprised look on his face.

The enemy soldier dropped to the ground out of sight and yelled something in Vietnamese. We still had not fired, and evidently the startled soldier had not been quite sure of our identity. There were answering shouts from all around the damn clearing as the NVA tried to sort things out.

We'd been on the ground for over five minutes by that time. Ordinarily it would have been dark already, but because we'd gone in early, there was still just a little light. I motioned for the tail gunner to lead us back the way we'd come. Once back in the center of the clearing, I gave the arm signal to get in our exfiltration formation, and we lay down in the tall grass.

I hurriedly dug the radio handset out of Derby's pack, said a quick prayer, and keyed the mike. "FAC, this is Team Four, over. . . ." I whispered.

No answer.

They've already left the area, I thought, and we're dead meat.

"Any aircraft, any aircraft, this is Team Four, over. . . ."

There was another silence, then suddenly a response. "Team Four, this is Infil One. Do you have a problem, over?"

Did we ever! I quickly told the pilot, Captain Conner, that we were surrounded on the LZ and asked if anyone could still pull us out. By this time it was almost full dark.

"I'll give it my best shot," Conner answered. "ETA about zero-four." I was listening on the radio as Conner coordinated things with the gunships, when the enemy finally began trying to kill us. A grenade exploded and several automatic weapons opened up over near the edge of the clearing where they'd last seen us.

"We're taking fire," I said into the handset. By then I figured it was no longer necessary to whisper.

I was on my back with the signal panel on my chest, watching over my boot tops for the choppers. First I heard their rotors, then suddenly there they were, flying low and fast, the slick in the center with a gunship on either side. It's the arrival of the Valkyries, I thought, and decided they were the most beautiful sight I'd ever seen. The gunships opened up with everything they had, making one fast, deadly run along the edges of the clearing. Captain Conner brought the slick right into the mouth of our V, and the next thing I knew, I was diving into the chopper's open door.

I took one look around, saw that we were all there, and wildly waved a thumbs-up. *"Go! Go! Go!"* everyone was yelling, and we took off again like we'd been shot from a catapult. The door gunners were already firing nonstop. My point man suddenly saw something and opened up with his carbine. We had just flown over the treetops on the edge of the clearing when there were three large explosions in the center of the LZ. "Too late, suckers!" I screamed, suddenly laughing, realizing I'd lived though it once again.

Chapter 25

When we got back to the MSS, we discovered that Team 1 had already beaten us there. It turned out that the other team had also seen smoke near their primary LZ, and so attempted to infiltrate on their alternate instead. Their chopper took ground fire as they approached this second LZ and the mission had been aborted.

After the brief-backs it became clear that the enemy was guarding all possible infiltration clearings in force. Plans were drawn up to begin staging a series of fake infiltrations, followed by immediate air strikes. Operation Tazewell was working under II Field Force, and we coordinated with them to make Psy War leaflet drops following these air attacks.

In the meantime, Team 3 was still in its AO, and still uncompromised. On the morning of September 27 they reported locating an enemy telephone line, new, yellow wire, the kind that could be purchased in most village markets. The team decided to follow the wire to see where it led. After following it for several kilometers and not coming to the end, the team made its night bivouac. The next morning, with several of the indigenous severely ill from flu, Team 3 was exfiltrated without incident.

That evening, two more teams attempted to infiltrate the AO. One team was again shot out of the LZ before the men could even exit the chopper. The other group, Team 2, exited the chopper at about ten feet over tall elephant grass. One of the indigenous team members landed on a hidden stump and was knocked unconscious, which caused that mission to be aborted too. At first light of the next day, however, Team 2 was successfully infiltrated into its alternate LZ.

Adding to all our other problems, some sort of mystery illness was affecting both the American and indigenous recon team members. The symptoms were high fever, nausea, chills, and so forth, followed by sudden fainting spells. One of the team leaders, SFC Wilbur, passed out right in the middle of his brief-back.

Sergeant Miller volunteered to take over as SFC Wilbur's replacement, and on the evening of September 29 this team was deployed. The other American on Miller's new team was a friend of mine from Okinawa, Leroy Park, who had recently transferred to the unit.

The team members were sitting in the open doors of the chopper in the usual fashion as it approached their LZ. When they were still thirty feet above the ground, Park was creased on the left temple by an enemy bullet. He was knocked unconscious and fell from the chopper.

When Miller realized what had happened, he led the rest of the team out of the chopper also. Miller found Park, still unconscious, lying on his back in the tall grass. It appeared that in addition to the head wound, Park had broken his left arm in the fall. This team never made it off the infiltration LZ either and was evacuated under enemy fire.

By the morning of September 30, Team 2, led by First Lieutenant Fitts, was the only unit still on the ground. In the early afternoon it too was surrounded by the enemy and extracted.

We were getting nowhere fast, but still had one last trick up our sleeves. The G-2 of II Field Force requested that Team 3 be reinserted into its AO for a special mission. The team was issued a tape recorder and given a crash course on how to tap telephone lines.

After several more weather delays, the team was once again successfully inserted in the AO on October 4. They found the enemy wire, tapped in, and recorded messages for the next twenty-four hours. At the completion of the mission they were once again exfiltrated without incident, and the tape recordings were turned over to the higher headquarters G-2 for evaluation.

On October 6 the mission-support site was closed out and all units returned home to Ho Ngoc Tao.

The day after we got back, all the American recon members went over to the field hospital at Bien Hoa to visit Menkins. He was awake and in good spirits when we got there, and told us he was being evacuated to the United States the next day. The bullet had passed completely through, just missing his femoral artery and several other important parts, so he considered himself lucky.

In the bed next to Menkins lay a kid who hadn't been so lucky, from one of the newly arrived American infantry units. The young man's right leg was gone from the knee down. One of the nurses told us later that the poor guy was a draftee and had only been in Vietnam for two weeks.

About a week after we'd come back from Operation Tazewell, I found out I was being transferred to Nha Trang. A new unit, the MACV Recondo School, was being formed, and I'd been selected to fill the slot of commo supervisor.

I had mixed emotions about leaving Sigma. On one hand, I was happy to be getting out of it alive. My nerves were almost completely shot by then, and I didn't know how many more close calls I could endure before completely losing control. On the other hand, I was emotionally attached to the unit and felt I was running out on the men.

One of the newer guys, an NCO named Mike Newbern, took my place on Team 5. The morning I was due to leave camp for the trip up to Nha Trang, I went out to the rifle range, where Anderson and Newbern were playing around with a couple of the Swedish-Ks. Andy and Newbern were both still confident and gung ho, their morale unaffected as yet. They told me that Sigma had already been alerted for the next mission.

"See, Wade," Andy said, "you didn't get killed after all. Now you get to go back to headquarters and fuck off for the rest of your tour."

"Yeah," I told him, "and at least now you have a running partner who's large enough to carry your big ass through the jungle when you get shot. Come see me if you get up to Nha Trang. You'll find me at the bar in Project Delta's NCO club!"

The last memory I have of Anderson is of him on the range, happily wasting government ammo.

Chapter 26

Good ol' Nha Trang, I thought as I stepped off the Caribou tail-gate. Once I got to 5th Group headquarters and had a chance to look around, I decided that it truly was turning into "Smoke Bomb Hill, East," as I'd been warned. They'd even started using white-washed rocks as decorative borders around things. Not only that, but there was all of that saluting, "yes-sirring" and "no-sirring," going on. I completed my in-processing as quickly as possible and hightailed it over to the Delta compound.

This was the first time since I'd been in Vietnam that I would be operating so close to the flagpole. Wisely, I knew enough to stay as far away from the headquarters building as possible. I had a bad problem with controlling my mouth in those days and was in the habit of saying weird things, such as the truth, that tended to get me in trouble in the rear areas.

I still had about three months left on that year tour, and I decided that if I could hide out over around Delta and the Recondo School area, I might escape without getting busted back down to Private, E1.

When I got to the MACV Recondo School that fall of 1966, it had just broken away from its parent unit, Delta, and moved to its own compound right next door. I realized that getting sent there as the commo supervisor could be considered a real plum assignment. Word was being circulated that all the original cadre for the school had been handpicked by Colonel Kelly himself.

The Recondo School was organized to train members of all the allied infantry units in Vietnam in long-range reconnaissance methods and techniques. The school had very high political visibility, and General Westmoreland himself visited us several times while I was there. Actually, the name "Recondo" had been dreamed up by Westmoreland back when he'd been in command of the 101st Airborne. In the late 1950s and early 1960s, the 101st had a similar training course, which taught recon and commando techniques, hence the name. In a tip of the hat to Westy, our MACV Recondo patch, which was worn on the right pocket of the fatigue uniform, even resembled the old 101st version.

Only about ten other guys were assigned to the school when I got there. Some of them had just arrived. These new guys were still fresh, energetic, and rarin' to go. Some of the cadre, however, were old, burned-out cases like me who for one reason or another found themselves assigned to the school for the last few months of their tours. Charlie Telfair, with whom I felt an immediate kinship, was fond of saying, "I'm just sick and tired of being sick and tired all the time!"

Sergeant Major Haleamau was the ranking NCO and did a great job keeping us in line. Our commander, Major Rybat, known as Batman, was an enthusiastic weight lifter and body-builder with shoulders about five feet wide. We had several weeks until the arrival of the first group of students, and in the meantime we began work on developing the periods of instruction (POI), writing the lesson plans, and completing construction of a large new classroom building.

As the commo supervisor, I also had to put together a number of signal-operating instruction booklets, build a couple of radio mock-ups for training aids, and make sure we had sufficient radios and other commo equipment on hand. Because we were next door to the SFOB, there was no necessity to operate a radio net with them, thus eliminating the need for things like the evening sitrep, which I'd grown to despise.

I enjoyed teaching classes and enjoyed the process of developing the POI and writing lesson plans. I did most of this work while seated at a table over at the Delta NCO club. I thought I probably resembled Hemingway, or maybe Sartre, who also did their best work in cafés, but several people thought I actually resembled a drunken, reprobate fuck-up, and I was advised to move my "office" back to the school.

Things ran pretty smoothly as those first few weeks rolled by. I managed to stay out of trouble by keeping completely away from headquarters and the other REMF units that had recently moved into the Nha Trang area. I could count on feeling welcome at the Delta or Omega compounds, and also had some friends over at the Nha Trang Mike Force. If I wanted to go into the city itself, which I seldom did in those days due to the town's crowded nature and the swarms of MPs, I could get there from our own gate without passing through "Little Fort Bragg" at all.

One day we were briefed on a new opportunity being offered. Special Forces enlisted swine with prior combat experience could receive direct commissions, we were told, and all you had to do was put in for it. There were a few strings attached, of course. The deal was, you had to extend for another year-long tour in Vietnam, and then, once you received your commission to second lieutenant, you would be transferred to one of the "leg" infantry units and take over a platoon. Some deal!

I actually seriously thought it over anyway but eventually decided against it. For one thing, I'd known too many men who'd received commissions during the Korean War only to be reverted to their old enlisted ranks after the fighting was over. Also, at this time there were many horror stories about junior officers being "fragged" by their own men in the regular infantry units. Besides, I didn't want to leave Special Forces.

One afternoon as I was elbowing up to the bar at the Delta club I overheard a couple of guys talking about some heavy shit that Project Sigma had just gotten into down in Binh Long. One of Sigma's recon teams had been shot up and both the Americans killed.

"Who were the Americans?" I asked.

"Guys named Anderson and Newbern," the man told me. "Did you know them?"

I had to wait several weeks to get the full story. One day I ran into Goad, who was in Nha Trang on business. After congratulating him on his promotion to first sergeant of the recon section, I asked him about my friends.

From what one of the surviving indigenous team members reported, the team was compromised upon insertion. This was pretty much a given by that time, and the team continued the mission anyway. During the first night, the team heard the enemy searching for them and decided to move bivouac locations. This was accomplished without making contact with the enemy, and the team thought they had successfully evaded.

When the team made their scheduled morning radio contact, they did not even bother to mention the previous night's activities, simply reporting that they were continuing the mission. At 0810 hours the team was ambushed. Both Americans and one of the indige were wounded by the initial burst of automatic weapons fire. Anderson was wounded in the leg and tried to crawl off to one side. Newbern managed to contact the FAC and request help before he died. Anderson was reaching for the handset when he too was killed.

Two of the indigenous team members survived and were extracted. Colonel Reish scrambled the commando company, which Goad accompanied, and an hour later the three bodies were recovered. When all friendly forces had cleared the AO, the entire area was saturated by air strikes from the helicopter gunships and seven sorties of Tac-air.

To me, it was all eerily reminiscent of the patrol Andy and I had managed to pull off during Operation Golf. We'd been lucky at that time. This time the luck had run out. Colonel Reish said he felt the disaster was due to American overconfidence.

Sometimes you get the bear, and sometimes he gets you. . . .

We began receiving students around Thanksgiving time, even though our new classroom building was not yet complete. Each class at the Recondo School lasted for three weeks. We had to teach the students an awful lot of stuff in this short period of time, and the training days often lasted twenty hours or more. We kept the students under constant pressure, and this was the only Army school I've ever heard of where the training involved pop-up/shoot-back targets.

The training at the Recondo School had a lot in common with other Army schools, such as the Ranger course and the jump school. During the first few days of training, the students were subjected to lots of verbal abuse, arduous killer runs, push-ups, and all of that. This was done more or less as an initiation and to get the students in the right frame of mind. It also immediately weeded out the weaklings and quitters, something that is definitely not needed on a recon team.

Toward the end of the first week we started training in the fun stuff like rappelling, use of McGuire rigs and rope ladders, range firing of special weapons, demolitions, and the patrolling techniques Delta and the other special projects had developed over the past few years. The students always enjoyed that phase of training the most.

The second week of training was much more cerebral, involving advanced map reading and land navigation, report writing, radio communications, and so forth. This week got rid of all the dumb-asses, of which there were always many. It was common for a man to pass the first, physical phase of training with flying colors, only to bomb out in week two. A recon man needed to be not only tough, but also smart.

Those who made it to the final week were fairly certain of passing the course unless they messed up on the final exam or got killed. Getting killed on the exam was a real possibility, because the exam consisted of an actual recon patrol in enemy territory. Members of the cadre accompanied each student patrol but acted only as graders, and would only step in if it appeared things were completely screwed up.

I was responsible for all of the communications training, which took up one full day, and I assisted with the weapons training and some of the air operations classes. I liked working with the students and felt like I had some important, hard-earned information to pass on that might save lives.

One of the exercises I developed involved close-distance radio nets. The students broke down into their training teams, spread out to different parts of the school compound, then practiced using the PRC-25s to call the "FAC" (me) and report intelligence or request help. In one drill, each team pretended it had been compromised. Each was required to call the FAC, request a fix to get their exact location, then call in some sort of fire-support mission.

The important point I was trying to teach them with this exercise was to always find their actual location on the ground before they started calling in artillery or bombs. Almost every time we did this drill I'd have a radio conversation that went like this:

"Arty, this is Team Alpha, I request one round of eight-inch artillery at grid coordinate 123456, over."

"Roger, Team Alpha, one round of eight-inch on the way."

"FAC, this is Team Alpha, request fix of my location, over."

"Roger, Team Alpha, your location is grid coordinate 123456. . . ."

Another Christmas season approached, my third in Vietnam. The usual phony cease-fires and bombing halts were announced by both sides. As usual, the enemy used the break in the bombing to flood the Ho Chi Minh Trail with fresh men and supplies. What the hell, at least we wouldn't run out of targets anytime soon.

Back on the college campuses the kids were really getting into the swing of things. The war was immoral and unjust, they said. The U.S. was acting like a colonial power and was trying to impose an American solution on a foreign people. We were excessively cruel. We were interfering in what was really just a civil war, and in doing so were violating international agreements!

In Vietnam we soldiers read all of this with great amusement. These whining college students were of our generation, after all, and we knew the *real* reasons they didn't like the war. Hell, having to go off and fight a war would cut into all the party time, drug-taking, and wild sex orgies. You had to cut your hair short and take orders. Besides that, you could get your damn ass greased over there fighting them Veet-congs. It was a lot easier to declare the draft and the war immoral than to admit that you were a chickenshit coward.

By New Year's 1967 there were almost 400,000 U.S. military personnel in Vietnam. Over 6,600 Americans had been killed, along with another 48,000 South Vietnamese. New units from the States were arriving almost daily. But so were new units from North Vietnam.

The Recondo School had been on stand-down during the holidays, but after the first of the year, we really got things in gear. All the cadre slots had been filled and the new classroom building was operational. We had a formal grand-opening ceremony, with Westy making a brief appearance to give it all his blessing.

I was getting short-timer pains and was anxious to get the hell away from the war for a while. At the same time, I was worried about what I'd find back in the ol' U.S. of A. Besides the specter of being spit on by some college punk, I really wasn't looking forward to returning to the spit and polish of Fort Bragg.

Even before I'd gone to war and discovered what it was that real armies did for a living, I hadn't much cared for the normal day-to-day bullshit of the peacetime military. Now that I knew better, I was sure it was going to be a case of, "How're ya goin' ta keep 'em down in Fayetteville, after they've seen Saigon?"

One day, several weeks before I was expecting it, Haleamau called me into the orderly room and handed me my orders. I was to report back to Bragg and had been assigned to one of the new groups, the 6th. I'd get a thirty-day delay en route, which began when I signed out of the replacement depot at Oakland.

For the rest of the day I actually entertained the idea of going over to the headquarters and extending for another tour. But that night we had a rather heavy enemy probe, and I decided it was time for me to get my ass home after all.

Epilogue

I guess I hadn't actually realized how much things had changed in Vietnam during the past couple of years until I started attempting to clear the 5th Group and get the hell out of country. In the earlier days, back when I'd arrived and departed Vietnam as part of an A-team, it had been no sweat. Clearing Nha Trang had been a simple matter of turning in your individual weapons, signing a paper or two, then saying good-bye to everyone at the bar while you waited for the plane.

By '67 it was a lot more difficult. I began making the rounds of all the offices, departments, sections, and clubs I was instructed to clear early one Monday morning. By noon of the next day there were still little blocks on my clearance form that hadn't been checked off yet. It amazed me how many levels of bureaucracy had been added around group HQs. Christ, I think I even had to clear through the Nha Trang Steam Bath and Massage Parlor.

It was 1600 hours of the second day of runarounds when I finally got to the end of my checklist, turned in my M-16, and was given one of those knives that the Project Delta NCO mess passed out as a reward for paying your bill. (I promptly lost this knife and have been kicking myself in the ass ever since because they are now a much-sought-after collector's item.)

It was too late to catch a flight by that time, so I had to spend another night in Nha Trang, now without a weapon. Bright and early the next morning I was over at the airfield, ready to catch a hop down to Bien Hoa. This too was a nightmare. The flight operations building was jammed with other American soldiers, and I discovered I had to put my name on a standby list that was over a hundred people long. Once on the list, you couldn't leave the area without risk of missing your turn. Guys were sitting and lying around everywhere, and one of them told me he'd been there two days.

213

When the last flight of the day was announced that afternoon around 1700 hours, I was still number 22 on the standby list. The plane was a C-123, and there was only room to take ten more passengers. An Air Force guy came out and told us he was required to inform potential passengers that the plane was carrying American dead. Because many men ahead of me on the waiting list refused to ride on the plane, I lucked out and got a seat.

All day long while waiting around, I'd been taking nips from a bottle of vodka I'd wisely packed in my handbag. By the time I finally got on the C-123, I was about half drunk and a little unfocused. I guess I expected to see dead bodies just lying around on stretchers or something, but all I saw when I got on the plane was equipment and some gray bundles strapped in the center of the floor. I spotted an empty seat on the other side of the plane and climbed over the bundles to get to it. As soon as I stepped on the dead guy in the body bag, I realized what it was, but by then it was too late.

There was a young, sad-looking Spec Four from the 25th Infantry watching me. "Hey, be careful," he said, "that's my first sergeant you're stepping on!"

That night at the replacement depot in Bien Hoa, I had a horrible nightmare about watching, unable to move, while in front of me a body bag was slowly unzipped from *inside* and a mangled corpse came crawling out, leering at me.

If I'd thought it was hard getting out of Nha Trang, it was nothing compared to the BS I encountered in Bien Hoa. Before I got there, I had a vague idea that I'd be able to slip away for a couple of days, run into Saigon for one last binge, say good-bye to Lyn and all the girls on Tu Do, then come back, sign in to the repo depot, and zip away to the States.

WRONG!

When I got off the C-123 at Bien Hoa, I was still a little fuzzy-headed and managed to let myself be herded over to the replacement unit to sign in. Once there, I was trapped in the big, mindless system and found that there were still more lines to stand in, more stupid, unnecessary forms and papers to fill out, and several more whole days of waiting around.

We were broken down into airplane loads, each group consisting of about two hundred guys. On the morning we were supposed to leave, our group was taken over to a big, empty hangar, where we were subjected to a detailed shakedown inspection. We had to dump out our duffel bags in front of us and then, as an "inspector" came around, go through each and every item while it was checked for contraband. The two main things they were looking for were "war souvenirs" and drugs. Anything that even resembled a weapon was confiscated, including the pellet pistol I'd traded a bottle of whiskey for back in Nha Trang.

Once through the shakedown, we were herded back in buses and taken to the Bien Hoa airfield, where we were kept in isolation, under guard, while waiting for our plane. We sat in the sun on the hot tarmac for several hours before the "freedom bird" arrived. It was a civilian 747, and it parked right in front of our group.

The doors of the plane opened and out came its load of FNGs, most of them young draftee kids with confused, scared looks on their faces. Poor bastards. Our group yelled them the traditional welcome: "You'll be sooorrryyyyy!"

There was another hour wait while the plane was serviced and refueled. The civilian crew, including several tight-assed stewardesses, were picked up in a staff car and whisked away to some air-conditioned VIP lounge to be entertained with war stories told to them by rear-echelon quartermaster officers. Finally we were ordered to board the plane.

"Well," we said to each other, "nothing can stop us now!" The plane started to taxi, and everyone cheered. We'd only gone a couple of hundred feet toward the takeoff point, however, when there was a crunching sound and the plane came to a sudden halt. Now what the fuck?

The plane taxied back to where we'd started, and we were all told to get off again. Seems that our plane had run into a piece of equipment parked out on the apron and had damaged the left outboard engine; we'd have another slight delay while it was repaired.

"How long a delay?" we asked one of the Air Force mechanics.

"Oh, I don't know, at least four or five hours," he told us.

There were about fifteen of us on that planeload from Special Forces, and we immediately noticed that this unscheduled accident had screwed up the repo depot's system. Our guards had already left, leaving us free to contact a Vietnamese slicky-boy who happened past on his motor scooter. We took up a quick collection of money, and within half an hour all of us guys from 5th

Group were sitting around in the shade eating fried chicken, drinking cold beer, and telling lies.

The rest of the poor men in our planeload watched us jealously, having to wait several hours before someone finally got around to delivering them a few cases of C-rats and some lukewarm, iodine-laced water.

Urged on by the civilian aircrew, who definitely didn't want to spend a night there, the mechanics did a fairly quick repair job. Four hours later we were finally airborne and winging our way back toward Travis AFB, Oakland, and the "World." Us 5th Group guys all sat in the back of the airplane and passed around the bottles of booze we'd smuggled on board. We sang our own special version of Barry Sadler's recent hit, "The Ballad of the Green Beret." It went like this:

> Back at home, a young wife clapped.
> Her Green Beret had just been zapped.
> She'll take his wings and all that trash,
> And trade it in . . . for ready cash!

Where They Are Now

Carl Hargus served several more tours in Vietnam, working primarily with Project Gamma. He retired from the Army as a command sergeant major, and currently lives with his wife in the St. Louis area. Carl works for the Missouri State Veterans Commission as a service officer. Carl and I have stayed in contact over the years, and he furnished many of the photos for this book.

George Emert got out of the Army after our tour at Camp Vinh Thanh. George continued his education, earning a Ph.D. After a very successful career in the corporate world, George entered the field of education. He is currently the president of Utah State University at Logan. I'm grateful to Dr. Emert for many of the photos in this book, and thank him and his wife, Bille, for putting up with my annoying phone calls and stupid questions.

Gunboat Smith eventually retired from the Army as a sergeant first class. He currently divides his time between Hawaii and his old hometown in Tennessee. The last I heard of Smitty, he was back home giving instruction to local law enforcement officers.

Most of the other men mentioned in this book also retired from the Army. If you wish to contact any of them, you can do so through the Special Forces Association. I'm sure they will all be glad to give you their own versions of the events I've covered here, and will probably tell you that I am full of crap.

Lessons Learned

A few weeks after I submitted the manuscript for this book, my editor called me. "You know, Leigh," he said, "what I wish you would add to the book are some of the specific things you learned in combat during the Vietnam War."

I told the editor that I was reluctant to do this for fear that people would think I was trying to set myself up as some sort of super-Rambo.

"Right off the top of my head I can rattle off the names of ten or twelve other guys who had more Vietnam combat experience than I did," I told the editor. "I can give you the names of men still alive today who had already served in two wars before they ever even got to Vietnam!"

"Yeah, but do they write books?" he asked. "If guys like you don't tell about it, who will?"

Back in the 1960s, young soldiers like me had some incredible role models and teachers. It is currently popular to talk about how much better today's military is than the one we had in the Vietnam War. This is true in an overall sense, I suppose. Today's troops are better educated and probably better trained. And today's military is an all-volunteer force, with no whining draftees to worry about. What the new Army doesn't have, however, is the *combat experience* in the senior NCO and junior officer ranks that was there in the sixties.

Glancing through a few current issues of the Special Forces Association newsletter, *The Drop*, and reading some of the recent obituaries, I came across this item:

COMMAND SERGEANT MAJOR (RETIRED) FRED E. DAVIS, SR. Fred served in Darby's Rangers during WWII. He was captured by the enemy, but managed to escape and return to friendly lines.

218

During the Korean War, Fred fought with the Airborne Ranger companies. He joined Special Forces in 1955, fought in Laos in '61 and Vietnam in '66 and '67. Command Sergeant Major Davis had three awards of the Purple Heart, the POW medal, and the third award of the Combat Infantry Badge.

I had the honor to serve with, and learn from, Sergeant Major Davis in Vietnam and Thailand.

Right next to the obituary of CSM Davis was one for another man I served with in Vietnam and Thailand. This one was for Sergeant Major (Retired) Gerald "Moose" Brannon. Brannon was also a triple Combat Infantryman Badge winner, and he too had served with Rangers in WWII and Korea before fighting in Vietnam with Special Forces.

In another issue of the newsletter, I read the obituary of yet another man I knew. When I was first assigned to the recon section of C-5/Sigma, my first instructor in long-range patrol techniques and tactics was Robert G. Grisham. "Pappy" Grisham was also a WWII and Korean War veteran. Grisham served a two-year assignment attached to the British SAS in 1961–62. In Vietnam, Grisham was at the hot A-team camp known as Khe Sanh in '64, and later served with MACV SOG—where I first ran into him—CCC and CCS. Bob Grisham retired as a command sergeant major with thirty-four years in the Army.

I also had the privilege of serving under some very experienced officers in Vietnam. Most of these were men who had prior combat experience as NCOs in either WWII or Korea, and served in Vietnam as lower-grade commissioned officers. Harry "the Hat" Munck was one of these. I worked for LTC (Retired) Munck for several years when I was in Thailand.

Colonel Munck was an enlisted infantryman in WWII, attended OCS after that war, and went to Korea as a junior officer. He joined Special Forces in the early fifties, and after spending many years of that decade in Germany with the 10th Group at the A-team level, went to Vietnam in the early sixties. Colonel Munck worked closely with the CIA during these years, eventually retired from the Army, and started a second career with "the Agency." Hell, I admired Harry so much that I ended up marrying one of his daughters!

In Special Forces during the Vietnam War, guys like these weren't uncommon. In those days, if you didn't have at least one star on top of your CIB, it was embarrassing to wear it. There were men with similar combat backgrounds in all the other services too. The Marines still had NCOs on active duty during Vietnam who had fought with Raider units in WWII, survived numerous beach landings in the Pacific, and frozen their asses off in Korea before they ever got to the jungles of I Corps. The Air Force had fighter pilot aces from both previous wars, and men who had served in the China-India-Burma Theater with the *original* Air Commandos. For young soldiers like me, these men were gods. They were, and still are, my heroes.

Compared to warriors like these, I'm definitely a lightweight. The trouble is, as my editor pointed out, this type of man doesn't talk much about his combat experiences, much less write books about them. Unfortunately, as these old hands pass on, a lot of their hard-earned combat experience dies with them.

Although I'm no Fred Davis or Harry Munck, I won't understate my own combat experience in Vietnam. Although there are many men who had more combat than I, there are a hell of a lot who had less too. All my experience was down "in the trenches," so to speak. I served in Vietnam in every rank between Spec. 4 and SFC, and it was all on A-detachments or in special projects. I was there off and on from the earlier days right up to the time the 5th Group rotated back to the U.S., so I had a pretty wide perspective of the history of the conflict and how things actually went down. Because I had a ten-year break in Army service and was still on active duty up until 1992, I can relate my experiences in the sixties to what is going on in the New Modern Army.

I've always been pretty outspoken and have never been afraid of making waves—which is, no doubt, one of the reasons I retired with twelve years in grade as a sergeant first class! What I'm going to say in this "Lessons Learned" section may piss off some people, but it's the truth as I see it. Some of it will undoubtedly not be politically correct, from either the standpoint of current official Army doctrine or as compared to society's recently accepted view of the military and war. To this I can only say, tough shit.

You should also keep in mind my limited perspective. Except for several months attached to the 173rd Airborne, all my Vietnam experience, and most of my Army career, was with Special Forces, and all of that was, as I mentioned, in units no larger than company size. One of the most important lessons I've learned is that combat experience is pretty unit-specific.

Although there are subjects such as "fear in combat" that are the same no matter what type of unit you fight with, there isn't much crossover between, say, the experiences of a fighter pilot and a combat infantryman. Unless a man actually served with Special Forces units, he just won't understand many of the problems we had—just as Special Forces men don't understand what the regular infantry units went through.

Killing the Enemy

I grew up watching those great WWII and Korean War movies. One of the popular Hollywood themes in those days was the one about the young soldier who is thrown into war for the first time, and about the great anguish he goes through the first time he must kill another human being. Most of the popular war books I read also had an antiwar theme woven through them and involved sensitive young men who were forced into battle and who experienced a lot of emotional suffering at the horror of it all. At about this same time, there had been studies done by the Army indicating that in combat, many men, for one reason or another, wouldn't fire their weapons.

When I went through basic and advanced individual infantry training at Fort Ord in 1961, there was a lot of emphasis placed on indoctrinating us to fire our weapons at the enemy. At that time, we were training to fight the previous war in Korea. We spent a good part of our days charging up hills, then lying in defensive positions and fighting off mass attacks by hordes of so-called "aggressors."

Firepower was the order of the day. The claymore mine was brand-new and had been invented just for this purpose. We interlocked our machine gun fire with our M-1 rifle and BAR fire and shot, shot, shot. The cadre went to great efforts in their attempt to turn us into aggressive killers.

This "kill-kill-kill" business still goes on, especially in units such as the Marines, Rangers, Airborne, and Light Infantry. Frankly, it's pretty damn embarrassing.

By the time I actually got to go to a real war myself, all this emphasis on aggressively engaging the enemy and killing him had planted a nagging worry in the back of my mind that when the chips were down, maybe I actually *wouldn't* be able to "pop a cap on some bastard's ass." Maybe something mysterious happened to you when the target was another human rather than a paper silhouette. Maybe having an enemy soldier in your sights turned you into a blubbering, sniveling Milquetoast.

Ha! Rest assured, young soldier, when you are engaged with an enemy who is doing his damnedest to kill you, you will have no hesitation about trying to kill him first. I certainly had no problem with shooting at the enemy, and I never fought with any other soldier, American or Viet, who had any trouble either. (In fact, it was just the opposite, a subject that I'll cover later on.)

I'm no crazed stone-killer, but I have to tell you that personally, I felt nothing but a euphoric elation when I shot and killed an enemy soldier. Hell, I felt good even when I shot and *missed* the bastards.

Civilians often ask stupid questions of combat veterans such as, "What's it like to kill a person?" The politically correct answer is, "It was horrible, just horrible," then the vet is supposed to tremble a little and maybe squeeze out a few tears. What I actually experienced was a feeling of relief and triumph.

I've always had a sort of primal fear of creepy crawly insects. One day in Vietnam I was sitting in a bunker when one of those foot-long, red, jungle centipedes came crawling in to join me. When I killed enemy soldiers in combat, it gave me the same feeling I got when I smashed that centipede with my rifle butt.

When killing the enemy, however, there was also that added feeling of triumph I mentioned. It is similar to how you feel when you successfully score a touchdown in football, or beat your opponent in any other sport. When it's a matter of your life and death, however, the feeling is much stronger. Winning in this situation arouses very ancient, deeply buried emotions in the male human. Remember how Tarzan put his foot on his vanquished opponent and beat his chest as he roared in victory? It's a lot like that.

Hating the Enemy

Having said all of that in regards to how easy it is to zap "the bad guys," it will probably sound a little odd to hear that I never hated the enemy soldier. In fact, I never talked to any other *professional* soldier who hated them. I don't even think that men who were prisoners of war and were mistreated by their captors felt any hatred for the enemy in general, although there might have been some hatred for individual tormentors, sadistic interrogators, and so on.

Oh sure, the other side pissed me off, and I sure as hell hated the stuff they did to us in their attempts to kill us. Mostly, however, if I felt anything for the enemy, it was grudging respect, and sometimes even a little pity. Only a soldier can empathize with the plight of another soldier—no matter what side that other soldier is on.

The VC and the NVA soldier was only doing what I was doing, which was putting his ass on the line in the attempt to kill his enemy and win for his side. During the course of the Vietnam War, the people I held hatred and complete disrespect for happened to be some of my own countrymen. You know the ones . . . those who sat in the safety of the U.S. soaking up the good life while smugly, stupidly, and viciously giving support, aid, and comfort to the enemy. I will despise these people to the day I die. On the other hand, I wouldn't mind going back to live in Vietnam, and would particularly enjoy talking to old soldiers whom I fought against. ("Remember when those jets dropped the cluster bombs on your sorry gook ass? It was me calling them in . . . pass the bottle, will you?")

Fear and Bravery in Combat

It seems like this subject is approached from different extremes, especially by guys who write war books. On one side you have the antiwar "Oh, poor, pitiful me" bunch who go on and on about how terrifying it is. On the other side are the tough guys who never mention being afraid at all but allude only to "adrenaline flow," being "fired up," and so forth.

Another one of those stupid questions civilians ask is, "Were you scared?"

If a person isn't scared in combat, there is something mentally wrong with him. Either he is mentally deficient or he is mentally ill.

You can't be "brave" in combat if you aren't scared. Bravery in combat isn't absence of fear, it is doing what needs to be done *despite* your fear. As a famous wannabe combat soldier once wrote, it's displaying "grace under pressure," and all of that.

I witnessed feats of selfless bravery in Vietnam that can still bring tears to my eyes today when I think back on them. I don't think I ever saw anything but courageous acts from *any* member of the U.S. military, whether in the air or on the ground. In fact, my personal opinion is that there was too damn much bravery by Americans. Too much bravery leads to too many friendly KIA. We'd have been better off, I think, if we'd taken more of a "survivor" attitude to it all, and hunkered down for the long haul.

In combat I tried simply to do a good job. The types of jobs I did entailed a lot of risk and danger, but I never tried to be especially heroic. I was actually as worried about screwing up and disgracing myself as I was about getting killed, which is, unfortunately, a common attitude among professional soldiers. If you aren't careful, this attitude can get you and, more important, the men under your command killed.

The bravest thing I ever did in the war was that after finding out just how scary and dangerous Vietnam was that first tour, I volunteered to go back there four more damn times.

Combat Training vs. the Real Thing

Since the Vietnam War, great advances in combat training have been made in all the U.S. military services. The current slogan in the Army is, "We train as we fight and we fight as we train." It's hard to argue with this theory. This is the way you should train whether you're talking about global warfare or some style of urban, "street-effective" martial art. The big problem is making sure that you're training to react and perform correctly in the first place.

I want to make just a couple of comments about this subject, although I'm sure they will infuriate many people whose entire military careers have been built around a particular style of combat.

Since my first combat tour, I've had certain reservations toward the old huhaa-huhaa, fix-bayonets-and-charge, advance-at-all-costs, damn-the-torpedoes, full-speed-ahead philosophy of fighting. Don't get me wrong. I understand that this style of blind, mindless, aggressive action is sometimes needed in a fight. And the types of units that drill in this sort of stuff the most happen to be assault or shock units such as paratroops, Rangers, and Marines.

What I'm trying to get at here is that there has to be some flexibility built into the system of fighting. I mean, after you make your heroic frontal assault, take your objective, evacuate your 60 to 90 percent casualties, what do you do for the rest of the war? Do you really think you'll be relieved by a fresh unit and sent back to a rear area to await the next call to storm another beach or make a night drop on another airfield? Not all wars are over in two or three days, you know.

Yeah, I'll admit I'm partisan toward Special Forces, but I always felt like we had the right idea. The guerrilla method of warfare is more practical. It is very similar to several martial arts that incorporate both a "hard" and a "soft" style.

Okinawan Goju karate is a perfect example. This fighting style uses both the hard, linear, straight-ahead, *go* techniques, and the soft, circular, giving-way, *ju* techniques.

"Oh, God," you're probably saying to yourselves, "he's going into Oriental mysticism. Next he'll start talking about yin and yang!" Okay, I'll put it this way: you got to know when to fold 'em, and know when to bet your ass off. In war you have to understand that knowing when to retreat, not fight, withdraw, cut your losses, and so on is just as important as knowing when to aggressively engage the enemy. Guerrillas attack where and when the enemy is weak or soft (a fist to the solar plexus), withdraw when the enemy is too strong (dodging the opponent's punch), and then counterattack or ambush when the enemy is again vulnerable (counterpunch).

In Vietnam I saw too many people killed by mindlessly following the huhaa-huhaa style of combat when there was no *reason* for it. Worse than just getting themselves needlessly killed, huhaa-huhaa-type leaders usually got some or all of their men killed too. As I mentioned in the section on fear, many leaders would rather get themselves and their men killed than risk having someone up the chain of command think they weren't being aggressive enough.

As Patton once said, the idea is not to die for your country, but to make the enemy die for his . . . and no one ever accused Patton of not being aggressive enough. There is such a thing as being too aggressive in combat, just as there's such a thing as being too cautious. No one thinks badly of a gambler for folding a losing hand or of a boxer for dodging a straight right.

First Time in Combat

It's something that's on every new soldier's mind. You've trained hard, and the training was supposedly as realistic as it could be, but what is the real thing going to be like? How will you react? Will you panic, freeze up, cry, break down, go crazy, shit your pants, or otherwise disgrace yourself? Or will you act out your fantasy of reacting heroically, perhaps leading the few survivors of your pitifully depleted squad in one last, glorious, futile attack on an enemy machine gun emplacement?

It will probably be none of the above. I can almost guarantee you, however, that it will be an "interesting" experience.

No matter how realistic we try to make combat training, it is simply impossible to make it completely real. This is because as you train, whether it is with MILES equipment or whatever, you know that no one is *actually* trying to kill you.

I'll have to go back to the martial arts training analogy because it is very similar. If you've trained in a dojo for twenty years but have never been in a "real" fight, you're going to be in for a surprise the first time you look into the cold eyes of an opponent who fully intends to hurt you very badly, or kill you if he can.

Hey, don't sweat it! This is where your training, or lack thereof, will come into play. You will pretty much start automatically reacting without thinking, and if the training was tactically sound in the first place, you'll probably get through it all without falling apart. If you have luck on your side, you'll also get through it all in one piece.

You might go through several of your first encounters in combat in just this way—simply reacting automatically. After a while, once you get used to being in these situations, you will be able to start *thinking* about what you're doing. This is both good and bad.

It is good because you are now becoming a true professional

soldier. Being able to think, react, and make sound decisions in the din, chaotic fury, and pure, goddamned terror of combat, is what it's all about, especially if you're a leader.

The bad part is that when you start thinking about it, it gets even scarier! Good combat leaders have good imaginations. Unfortunately, the better imagination you have, the more scared you can get. I have an excellent imagination, and I often admired the occasional dumb ox I ran across who was "brave" because he was simply too damn unimaginative to figure out all the possibilities of the situation he was in!

To sum it up, believe that your first combat experience will actually be the easiest one you go through. If you're a paratrooper, you'll understand me when I say it will be pretty much like your first jump—the first jump is usually the best one you ever make.

The Role Luck Plays in Combat

One of the most mysterious aspects of combat survival is the part that pure, random luck plays in it. This is one topic every soldier starts to wonder about after his very first battle.

Why did Sergeant Joe Blow, who was standing next to me, get hit ten times in the chest, while I never got a scratch? Why did Private Schmoe, who spent the entire battle huddled down in his fighting position, get killed by a direct hit from a mortar, while Sergeant Rock, who spent the entire time exposing himself to the enemy, come through with a minor wound?

It is no big wonder to me that after every war, various versions of the philosophy known as existentialism become very popular. One of existentialism's major themes is that there is no rhyme or reason to life—that it is all completely absurd!

It's this uncertainty factor of war that has always made it so . . . "interesting." From generals on down to fire-team leaders, combat soldiers have learned to go by the maxim "hope for the best, but plan for the worst." Combat is all one big Murphy's Law. Because of all the variables involved with combat, it is as hard to predict and control the outcome as it is to forecast the weather.

I suppose the best way to look at combat is the same way a professional gambler looks at a poker game. You can't take the element of chance out of poker, but you can do everything you can to increase your odds of winning. You study the game, learn how to quickly do the math for figuring the odds, study the people you're playing against, and so on. A combat soldier does the same thing: he tries to work every angle to get the odds on his side. Both the gambler and the combat soldier try to eliminate the element of chance as much as he can. What both really want is a sure thing.

Although every combat action you are in is a new toss of the dice, old soldiers begin to wonder if their odds don't get worse each time they once again cheat death. I don't know what a statistician would say about this. In theory, the more combat experience one has, the faster, smarter, and wiser one should be, thus *lowering* one's odds of getting killed. However, from my experience, and from my own gut feeling, I believe that the longer one is exposed to combat, the lower the odds of survival become.

A lot of this is a psychological mind game you have to play with yourself. The Vietnam War was pretty long, but we were sending men there only for twelve-month tours of duty as opposed to "the duration," as we did in previous wars. I tried to convince myself that each tour I performed reset the odds. I tried to serve "one tour at a time," sort of like the alcoholic's "one day at a time."

This didn't really work. I knew deep down that I would keep volunteering to go back over there again and again until the war was either over or I was killed. Psychologically, I was "in for the duration," just as most other professional soldiers I associated with were. I'm fairly certain that had the war gone on much longer, I would have used up my remaining luck.

Wounds

One night in 1970, at Camp Dak Pek, we were under siege. Everyone was on alert in our trench lines. We'd just retaken the camp after being partially overrun the week before, and were still repulsing nightly probes and attacks. Needless to say, everyone was slightly trigger-happy. About 1200 hours one of our Yards had to take a dump. He didn't want to shit right there in the trench, so he foolishly moved out *in front* of our lines, to the edge of the wire, and relieved himself there. On his way back in, one of our own troops shot him through the head with an M-16.

It took a few minutes to figure out that it was not an enemy sapper we'd shot but one of our own. The wounded Yard was lying out there yelling for help, so a couple of guys went and dragged him back to our lines. The wounded man was still conscious for about ten minutes, although drilled neatly through the brain. The round had gone in a little off center, entering in the forehead above the right eye and exiting from the back of his head without making the usual nasty exit wound.

Although still alive, the man had obviously had it. Our chopper pad was zeroed in by enemy mortars, it was night, the wounded was an indige, so trying to get a dustoff was out of the question. We put him on a stretcher and lugged him down to the medical bunker. The wounded man was no longer conscious by then, although still breathing, so our medics put him over in one corner, out of the way, while they continued to work on the other wounded who might still be saved.

Sometime after it got light, one of our Yard nurses happened to check the head wound case, and to everyone's amazement, discovered he was still alive. He lasted until noon before he finally gave up and died.

After you've been around a lot of dead and wounded, you stop taking things for granted. Sometimes you see men with ghastly wounds who are still up and moving, at times still fighting, who you think should be long dead. We had a wounded Striker at Camp Tan Phu once who had taken a round right through one of his balls. The Striker's main reaction to this was embarrassment at the wound's location!

Just when you start marveling at the toughness of the human body, however, now and then you find dead bodies with what appear to be only very minor wounds. I found one dead soldier who had a tiny hole in the chest of his fatigue uniform that was surrounded by only a small splotch of blood. Evidently, a tiny piece of frag had entered the wounded man's chest and done some sort of fatal damage to his heart.

Shock is a big killer, and something you need to be particularly careful of. A wounded man can go into shock simply from fear, so when treating a wounded soldier, you need to be careful how you react to his condition.

If you go running over to the downed man, take one horrified look at him, scream, "Oh, my God!" and then throw up, it isn't going to do much for your buddy's emotional state. A very experienced

Special Forces medic once told me that he tried to approach each patient in a nonchalant, casual manner, no matter how critical or urgent the situation seemed to be. The few seconds you lose by doing this will probably do more for the wounded man than excitedly running over and feverishly going to work on him.

You will also live longer yourself if you take a few moments to check out the tactical combat situation before you go gallantly running to the wounded man's aid.

Sometimes you have to watch men die. In antiwar movies there's usually one of those "stark reality" scenes where a horribly wounded man is screaming, thrashing around, throwing blood everywhere, begging for his mother, and all of that sort of thing. I suppose this occasionally occurs, but I never witnessed it. The men I saw die usually knew they'd had it, were resigned to their fate, and went out bravely and peacefully. Time and again I heard stories of men who were wounded while on small SOG patrols. In cases where they knew they were slowing their comrades down and needlessly jeopardizing their friends' lives, they begged to be left behind.

Marksmanship

One thing that I'm certain of is that rifle marksmanship in combat is still just as important today as it has always been. In Vietnam, one of the first things I became aware of was that the South Vietnamese troops were lousy rifle shots. Luckily, it soon became obvious to me that the enemy weren't any better.

Many noncombatants think that the Vietnam War was all fought in thick jungle terrain. In actuality, there were many open areas too, such as the Mekong Delta, where I found myself during my first tour. It's when you're traversing these open areas that you really start to worry about enemy sharpshooters.

I'd been taught to shoot at a very young age and had been a real gun nut in my teens before I ever joined the Army. I was a good shot and knew I wouldn't have much trouble hitting a man at two or three hundred yards when armed with something like the basic M-1 Garand. I assumed the enemy was probably as good as I, so you can imagine the feeling of vulnerability I endured the first few times I stepped out into those wide-open rice paddies.

It didn't take me too long to discover that I didn't have much to fear from enemy sharpshooters. The VC and NVA all pretty much used the old "spray and pray" method of engaging enemy targets—just as the South Vietnamese did.

Although large volumes of poorly aimed fire can be just as deadly as small volumes of carefully aimed, accurate fire, somehow it's not as scary to face. In the first case, you figure it will be simply bad luck if you're hit, and in the second case you know you won't stand much of a chance if and when an enemy soldier picks you out as his target.

There were very few instances in Vietnam when friendly troops were killed by single, carefully aimed rifle shots. When this did take place, it sent goose bumps up everyone's back.

Camp Dak Pek was in the jungles of the central highlands, near the tri-border area. The camp itself was down in a valley, however, and before our operations could reach the cover and concealment of the surrounding mountains, we had to traverse about a klick and a half of completely open terrain. When I got there in 1970, people on the team were still talking worriedly about an incident that had occurred at least a year before in which an American Special Forces officer was killed while leading a patrol out of camp.

Only one shot had been fired, it had come from several hundred meters away, and it drilled the unfortunate American in the center of the chest. There were only two Americans accompanying the hundred or so Montagnard troops. The American officer had obviously been the victim of a trained sniper.

From intel collected, it was determined that the sniping was done by a specialist, probably a Russian adviser using a scope-sighted rifle. We suspected a Russian because by that point in the war most American Special Forces had decided that the Vietnamese were incapable of learning how to shoot that well. Thankfully, there were no further incidents of this kind, but just the threat of a repeat performance was still making team members jumpy a year later.

Marksmanship vs. Volume of Fire

I didn't fire my weapon, whether it was an M-2 carbine or an M-16, too many times in Vietnam—at least not compared to many soldiers I fought with—and during the entire time I was there, I never fired at the enemy on full automatic. On the other hand, I usually hit what I shot at.

By the time I joined the Army in 1961, there was already a huge battle going on within the infantry branch concerning how soldiers should be taught to shoot, and as to whether true rifle marksmanship wasn't an obsolete skill.

The Army had just begun using a method to teach combat rifle skills known as "train-fire." Train-fire involved engaging pop-up silhouette targets that appeared, then disappeared, at different ranges. If the shooter hit the man-size silhouette anyplace on the target, it would fall down. In those days we were still issued the eight-shot, semiautomatic M-1 Garand, the primary infantry weapon of World War II. We sighted the rifles in for two hundred yards, then didn't move the sights. We were instructed to use so-called "Kentucky windage" to rapidly engage the variable-range targets. This involved spotting the target, making an immediate estimation of its range, then either aiming high at the ones farther away than two hundred yards or low for the closer ones.

The Army thought, correctly, that this type of shooting was more realistic than the Camp Perry type of training that had been the model up until that time, and I'll admit that train-fire had a lot going for it. It taught the soldier to quickly spot and engage targets and to properly estimate range, and the trainee was shooting at a simulated human form rather than a bull's-eye. The trainee also received immediate feedback on his accuracy because after each shot he could see how he was doing rather than having to wait for the target to be pulled and checked by the pit crew. What train-fire unfortunately didn't do was turn out expert shots.

In the early sixties there was no longer any specific sniper training in the Army, and though there were still sniper rifles in the inventory, such as the '03 Springfield with the Weaver scope and the sniper version of the M-1, they were no longer issued.

Snipers were considered to be obsolete, and many people in the higher echelons figured that, as far as that went, so was the entire infantry. As I mentioned earlier, heavy firepower was the order of the day, and the "experts" were more concerned with ensuring that soldiers put a lot of rounds downrange than they were with training them to aim and hit their target with pinpoint accuracy.

The new infantry basic weapon, the M-14, was coming on line just then. This weapon was designed to appease both the "volume of fire" side and the dwindling, politically incorrect bunch who still thought that accurate rifle fire was important. Like most compromises, the M-14 wasn't very good at filling either role.

The M-14 was basically a reworked M-1 with a twenty-round magazine and a selector switch. Because of the relatively light weight of the weapon, the heavy caliber it was chambered for, and the drop-combed stock, which was not designed for full auto fire, the M-14 was pretty much worthless when fired on full auto. Because of the light, wispy barrel, which tended to bend easily and distort when hot, it wasn't as good at driving tacks as either the '03 or the M-1.

Meanwhile, back in the Corps . . .

Ah, the good old Marine Corps. Always more conservative and traditional than the Army, the Marines have never felt it necessary to jump on each and every bandwagon that comes along. By the time the M-14 was replacing the M-1, there were still many Marines who bemoaned the fact that the M-1 had replaced the '03 Springfield. Nor had the Corps bought into the Army's spray-and-pray argument but continued teaching their men to be expert rifle shots. They trained the old way, using the tried-and-true methods of marksmanship training, which involved lots of dry-firing, sighting in, and many hours on the known-distance range.

So what were the results of the Marine's old, conservative ways? Well, besides keeping the best-looking dress uniform of all the services, they also continued to turn out infantrymen who could shoot. Although it pains me to say it, today's average Marine can still outshoot the average Army soldier.

When the first elements of Special Forces went to Vietnam in the 1950s, both the South Vietnamese Army and ours were armed with the same family of WWII and Korean War vintage small arms. By the time I got there in '63, the United States had rearmed with the M-14/M-60, but to simplify the supply problem, our men in Vietnam continued to use what was being issued to the ARVN.

The Marines hit the Vietnamese beaches for the first time armed with the M-14, which they had finally decided was an okay rifle. When the 173rd arrived several months later, they were all armed with the M-16, and this soon became the new individual weapon for both Marines and Army.

I think that the military agreed to accept the M-16 because they figured it would just be a temporary stopgap measure. The M-14 had proved unsuitable for the type of terrain and the highly mobile warfare in Vietnam. The M-16 was lighter weight, smaller, easier to control when fired on full auto, and the ammo was lighter, which meant more could be carried. This ability for each soldier to carry more ammo was important due to the new spray-and-pray mind-set.

Of course, the Marines hated the M-16 from the word go. The weapon was obviously never designed for long-range accurate fire. It was too lightweight, the barrel was too short, it had lousy balance and feel, and it came with rudimentary sights. In the early days, there were also complaints that the rifle was prone to jamming often and that it was hard to clean.

By the mid-sixties, the Army had pretty much completely given up on the idea of training its men in true marksmanship. What with this newly issued M-16—which was obviously designed not for accuracy, but full auto—and the availability of massive artillery and air support, the handwriting was pretty much on the wall, wasn't it? The old idea of controlling fire, conserving ammo, and all of that, pretty much went out the window in Vietnam too. Hell, if you did manage to shoot up all the thousands of rounds the troops were carrying into combat, you could always get an immediate air resupply.

Luckily, the Marines never gave up on the importance of carefully aimed, accurate rifle fire in modern combat. In particular, they never gave up on the importance of the sharpshooter or sniper. The Marines should get most of the credit for the development and issue of the modern sniper rifle. In Vietnam they proved the point that a well-trained man with a good rifle is a much more cost-effective means of killing an individual enemy soldier than an air strike.

After Vietnam, the Army's focus of interest returned to the European theater, which involved terrain with lots of open spaces. We somewhat grudgingly admitted that snipers might come in handy in such terrain, developed a few true sniper rifles, and initiated courses of specialized sniper training that were modeled on the Marine version.

Although not really suited for combat in the European theater, the M-16 was not replaced as the basic weapon, but has gone through several modifications, and has now been around for over thirty years. The current version, the A-2, has a heavier barrel, which gives it better balance, a fully adjustable rear sight, and a redesigned front handguard.

It seems ironic that the U.S. military has spent jillions of dollars developing high-tech missiles, smart bombs, and so on, that are capable of pinpoint accuracy, while continuing to devalue the importance of accurate rifle fire. Now that we have a standing, professional Army that spends its time training for combat—rather than depending on a flood of draftees who must be trained as quickly as possible and rushed into action—we have no excuse for not taking the time to teach them how to shoot better. A battalion of infantry can spend a month shooting on the rifle range for less than it costs to lob off one of those cruise missiles.

The bottom line is: spray-and-pray doesn't cut it.

Indirect Fire

Like all infantrymen, I immediately developed a great respect for artillery. Artillery has always been one of the great killers in ground warfare, and although the enemy in Vietnam never had a whole lot of indirect-fire assets, what they did have they used very effectively. It is odd that although the Viet Cong and NVA were lousy rifle shots, they were sometimes wizards with indirect-fire weapons.

Part of their wizardry came from the fact that they didn't have unlimited rounds to burn up as our side did. Each rocket or mortar round they shot at us had come from the north on some poor bastard's back, so they did everything they could to make each round count.

The enemy did particularly well with their limited artillery against our fixed locations. This was because they could work out exact ranges, angles, preselected firing positions, and so forth. They didn't do so well when attempting to engage our troops who were moving and in random locations. The enemy usually tried to figure out good, likely targets, such as possible landing zones, zero them in, then wait for us to arrive.

Our friendly artillery faced the opposite problem. Although our cannon-cockers could immediately react, re-lay their guns, and hit a dime at ten kilometers, we most often didn't know if there was really any enemy there or not. We often used spray-and-pray techniques with our artillery, just as we did with our small arms. We called this "H&I fire," meaning harassment and interdiction. I don't think it usually did much interdicting, and about the only people it harassed were friendly troops near the guns who were trying to sleep.

One of the techniques we used when patrolling around our A-team camps was continuously covering the route of the operation with the camp mortars. Each time the unit stopped, we would call our location back to camp and give the mortars the coordinates of a few likely avenues of enemy approach, retreat, and so on. The guys back at camp would do sort of a "quick and dirty" lay on these and, if needed, could start bringing in rounds with little delay.

In the early days of the war, the enemy used mainly captured 60mm and 81mm mortars against us. As supplies from the North increased, we started seeing more of the Russian 82mm and 120mm mortars, along with the 122mm and 140mm rockets. To counter these weapons, we simply built deeper and better bunkers. The bad guys didn't seem to have any rounds with delay fuses—which would detonate their shells after they'd penetrated well into a target, rather than on its surface—so it was fairly easy to defend against even something as big as a 140mm.

The enemy used their limited artillery with best effect as terror weapons against "soft," unfortified targets such as cities and villages. Out at the A-teams and fire bases, life wasn't nearly as bad as it would have been had the NVA been able to employ actual heavy artillery pieces against us, such as they were able to do against the French at Dien Bien Phu. Those of us in the American Army whose only combat has been in Vietnam (or later) have never had to suffer though an honest-to-God artillery barrage.

Air Support

Direct air support really came into its own during the Vietnam War. Because we were airborne troops and trained to depend on air insertion and resupply techniques, Special Forces naturally used air assets heavily from the very earliest days.

Most of the A-team camps in Vietnam were entirely dependent on air resupply and reinforcement. We also depended more on Tac-air for fire support than the regular units, because we were usually outside of friendly artillery range. This was especially true in the early days before the arrival of large American units, and later on when SF became more deeply involved with cross-border operations.

I never had anything but positive experiences with our air support, whether it involved Army or Air Force aircraft and pilots. Occasional mistakes were made—so-called deaths by friendly fire—but considering the extent to which we used close air fire support, these incidents were extremely rare. Personally, I had absolute faith in our pilots and had no qualms about bringing in air strikes very close to my position.

The helicopter gunships, which were constantly under development and improvement during the entire course of the war, could work especially close to friendly troops. I called them in as close as twenty-five meters from my position on several occasions.

As the war went on, the Air Force got better and better. Not only could one depend on close support from the planes such as the prop-driven Skyraiders, which were specifically for Tac-air support, but we thought nothing of calling in jet fighter-bombers to within almost hand-grenade range. During the battle of Dak Pek, when we were trying to retake the half of the camp held by NVA, we brought numerous fighter-bomber sorties to within fifty meters of (well-dug-in) friendly troops with no ill results. . . . I'm talking 750-pound bombs and napalm here, not just strafing.

Special Forces also worked often with the Air Force's armed transport planes such as the original AC-47, nicknamed "Puff," or "Spooky," and later the AC-130s. These planes not only provided flares for nighttime illumination, but very accurate and devastating fire from their electric miniguns and cannon. These planes were especially useful when the friendly troops were all in bunkers with overhead cover and the enemy was attacking out in the open. The fire could be called down directly on top of the defender's position, killing everything that moved above ground.

Coordination between the Air Force and the infantry eventually developed to the point that we were practically able to call in a B-52 strike as tactical air support. If there was a really good target, it was usually possible to get some B-52s in on it within a couple of hours, sometimes sooner. If you want to see something impressive, you should see what it looks, sounds, and feels like when one or two B-52s are dropping cluster bombs!

Napalm and Other "Cruel" Weapons

Remember that old, unanswerable question from childhood: "Would you rather suck the snot out of a dead body, or slide down a forty-foot razor blade?"

I'm reminded of that stupid question when I hear civilians talk about "especially cruel" weapons of war. I mean, would you rather get blown to bits by a 105 howitzer or vaporized by a tactical nuke? Would you rather die painfully from a bullet to the groin or painfully from a napalm bomb?

War is *supposed* to be hell, and trying to enforce a bunch of dumb, unenforceable rules won't change it. For some reason, probably simply because our side was able to use it and the communists weren't, during the sixties napalm was especially singled out by the anti-American, antiwar protestors to whine about. I didn't hear much complaining about its use from our combat troops in Vietnam, however.

When a pilot of a Tac-air sortie radioed that he was coming to my aid with a full load of napalm, the response from me and the other beleaguered troops was always, "All right! Sock it to 'em! Burn-baby-burn!" I never saw anyone start crying and wringing their hands about the cruelty we were about to inflict on the "poor, agrarian, patriot freedom-fighters" who were doing their damnedest to kill us.

Communications

A couple of years ago I wrote an article about the types of radio communications Special Forces used during the Vietnam War. I sent the article to a popular magazine that states that it is "the magazine for professional adventurers." The article was rejected by the magazine, the reason given being that the editors thought the subject was boring and that the article was "just about a bunch of radios." So much for the claim that the magazine was for professionals. On the other hand, if you ignore the importance of communications in combat, I can just about guarantee that you will get all the adventure you can handle!

I'll admit that communications is pretty boring. I think it's boring too, and it was one of my primary jobs in Special Forces.

Unfortunately, most infantry types are either bored or intimidated by the subject of commo, and when a leader gets to the paragraph of the operations order that addresses the subject, he usually mumbles something like, "Current signal instructions are in effect," and hurries on to something more interesting.

I learned the importance of commo in combat early on in Vietnam, because in those early days our commo was piss poor, and I got to see the results. We not only had very tenuous communications with higher headquarters, but also with our combat operations in the field. This caused us a lot of unfortunate casualties.

Today the radios are much more reliable, but I advise carrying backups for everything. I know the crap is heavy, but when dealing with commo, you must always remember the corollary to Murphy's Law, which states: "In combat, communications is always perfect until you really need it." In modern warfare, commo is more important than ever. It doesn't do any good to have all that air and artillery support if you can't communicate with it.

Besides having backup for the equipment itself, you need to make sure that everyone on the patrol or operation knows how to use the equipment. Modern, tactical voice radios are simple to use, but sometimes the younger troops develop a tongue-tied condition known as "mike fright" when it comes time to use one.

During the Vietnam War, at least in Special Forces units, junior NCOs and even Sp.4s and PFCs routinely led operations and called in artillery and close air support. If you're a young soldier and the situation is such that it's up to you to get on the radio and call for help, don't sweat it. When your shit is in the wind and it's a matter of true life and death, forget about trying to remember the proper radio procedure, correct forward observer techniques, and all of that.

When things get really tight in combat, it's just like in one of those airplane disaster movies when one of the passengers ends up having to fly the 747. Simply get on the damn radio and talk. Someone will help you. Remember that to call in air or artillery support, all you really need to do is communicate the two following pieces of information: (1) the location of your friendly troops, and (2) the location of the enemy. And when you come right down to it, all you need to communicate is *your* location, whether this is done by radio or some visual means such as a smoke grenade.

I killed a hundred times more enemies with a radio in Vietnam than I did with my M-16.

Security, Enemy Agents, and "Friendly" News Media

During the Gulf War, some of the news media there were complaining that they were not allowed enough freedom to cover the action. One of them reminded the command that during WWII, members of the press had accompanied the Normandy invasion. "Yeah," someone replied, "but back then the media was on our side!"

Unfortunately, that about sums up the situation. One of the first lessons I learned in the Vietnam War was that most of the U.S. news reporters were more friendly to the enemy side than to our own. Although some reporters were good guys and showed a lot of courage in reporting the war, too many of them were no better than enemy agents or propagandists.

Actually, you guys fighting the Gulf War had it easier with the press than we did in Vietnam because in the Gulf you weren't fighting communism. Many American news reporters are left of center politically, if not outright crypto-Marxists or Socialists, and they tend to support various "workers' revolutions" wherever and whenever they occur. During Desert Storm, all you had to worry about was the usual assortment of peace freaks and those who, for one reason or the other, loathe the U.S. military on general principle.

My advice in dealing with reporters is to treat them like mushrooms. You know, feed them shit and keep them in the dark. Don't tell them anything you don't want the enemy to know, because anything you say, especially if it is unflattering or detrimental to our side, will end up on the front page of the *New York Times* or on the nightly TV news.

Maybe someday the U.S. press corps will once again back up our military during wars, but don't hold your breath.

The Creative Nature of War

The U.S. military establishment has always had a love-hate relationship with creativity and creative leaders. In a light infantry type of war such as Vietnam, many of us discovered just how important independent, creative thought and action was, however.

I think it's ironic that being creative in war is tolerated either at the lowest levels or at the highest, but seldom in that huge, bureaucratic middle section. Personal initiative and cleverness is expected and appreciated if it's shown by the leader of a six-man, long-range patrol. If the same creativity is shown by a member of a general's staff, however, it usually doesn't go over so well; only the general himself is allowed that privilege, if, that is, he's capable of it.

It's too bad that many military men who are very successful during peacetime are next to worthless during war. During long periods of peace, the bureaucrats and expert managers rise to the top of the heap, and the real warrior types are either driven out or simply quit in disgust. Luckily, I'm not the only one who realizes this. In the last ten years or so there has been an effort in the Army to imbue leaders with a "warrior spirit and attitude," as opposed to simply allowing them to remain successful managers who are masters of intra-Army politics and intrigue.

The thing I loved about being in Special Forces during the Vietnam War was that I was given the chance to think, to be creative, and to take both the responsibility *and* the credit for the results of my actions. In Special Forces this chance to show your stuff in combat, to make life-and-death decisions, was extended to anyone who wanted to take it, whether he was a PFC or a colonel.

In the peacetime Army this chance is seldom offered to young enlisted men.

The Importance of the Basics

One of the last conversations I had with Colonel James "Nick" Rowe* was back when he was the commander of the Special Forces Survival, Escape, and Evasion course. I had just asked him

*We had served together—until his capture in 1963—in SF Team A-23 at Tan Phu, in the Delta. He was then a lieutenant.

about the current training standards for Special Forces radio operators. "Morse code is just about a thing of the past," he told me. "The operators learn it, but they only have to be able to send and receive about eight words per minute. Because of the new, whiz-bang equipment, SATCOM, and all of that, no one thinks it's needed anymore."

"Yeah," I put in, "not needed until a few nukes go off and the high-speed satellite crap doesn't work anymore."

"Exactly," he said. "We all know that nukes screw up short-wave and microwave commo, and that long-wave AM is about all that will work—but everyone is trying to forget about that."

High-tech gadgetry is neat, makes the civilians cream their jeans, and is good for recruiting, but when you get right down to it, a light-infantry war is won or lost on a very primitive level. When you have small units of men sneaking around in the woods trying to kill each other, skills such as using all your physical senses, knowing how to read signs, navigate with a map and compass, outwit and outshoot your enemy, are more important than the most sophisticated, expensive guided missile ever made.

If you let yourself depend on high-tech equipment for your survival in this sort of combat, you'll be in for a rude surprise. Remember the Murphy's Law I quoted pertaining to commo? The same goes for such things as global-navigation devices and any piece of equipment that has the word "computer" connected with it. If you don't learn the basics of land navigation—preferably without even so much as a map and compass—you'll be up the ol' shit creek when your electronic aids fail.

The situation light-infantry soldiers and leaders face today is the same one faced by teachers and students in our grade schools. With pocket calculators so common these days, it's very tempting to take the lazy, easy way out and forget about trying to teach kids how to do basic math the old-fashioned way, using paper and pencil. The difference between you and the grade-school kid is that while the kid simply risks spending the rest of his life dumb, you'll probably end up dead.

One of the first lessons I learned in the Vietnam War was that the more high-tech a weapon or piece of equipment was, the more likely it was to fail when you needed it the most. In war, your best high-tech weapon is your brain, and that's what you must learn to use and depend on.

Glossary

Air Commandos The Air Force's unconventional warfare unit. They date back to WWII, when they were involved with operations in the China-Burma-India Theater. They were reactivated in the early 1960s and often worked directly with, or in lieu of, Air America, which was the CIA Air Force.

AO Area of operations. This refers to the geographical area that a particular unit is assigned to conduct their combat operation in.

ASA Army Security Agency. This unit was disbanded some years ago. Its mission used to involve electronic warfare, particularly radio-intercept of enemy signals. Special Forces radio operators often worked against these guys in war games when we were training for our clandestine missions, and there was a lot of rivalry between us and them.

CID Criminal Investigative Division. These are the investigators for the Military Police.

CI Counter Intelligence.

FOB Forward Operations Base. Often used interchangeably with MSS.

"leg" Derogatory term used by paratroopers when referring to anyone who is not a jumper.

MSS Mission Support Site.

PCS Permanent Change of Station. A long-term assignment.

per diem A daily allowance paid when quarters and rations must be purchased on the civilian market. Special Forces soldiers prefer fighting "low-intensity, high–per diem" wars.

REMF Derogatory term used by frontline troops to describe the rear-echelon boys. It stands for Rear Echelon Mother Fucker.

S-1, S-2, etc. These are the designators for the staff sections in military units. S-1 is personnel, S-2 is intelligence, S-3 is operations and training, S-4 is logistics. In today's Army the lowest level of staff section is at the battalion, where you might find a major in charge. At higher levels you start running into the G prefix, which designates the general's staff.

S-3 Air As used in the book, this is the officer in the operations section who coordinates things with the flyboys.

SAS The British Special Air Service, one of England's crack unconventional-warfare units. The Australian SAS was modeled on the British unit and often fought alongside U.S. Special Forces units in Vietnam.

SEALs The now-famous Navy unconventional-warfare unit. Stands for Sea Air Land. Back in the 1960s this unit had managed to stay out of the spotlight of publicity, and most civilians didn't even know of their existence. (The same can be said for the SAS.)

SFOB Special Forces Operational Base. This is the support site for deployed Special Forces A-detachments. The SFOB is located in an area near the A-detachment operational area and usually consists of a C-detachment. In Vietnam the headquarters for all Special Forces was in Nha Trang and was sometimes referred to as the SFOB.

sitmap Situation map.

sitrep Situation report. One of these was transmitted daily by Special Forces A-detachment radio operators to higher headquarters.

TDY Temporary Duty. This sometimes results in being paid a per diem rate in addition to one's normal pay.

TO&E Table of Organization and Equipment. The official description of a unit, including organization, manning, and equipment authorized to it.

"If you enjoyed getting shot at,
Tan Phu was a great place to be. . . ."

TAN PHU
Special Forces Team A-23 in Combat
by Leigh Wade

Vietnam, 1963. Leigh Wade was a radioman for Special Forces Team A-23, a twelve-man unit sent to Tan Phu, a hell on earth in the Mekong Delta where the VC had the advantage of knowing the tangled terrain. In those early days, Special Forces didn't have the "luxury" of proper air, artillery, and logistical support, so patrols moved through the black tropical night with the danger of death lurking in every shadow. Wade left Vietnam thinking the Americans would pull out within twelve months, unaware that he would see five more years of bloody combat. . . .

TAN PHU
Special Forces Team A-23 in Combat
By Leigh Wade